BEHIND THE SCENES AT THE OPERA

Intimate Revelations of Back-Stage Musical Life and Work

BY

MARY FITCH WATKINS

Author of
"FIRST AID TO THE OPERA-GOER"

NEW YORK
FREDERICK A. STOKES COMPANY
MCMXXV

Printed in the United States of America

To all those artists and other workers behind the scenes at the Metropolitan Opera whose interest and help have been invaluable in the preparation of this book, my grateful appreciation.

M. F. W.

New York
1925

CONTENTS

v

BEHIND THE SCENES
AT THE OPERA

CHAPTER I

THROUGH THE STAGE DOOR

WHAT is Opera, and—still more important—*why* is it? The first is easier to answer than the last, so let us dispose of it at once.

Every one knows that Opera is a unison, or at least an earnest attempt at uniting Drama and Music, wherein each must forego its best qualities in sacrificing its independence, but which, as a completed achievement, is so ostentatious about the fact that it claims the prefix "grand" as the only thing at all suitable. At its best Opera can be, as Mr. Henderson says, "a great and moving art"; at its other levels it may be any number of things, among them something "stuffy, artificial, Victorian, and puerile," as a certain modern hurler of diatribes insists. But whatever it attains, it certainly more than holds its own against any other form of amusement offered to the public. The Man in the Box Office will prove this to any one's satisfaction. But it is not necessarily to financial evidence that we

1

refer; rather is it to that palpable appeal to the popular imagination which it possesses in such abundance. It always has held its own and it always will, please God, although even its most ardent upholders must candidly admit that as an art it often falls sadly out of step with the march of modern progress.

Right here, however, we find the answer to the second half of our question. The last-mentioned fact and that obnoxious word "grand" is the explanation. Opera is an institution to which we cling with a sort of desperation because it is our precious Museum of Romance. Pageantry and processions, kings and courts, swords and plumes—displaced in our lives by subways and typewriters and radios! Playwrights and authors do not dare purvey to us the romantic commodities any more—they have all become vivisectionists and bacteriologists. The ebullient "movies" have made, to be sure, a banal and saccharine effort to fill the void, but it is to the dear old red and gilt opera houses that we can always turn, without shame, for this much-needed refreshment, sustained by the unassailable and virtuous plea that we like music.

Once within the enchanted doors, however, the component parts of the spell set to work upon us. The great distances, the general atmosphere of lavishness and luxury, the enormous audience, the warm scents and pleasant stir, the vast stage, separated from us by that chasm full of industrious fiddlers and pipers: then the stimulation of color, movement and pictorial beauty, the direct appeal of magnetic personalities and, above all, the sensuous beguilement of our ears, our emotional seduction through the most responsive of our five senses . . . even the Cynic capitulates.

Opera is as it is because we fundamentally crave romance. We want plumes and velvet somewhere in our lives, and we get them. It is a fact that no one has ever made much of a success with an opera too much stripped of tinsel. *Louise* is the unique example of the gingham-apron school that ever came to stay. We never liked much the miners in the *Girl of the Golden West*—we even feel a slight shock when Sharpless comes to see Madame Butterfly wearing tweeds and a panama, and we hate the second Mrs. Pinkerton with a fury not unconnected with her modern frock. The dress coats and sport clothes in *Fedora* may be a factor threatening that opera's immortality. In all events, it has ever been so. In the early 50's a Viennese audience required the management to re-costume an entire production in wigs and farthingales before they would accept Verdi's "new" work of *La Traviata*.

The artificiality of Opera has always been the vulnerable point thrust at by its assailants. "Unreal!" rings the cry of derision. "Of course!" agree the complacent defenders. "That is why we like it!"

Could anything be more utterly absurd than for a great symphony to be shackled to the whimseys of a puppet show; for a noble drama to be mauled and mutilated by the exigencies of musical forms? A talented actor can rarely sing—and why harass a fine singer with alarums and excursions? When lovers voice their protestations in elaborate musical cadences that should be mere sighs and whispers— when townsfolk interrupt the business of their market days with dancing and choruses—when heartbeats are heard on drums, and blood-drops on plucked violin-strings—when melodrama is halted by a *bravura aria,* or an inspired melody tailored to the limitations of the human throat—an intelligent audience should reach for its hat. But does it? We all know that, instead, it stays on shouting and clamoring for more. And simply because they find it as delightfully fantastic as Mother Goose, as "grand" as the Golden Age, and as romantic as first love—all of which may be in fact the *real,* for aught we know.

Not the least of Opera's magic is the wonder and bewilderment of its creation. The blazing barrier of the footlights and the firmly descending curtain separate us from quite another world than the one we know. Its inhabitants appear to us somewhat akin to gods and goddesses, or perhaps only "those queer, interesting artists"—according to our temperaments. Their lives, when we pause to wonder about them, seem as remote from ours as the Eskimos or the Knights of the Round Table. That they are really just people, and that the opera house is merely their workshop, is a startling point of view which may or may not be true. The only way to find out is to forsake for a while the comforts of the orchestra chair and make an excursion around the corner or down the alley, as the case may be, to an unimposing little door, a door whose knob may be a trifle loose, and its paint scarred and worn: an entrance without honors or distinction, which one might pass a hundred times without any excitement whatsoever. It is, nevertheless, the Gate to Olympus, or the Service Entrance, whichever you choose, and it is an alluring door, say what you like, for it marks a distinct frontier. It is an outpost of that strange civilization whose business hours are concerned only with phantasy and dreams, whose relaxation—if any—is of sterner stuff.

Try to pass over the border without credentials and see what happens. You will be immediately challenged—not by crossed bayonets, but by the overwhelming sense of not belonging. Curiosity may help you hold your objective for a short time, but eventually the regretful retreat begins. An alien cannot exist in that rarefied atmosphere unless the workers' heritage is in his blood. As to qualifications for citizenship, one might mention first a language—and be laughed at. Only in the plural can the matter be considered at all: one tongue is as crippling as one leg or one arm. Four is the standard equipment, although the average runs far above. As to racial characteristics: enthusiasm, endurance, tenacity, ardor, and prodigality appear first in the list, to be immediately followed by the apparent derogatives of unreasonableness, inflammability, sensitiveness, pride, and self-indulgence. He who does not find this a perfectly normal and even an admirable blend is an alien without hope. He may not walk with artists.

Great and small, all the denizens of this world must sometime pass this little door. A large limousine draws up before it now and an opulent brunette emerges, clutching a fur collar over her throat and mouth. This is, without a doubt, Margarete Matzenauer, who will presently sing dark Ortrud, the Sorceress. She is accompanied by friends in evening clothes, whom she sends through into the "house" with a pat here and an affectionate kiss there, for all the world as if she were about to sail for a foreign shore. And in truth she is. From Broadway or Michigan Avenue to medieval Antwerp is a fantastic journey indeed. She nods to the mail-clerk, grasps a fat bundle of letters, and goes her mysterious way, to be almost immediately followed by Jeritza-Elsa, who has come up unobtrusively in a cab, with only a valise or two, and her faithful *fräulein* in tow.

Maria Jeritza, the queen, the glowing, golden-haired, golden-voiced incarnation of youth and beauty and success, has come to work, come in an ordinary taxi, wearing a modest dark coat, and a thick white veil over her radiant face. Her hand pushes against the battered panels with an impatient eagerness that is thoroughly human, but on entering she is at once lost to sight in the fragrant mists which advance to wreathe her feet; the incense clouds of sentiment which cling about the name of Elsa.

Down the street comes a stoutish, red-faced man, hurrying a little, but walking carefully to avoid slipping. He wears a greatcoat collared in astrakhan and ornamented with braided frogs; he carries a cane, and his hat is just a shade too small. That this is the Lohengrin of the evening need cause you no qualms, no clutching at shattering ideals. His overcoat does not detract from the glamour of the Silver Knight, rather does a bit of Mont Salvat's glory shine upon and ennoble the overcoat. This man knows the secret of *Abracadabra* and of transmutation—what are coats to him?

A greater magician than he, however, follows hard upon his arrival. A tall, dark, nervous man, with beaklike nose, and head bent forward as if habitually peering over to discover what the second 'cello, or the third English horn can be about. Is his wand in his pocket under the flying coat-tails, that artful wand which will presently bring a dream to life, and pull so taut a hundred vibrating puppet-strings? *"Maestro!"* breathes a respectful underling as he flings open the door. "Bodansky's here!" says the telephone girl into her instrument, to some one waiting to know.

And now, from every direction advance upon that innocent portal little groups of twos and threes, wearing nondescript garments and hopeful expressions. They enter the door with firm, bold step, bow to each other frigidly enough and dispose themselves upon the leather benches along the wall of the constricted lobby. Their eager eyes are fixed alternately upon that portal to the "house" and a door marked "Press." They converse in low tones and smile ingratiatingly on all who pass. The tension is palpable. Suddenly, with one accord, they spring to their feet. From the "house" has arrived the man of the hour, "Bill" Guard. A tall, spare gentleman in evening clothes, and a cravat of unique distinction. His erratic, forbidding manner is belied by the most genial of smiles; he is at once their patron, friend, and dispenser of gratuities. He swoops through their ranks swiftly, pretending to recognize no one, but once reaching the sanctuary of his den, turns in the doorway and beckons. Many are the slips of colored paper doled out to the deserving—the little crowd dwindles and flows like water toward the coveted gates, only one or two turn sullenly and go out the other way. This diplomat, this Machiavelli of Operaland, rarely makes a mistake. There is no more discriminating and helpful ally to the young journalist or musician, no more stern or relentless foe to the pretender or the mere hanger-on. He is Guardian-in-Chief of opera traditions, and they are safe in his hands. Other companies have, in so far as possible, his counterpart, gentlemen worthy, clever, and to be conciliated, but they are to "Bill" Guard as were all contemporary tenors to Caruso.

But why linger about this door ourselves in idle contemplation? Let those whose imaginations have as yet received no fillip go home forthwith, while the rest push on "strange marvels for to see." There need be no dread of disillusionment, no clay-footed idols. For every dream disturbed, a dozen wonders will take its place. Wiping off gilding and peering behind thrones is the most engaging occupation in the world.

CHAPTER II

THE SINGING ACTOR

IN the operatic world there are many thrones and principalities and powers, but the greatest of these, beyond all count, is the singing actor (in professional terms, "the artist"). Of him, for him, and by him was this delightful if bastard art created, and around him pivots the busy life behind the scenes. To know him is to hold in one's palm the key to many doors. Setting out upon a rainy afternoon to capture in a journalistic net the secrets of his great art resulted, however, in an immediate and disconcerting discovery. The thing could not be done! Therefore it seems best to record merely what actually happened in the course of one of the most illuminating of interviews, and so let the reader do his own selective netting from among a quantity of colorful detail.

Successfully to confine the suave and yet naïvely eager personality of Mr. Antonio Scotti upon the printed page is an achievement at least within the realms of possibility, but to attempt a transcription of his quaint and picturesque use of the English language is regrettably hopeless. The subject of the chapter seemed to meet with his instant approval, however, and it is extremely fortunate that chance

10

led us to arrange the words of the title thus instead of "The Acting Singer," for, in spite of the obviously debatable sides of the question, he declared his platform boldly.

"Me, I am first, last, and all the time the Actor!"

And in order to prove his point he proceeded to give forthwith a series of the most diverting object lessons. He left the room and entered it again in the spirit of Scarpia, or Chim Fang. He fell upon the floor as it should, and should not, be done; he brooded darkly in one character; he rejoiced profusely in another. He courted, he loved, and he cursed invisible associates upon an imaginary stage. He sang such snatches of rôles as would put him in the mood, and knitted his mobile features into sardonic evilness, haughty contempt, or desperate woe, demanding ever and anon of the delighted audience of one, "Do I make plain?"

But this carries us too far along for an introduction. He began the whole thing with the calm statement that upon the lyric stage the drama takes precedence over the music; and if the ardent adherents of the traditions of *bel canto* wish to challenge him they had best remember that he is not only an Italian himself, but has been leading baritone of the foremost opera house in the world for twenty-six years, and ought to know what he is talking about. If he is forced, in the course of a rôle, to make a decision between voice and action, he sacrifices the voice every time. That, however, in his

opinion, rarely happens. He seems to have infinite
faith in composers, and as operas are dramas set to
music, he claims that the latter helps more than it
hinders.

However, *acting* is the thing under consideration
for the moment, and apparently it is either quite
easy or almost impossible. In other words, the real
test begins in the cradle. It is a trifle too much to
ask of biology that one be born knowing how, but
a certain inner aptitude and natural inclination can
be remarked, he claims, in the tenderest of infants
destined to be great actors, and nothing short of
the hand of God can restrain them. For them the
arduous studies of their profession will be play.
Others may indeed toil up the ladder to considerable heights by the sweat of their brows, but these
chosen ones sail blithely by them on wings. Some,
like the great Duse, have advantages of growing up
in the thick of the right atmosphere, for she, as you
know, went about as a child in the painted carts of
the strolling band of players to which her parents
belonged; but Mr. Scotti had to make his decision
all by himself, at about the age of nine.

Not one of his estimable family had the least
dramatic leanings in the world, and when the young
Tony began to spend all his time organizing amateur theatricals, they thought little of it save to mark
with some gratification how very popular this enthusiasm was making him at every social gathering
he was allowed to attend. However, when one day

his uncle, who was a bishop, heard the precocious youngster intoning from his own Mass Book in exact imitation of his Reverence's particular unctuousness, the family suddenly awakened to some interest. It was not the delicious mimicry of the worthy uncle which concerned them, but the richness of the voice which the boy revealed. The making of music in Italy is a serious national business and he was immediately put to work under the best masters available. As for Tony himself, he regarded the discovery of his voice with a good deal of satisfaction, for well he knew that it was the first big step along that road which was to lead him swiftly and inevitably straight into Grand Opera. There have been no regrets, no indecisions, for him.

Having succeeded in being born correctly and endowed while in the cradle, having progressed without interference, and eventually landed upon a stage, what does it entail in the way of study and method, if one is to keep faith with Nature and the public?

Mr. Scotti goes to the theater, and goes again— to see everything, good, bad, and indifferent. He claims that even in a poor company there may be one finely played bit that is worth observing, or if not even this, then the whole thing can serve as a warning of what not to do. When he sees a good individual performance he catechizes himself by means of it. "Would I, in ACT II," for instance, "have sat down while talking to Maude? And if not, why not? Would I have shown so much emotion here, or less there? Does the Count's anger carry conviction? How could a different note have been struck?" And so on, into infinite detail. All is grist for his mill. The American movies, which he claims are so popular in Europe because the action reveals to the habitually gesticulating foreigners a repose and restraint which fascinate by their effectiveness, he finds as instructive as the Comédie Française, where he sits absorbed before an intensive method that has founded an art almost too perfect in its meticulous technique. The Grand Guignol for melodramas, the Odéon for classics, the boulevards for the modern types. Oh, Mr. Scotti ekes out an amusing existence in Paris, or anywhere he happens to be. "Whatever starts me thinking is good!"

Much of that thinking, however, goes on in the restless brain when sleep should be knitting up such of his raveled sleeves as are in need. When asked how he studies his rôles, he unexpectedly replies, "In bed!" and this is literally true. When all is quiet and the lights are out, he discovers, like many other people, that ideas come humming thick and fast through his mind. A dozen times before he goes to sleep he will turn on the lamp and jot down some inspiration upon the paper he always keeps there in readiness. And this is not only his method with new rôles, but with the old ones too. Some effective bit of new business you may have noted in his Scarpia, or his Sharpless, was probably conceived on a weary night when he had sung the part, and lain down to take a well-earned rest. As he closes his eyes, he has a vision of himself crossing the stage. He sees a chair in his path, let us say; he clutches it to steady himself a little. "Ah, but excellent!" cries the actor, now wide awake. Snap, the light is on! *"Lean on chair Scene 2,"* he scrawls triumphantly. Then, snap, off goes the light, and in a moment he sleeps like a baby!

Another method of developing a rôle cannot be recommended for general practice, but has sometimes resulted in moments of intense dramatic value which could not have been better if carefully planned. As every one has lately begun to realize, the operatic stage is fraught with hazards. Mr. Scotti, however, has a perfect genius for turning his mishaps to account. One night in the second act of *Tosca,* when he was singing for one of the last times opposite Geraldine Farrar, he pursued her a trifle too ardently when she attempted to make her escape through the doors at the rear. His foot caught in some way and he fell suddenly off his balance, plunging forward to his knees. The shock was great, but his presence of mind was greater. The thing was *good*—he knew it instinctively, and held the pose for several moments to great advantage while he poured forth his irony mockingly at Tosca's feet. After the act Farrar congratulated him upon the innovation, and it was not until long afterward, when the business had become a routine part of many of his performances, that he ever admitted the haphazard origin.

Another almost similar story concerns one of his favorite characters, the rollicking, debonair Marcello of *La Bohème*. Snow in real life is a slippery affair, and its paper counterpart on the stage is quite as bad. In the third act, at the gate of Paris on an early winter morning, stage-hands on the bridges above liberally sprinkle the scene with these feathery flakes. The audience out beyond is always much impressed with the naturalness of the picture. Once when Marcello, making a hasty exit from the inn in pursuit of his flibberty-gibbet young wife, suddenly sprawled his full length on the ground, they unconsciously gave vent to delighted and amused guffaws, forgetting that this was grand opera and not the movies. Now it happens that laughter is not in key with the act that is to follow, and of all the operatic *contretemps* calculated to dismay a singer, it is the most dreaded. Scotti had no intention whatever of skating in this undignified manner upon his ear, and when he heard the public's mirth he could have wept aloud. Once more his actor's instinct, however, triumphed over his very human one of trying to pick himself up. With superb self-control he lay where he had fallen, rolling over just enough to shake his fist at the fleeing Musetta, and to shout his rage from this ignominy to which passion had apparently plunged him. The laughter stopped as if by magic. The audience held its breath. This was *great acting* it was privileged to see!

Many such accidents would occur upon that vast stage where movements must be swift and often violent, were it not for the tray of powdered rosin which stands in the wings for the wise ones to step in, as do the ballet, before venturing out. There are other things, however, which rosin will not help. One of these is the infallibility of the human machine. The assistant stage manager, whose duty it is to warn the principals in plenty of time for their cues, once, after a long and almost perfect record of many years, somehow blundered. Again it was a performance of *Tosca*. Scotti, summoned from his dressing-room to take his place at the little dinner-table where the parting curtains should reveal him, and casually sauntering through the rear door of the apartment, was paralyzed to see that the act was already on, and to hear the last notes of his musical cue just as he appeared. Some sixth sense prompted him, and without a moment's hesitation he began to sing, continuing his leisurely way to the table, and finishing the concluding bars only, in the place where he ought to be. It was so astonishingly effective that for a while they seriously considered adopting it as part of the regular stage directions for that scene.

This would seem an appropriate cue upon which to take up the *difficulties* of the singing actor. If, for instance, the music had not been inexorably insistent that he do a certain thing at a certain time, he would have had no such emergency to face. But Mr. Scotti has no sympathy with this viewpoint. To him the music was the saving grace. It brought him to his senses. If he had been an actor upon the legitimate stage, it would probably not have occurred to him to begin his speech before he got to his table, and there would have been a very awkward moment indeed. The hardest thing to do, upon any stage whatever, is to do nothing. He is severely put to the test in this respect in the second act of *Butterfly* when the wretched Sharpless comes to call with his unwelcome news. (Here it is really deplorable that we cannot set the stage for the anecdote as did Mr. Scotti, who became in turn Butterfly, the baby Trouble, and Zuzuki, the nurse, while explaining the situation.) You will remember, however, Butterfly's indignation at his question as to what she would do were the faithless Pinkerton never to return, and the long and pitiful recital to the maid and the little boy of exactly what would be her fate. During all this time the Consul has nothing to say or do, not even anything to lean against. He must listen, and his face must show that his heart is being wrung—that is all. "I am told," says Mr. Scotti, with a touch of pardonable pride, "that I am very fine just here. I will show you!" Whereupon he fastens a look of such unutterable sorrow and sympathy upon us that we feel an overwhelming impulse to sob.

"The next most difficult thing is to be a nice gentleman. It is much easier to be a villain. And when that gentleman is in usual evening clothes . . . oof!" His special resentment falls upon the rôle of De Siriex in *Fedora,* which, in spite of his dislike, gives a very fine opportunity to show his voice in an aria noted as one of the highlights of the score. A modern ballroom and a starched shirt-bosom do not lend themselves to the traditions of the grand manner. To rise, place one hand upon the heart, and advance toward the footlights would be unthinkable. . . . Mr. Scotti here lights a cigarette, swings one leg carelessly over the other and leans back comfortably in his chair. We feel subtly flattered that he should so take his ease in the course of an interview . . . but no, he is only showing what he does while singing that aria. And then he gets up and crosses the room talking and laughing genially with the invisible Jeritza. "That is what I do while they applaud," he states solemnly, coming back to where he started from.

It appears that one of the things that irks him most in all the world is the habit certain of the old-school disciples have of stepping blandly out of their rôles and acknowledging the tributes of the multitude. In his eyes it is the unforgivable sin, and a trap into which grand opera is very liable to lead the unwary. Just in case we cannot remember any such incidents, he dramatizes one for us then and there. The singer finishes his last high note and pauses while the sound of the "clack" is supposed to greet the ear. Two modest, pensive inclinations of the head are given with some pretense of being in character, then, as the tumult and the shouting do not die, he abandons discretion and bounding to the footlights throws appreciative kisses to his admirers in the auditorium. This seems to relieve Mr. Scotti's feelings upon the subject, and he comes back to business again with a thought which he captured during this last imaginative flight.

"Here, I will tell you the whole thing, if you would know! How many walls this room has *now?* Four you say? Well, *so has also the stage!* There you are. That is all there is to it for me!"

How superbly simple it sounds, for a great secret! Merely forget that the footlights, and the orchestra pit, and the big black hole filled with audience are there! Nothing but a mental attitude. Oh, quite easy! As for traditions, Mr. Scotti does not snap his fingers at them; far from it. He learns them letter-perfect and then freely discards any or all of them upon which he cannot build. That fourth wall of the room will do away with some; for instance, that time-honored rule about the back toward the audience. If there is no audience in one's consciousness, one turns here and there as one feels most natural. "Fancy this" . . . he jumps up to show a sidewise, crablike exit in an effort to keep his face to the footlights, and laughs immoderately at the spectacle he makes of himself. "But, on the other

hand, I could not do *so!*" . . . wherewith he drops
in a supplicating attitude before us, the knee toward
the imaginary spectators flexed. He then changes
quickly to the reverse position, and we must acknowledge that the effect is by far more graceful. "It is
—how you say?—*instinc'* . . . I feel sure of
that."

And this reminds him of something else, perhaps
even more important, after all. One must have, in
order to be an actor, such a highly developed talent
for observation and imitation that one could dupli-
cate the following extraordinary anecdote in kind.
When touring with his own company on the Pacific
coast a few seasons ago, Mr. Scotti was invited by
Mr. Healey, the local manager at San Francisco,
to visit Chinatown, and he accepted with pleasure,
because he was giving several performances out
there of his great success as Chim Fang in *L'Ora-
colo,* and he had not had an opportunity to observe
the Chinaman on his own ground in all the time he
was studying the rôle. So, after *Tosca* one night,
Mr. Healey brought several friends around to the
stage-door, and among them was a police detective
whom he introduced as the "Scarpia" of Chinatown.
Mr. Scotti was "ver' delighted to meet this colleague," and almost immediately the group started
on their journey.

When they reached the first of the oriental alleys,
they got out of their taxis and proceeded through
on foot. Scotti and the detective were together, the

others ahead. Suddenly two silent-footed Chinese came along the sidewalk, nodding and talking together in their outlandish jargon. The Americans stood aside for them; but as soon as they had passed, Scotti assumed a walk exactly like theirs and, turning to the detective, mumbled something in a high-pitched voice which sounded somewhat like "Choca-taw-chee-chu-wah-we-ha!" Immediately the two Chinamen stopped dead, turned about with a startled expression, stared for a moment with intense astonishment, and then hastened away in the opposite direction.

"Say," said the detective admiringly, "what did you tell those guys? I didn't know you spoke their lingo!"

"I don't spik it at all! Tha's a funny thing!" exclaimed Scotti, prodigiously pleased with himself. "I jus' maka some sounds lika they do. . . . Now what do you suppose, I 'ave *insult* them?"

This is indeed acting, but it is perhaps fortunate that such prodigal endowment in the profession is rare, otherwise what countless beguiling and precarious scrapes Thespians would constantly be getting into in Leningrad or Constantinople, or even Paris and Berlin if they did not speak the language. And that leads us back again by a gentle association of ideas to the opera stage, where Mr. Scotti finds our own linguistic limitations subtly influencing his art, and explains it somewhat thus: "You see I must act leetle more here where the words are not un-

nairestood!" Which starts a whole train of thought
in our own mind. Naturally if words convey a
meaning, it is not necessary to emphasize them so
generously with interpretive action. Are we, then,
by our polyglot operatic institutions, training for the
world a race of mighty pantomimists? Mr. Scotti
lays much of the subtlety of his Falstaff to this very
necessity. There are all sorts of *double-entendres*
and impressions which he must convey wholly without the help of words, which, if spoken in English,
would carry themselves.

Singing the big arias in the old-fashioned operas
is one of the hardest trials the modern singing actor
is put to, but both Mr. Scotti and Mr. Chaliapin
seem to have overcome that difficulty with distinction. "Every one must help me, however," Scotti
declares, and goes on to explain that a solid wall of
perfunctorily advancing and retreating chorus, and
other traditional features, must be swept away if
real effectiveness is to be obtained. If they stand
about in natural little groups he finds it easy to sing
while wandering among them, or while sitting or
otherwise behaving with some degree of artlessness.
He never presumes, or intrudes his own spontaneous
inventions without due consultation with the stage
manager and the conductor. This is one of the unwritten laws of the music theater. The singer may
come first in consideration, to be sure, because the
voice is not a mechanical instrument, but the conductor of the evening holds all the reins in his hands.

However, who could resist an amiable and exuberant baritone, who sometimes calls for a little consultation in his dressing-room just before the curtain, and who says in pleading tones, "Maestro, I feel ver', ver' good to-night. You please give me leetle more freedom perhaps here and there, eh?"

The stage manager, too, must have his say, and the wise singing actor always listens to advice, even if he does not take it. Conference and conciliation have won more operatic battles than all the fabled temperament of all the press-agent stories in the world. As for the coöperation of the other artists, that is a subject upon which too much or too little might easily be said. Mr. Scotti claims that nothing in his experience is so inspiring as to play opposite an artist of intelligence and true dramatic instinct, who knows the value of give as well as take. With such a partner, a scene is actually capable of working up to white heights without even one rehearsal. But alas, there are always the others, those who can offer one no help, who stand stock still and let the fiery actor go around them in futile circles. That tries the mettle of the most seasoned veteran, for there is something insidious about it which lets down and unkeys a scene almost beyond redemption.

"And right there *music* steps in and saves everything *just the same!*" says Antonio Scotti. "He is not so bad, that actor who sing, eh?"

CHAPTER III

INSIDE A PERFORMANCE

It is *Tosca* to-night, with a distinguished cast, and, although the curtain will not rise until a quarter past eight, we must enter the stage-door promptly at seven if we want to see everything from the beginning.

In France during the late war it was noticeable that the nearer one got to the actual firing-line, the quieter and more orderly did everything become; and so, apparently, it is at the musical front—the hour before the battle is serene. Only the telephone girl is on duty, and incidentally she is the most wonderful of the species in existence, the perfect answer to one of Kipling's "Ifs," for

> . . . she can keep her head while all about her
> Are losing theirs, and blaming it on her!

even when it happens in six different languages. She knows every comet, planet, star, or bit of star-dust in the whole organization, and their telephone numbers; she recognizes you instantly after ten years' absence, or she forgets when she should forget; she is able to do four things at once and a fifth on the side; above all, it is she who controls at her discretion that magic button which opens the door for you into the "house." However, like the shoemaker's barefooted children, she herself hears very few operas, although I should say that she is amply compensated by the amount of life which she daily witnesses in dramatic intensity. She is smiling, good-natured, and of comfortable proportions, a friend worth having. We always linger for a chat at her desk before penetrating farther.

While we are standing there the singer who is to interpret Scarpia comes in and stops for his mail. He is a handsome man, with a humorously saturnine cast of features, and, no matter when or where, he is always extremely well dressed. To-night he is in faultless evening clothes, not the usual attire of the performer, but as we go through the door together he confides to us in that delightfully broken English which twenty-six years have failed to repair:

"Beeg party to-night—ees not good for me—maybe don't go if I can!"

We get his meaning quite clearly, and express a hope that he will be successful in his evasion, although we doubt it. He is socially much in demand and occasionally has to break that iron-clad rule of all successful singers which takes them straight home and to bed after a performance. But Scarpia dies punctually at 9:45, so perhaps the hostess' chances are fairly good for this evening. His dresser and wigmaker are waiting for him, so we leave him at the door of his room, and pass along the short corridor and down the steps to the stage under a large sign requiring one to be silent in French, German, and Italian, as well as in English.

Between us and the women's dressing-rooms the nave of Sant' Andrea della Valle now spreads its Renaissance proportions, empty of all save the simpering statue of the Madonna on her fountain and the shrouded canvas on the easel at the left. The gray, sound-proof curtain is down, and the only illumination is a single pilot-light upon a thick cable. No "regular" church ever enjoyed a quiet more profound. But it is the calm of taut nerves, of suspended animation, for these planks upon which we so lightly tread have probably sustained more weight of woe, more spilled emotions, more passion and joy, madness and exultation, than any floor extant. Our steps become reverent. We walk the length of a city block and arrive in the opposite wings behind the Attavanti Chapel. A muffled soprano trill meets our ears—we are now upon the distaff side; the opera house separates her members as rigidly as a Quaker meeting-house.

Up five steps again, through another padded door, and we are outside the prima donna's dressing-room. We have missed her arrival, but we know better than to disturb her now. Through swinging glass doors we can see the timekeeper, a distinguished individual with a carnation in his buttonhole, who presides at a desk beside the clock and shepherds the arriving chorus and supers. They are beginning to come in already; there is a constant slamming of doors and a scurrying up the iron staircase. There is a faint tang of abandoned tobacco in the air, for smoking is also forbidden in all languages. The transoms of all the rooms but the star's are dark; there is no other woman in the cast to-night except the shepherd in ACT III, who will come in at the last possible moment and stand behind a protecting bit of scenery in her hat, coat, and gloves, allowing her voice alone to impersonate the tattered lad out on the Roman hills—this is her easy night.

There are six dressing-rooms on this corridor. Two large ones for the principals, and four smaller ones for the lesser lights. The smallest and stuffiest of all has a history. There are screw-holes in its panels, and it once bore a shining brass plate upon which was engraved the proud name of "Farrar." It is doubtless the least desirable room of the six, but the last shall be first, and it has been the scene of much grandeur. Even now, when one pokes an inquiring nose into its emptiness, a vague yet familiar perfume rushes to meet one—the walls, the curtains, the carpet, all breathe "Geraldine"! It was once the only privately owned dressing-room in the annals of the house, and the way of it was this:

The two large rooms are almost identical in convenience, size, and arrangement, but custom has always bestowed Number 10 upon the leading lady, and Number 11 upon the secondary. Very naturally this led to some heart-burnings and not a few

rather fiery and dramatic moments, especially on
nights when the assignment hung upon a nice decision as to the relative importance of the Countess
or Suzanne in *Figaro,* Venus or Elizabeth in *Tannhäuser,* Brünnhilde or Sieglinde in *Walküre.* Such
strained relations resulted in one particular instance
that blood flowed during a dark moment in an act
of the last-mentioned opera, and an indignant and
stricken Sieglinde had to be bandaged up before she
could take her curtain calls. The astute Geraldine,
not wishing to let herself in for any such imbroglio,
discovered that one little room was not much used
because of its size and airlessness, and somehow
cajoled the right to its exclusive use from an in-
dulgent manager. She turned it into a charming, if
constricted, bower, hanging it in gray and rose, over-
coming its lack of ventilation with scent and vapors,
and fitting it up with every luxury to suit her personal taste. She then put the key firmly in her
pocket, and smiled sweetly as she watched the
other prime donne across the hall in their bi-weekly
packing and moving of their costumes and chat-
tels.

Now suddenly a bell rings, and strident echoes of
it are heard in the vast regions above our heads.
It is the half-hour. A boy with programs appears
and knocks at Number 10. We crane our necks for
a glimpse, but only an austere *fräulein* in a black
apron opens a wary crack, and straightway shuts it
again. We caught momentary sight of a basket of

roses and the flash of a shining gown upon a nail, but "Do-re-mi-mi-mi!" sings a luscious voice, and there is a sudden ripple of a soft and foreign tongue. We linger for a moment, enthralled, then open the glass doors and mount the stairs.

These are already populated by a strange motley. This is an Italian night, and it might be Florence or Milan rather than New York, for all the English one hears, and likewise on a French night the place has a chameleon ability to become Paris, or, with a German opera, Vienna. Soldiers, monks, choir-boys, gendarmes, and peasants line the stairs and landings, all talking and laughing and humming at once and having a most sociable and pleasant time. They are carelessly made up, if at all, and their wigs are ill-fitting and casually adjusted, but their costumes are fresh and correct, and they wear them with an accustomed acceptance. It does not occur to any of them that they are dressed up or objects of interest; they wear with equal indifference toga or small clothes, armor or kimono, it is all in the day's work; and somehow they always manage, no matter what they wear, to look exactly the same. The ladies are a trifle more interested. As we peer into their long room on the third landing we see them bending carefully to look into their mirrors, adjusting a ribbon here, a curl there, or adding a deeper note of rouge upon the cheek-bones; but the net result is persistently the same as with the male forces—they cannot change their spots, and a lady of the chorus always resembles a lady of the chorus, no more, no less.

Another bell rings, this time right over our heads. Already it is the quarter-hour! Our pulses quicken, we scurry out to the iron bridge in the flies and look down. Far below us is the once deserted church, but what a scene of animation possesses it now! Its true acolytes wear shirtsleeves and overalls, its priests the soft hat or the derby.[1] Orders are being shouted, border, cluster, and spot lights snapped on and off, flats are moved an inch to right or left and feverishly screwed down, borders are lowered a trifle, then raised. Three or four little men with open scores under their arms are running about as if frantically seeking some one, and a tall individual stands quietly at one side talking continuously into a telephone. There comes a curiously foreshortened Cavaradossi to inspect his brushes in consultation with the Sacristan. Angelotti joins them and they go across and try the chapel gate. A preoccupied person, checking up a list, almost collides with them. It is high time for us to go down. Every last member of the orchestra has long ere this punched the time-clock and descended to his subterranean green-room to tune up. Pushing our way through the throngs at the foot of the stairs, we cannot resist a final peek into the prima donna's hallway. This time we are rewarded.

---

[1] Very recently a new rule has appeared in one opera house forbidding this picturesque headgear upon the stage.

Her door is flung wide, and there in the opening, against a background of light and warmth, and the heavy fragrance of powder and grease-paint, stands the radiant Tosca herself, all ready to go to church except for her staff and garland. In spite of the strange condition of her face, which is now ready for long-distance scrutiny from six thousand eyes, she is beautiful. In fact, the chalk-white forehead, chin and throat, the carnation cheeks with the lavender bloom upon them, the purple eyebrows, reddened nostrils and ear-lobes, the beaded lashes and carmined lips give no effect of a hideous mask, as one might suppose, but are on the contrary quite becoming. It seems perfectly appropriate for her to look that way, for she is one of the goddesses, and we should not expect her to—in fact would be vastly disappointed if she did—look in any way normal. Being, however, a very great artist, and mistress of all the mediums she employs, she has, in making herself unreal only increased her allure.

At this moment she is talking earnestly, in curious muffled tones, to a gentleman in evening clothes with padded shoulders and a foreign air. When he turns for a second, we see that it is the conductor of the evening. We might have known it by the restless left hand that is beating time along the lapel of his coat. He always seems to be hurrying somebody through something a little faster than they will go. Tosca hums a measure softly, takes a step, makes a half gesture, and turning to an unseen companion demands her score. It is brought and quickly opened. For a moment her shining head and the conductor's gray one are bent together over a passage. "Ta-tara-ta-ta" he sings to her in a funny, raucous voice; then suddenly he kisses her hand and is off like the wind toward the stage. We follow him as best we can through the groups which block our way, only to see him disappear down a little staircase to his rabbit warren, from which he is soon to emerge into the orchestra pit and tap peremptorily for attention, as the lights are lowered.

We run up into the south corridor to see how the numerous gentlemen who populate the cast are faring. We just met Angelotti out on the stage. His moment is to be brief, and his make-up exactly the sort of fungus one would be apt to acquire in the dungeons of Sant' Angelo. We do not feel drawn to him.

Cavaradossi, however, is quite superb. He is sitting now before his mirror slowly sipping something from a thermos bottle, while his wife, charming and helpful lady, walks about examining him from every angle with a calm but concerned eye. Somewhere in the background is a dresser or valet, brushing a coat. The tenor puts down his cup, holds the tip of his nose between thumb and forefinger, and tries his upper register. He then pulls his wig a trifle farther over his brow, places his hat jauntily upon it, and clicks his heels—he is ready! A most immaculate, dapper Beau Brummell, this Roman painter Cavaradossi. We suspect he must have been either a *dilettante* or else the most successful man of his day. He saunters into the corridor and joins the group of his compatriots around the entrance to the room where Scarpia is seated, a bib under his chin, engaged in sketching the vileness of his character into the corners of his nose and mouth. Spoletto and the police are up one flight. As we gaze, wondering if we have time to seek them out, there comes over everything a sudden electric stillness.

We glance behind us. The stage is as empty as when we first arrived, but the gray asbestos drop is slowly lifting and now only the famous yellow brocade separates us from a strange roar and clatter that sounds like a busy mill in full operation, but is really the clack of many thousand human tongues. Two Louis Seize pages stand alert, the golden cords in their gloved hands. The technical director, *deus ex machina,* with the chief electrician, and two slender, nervous gentlemen with scores, stand in a tense group before the big switchboard. An elderly assistant peers anxiously through a sort of tubular peephole in the proscenium. Suddenly he snaps his fingers, and the tap of the conductor's baton outside is distinctly heard. Then the three sinister chords crash out from the hidden orchestra—some one touches a buzzer—there is a faint sigh of "Curtain!" from every one and no one—the elegant pages spring back just in time to escape observation, and, as the gold fringe folds up gracefully out of the way, take their places in the first *coulisse* just where they can best obstruct our view.

But we can feel, even if we cannot see. With the parting of those curtains there is a strange and powerful psychic wave which strikes us and sends our hearts into our throats and sets our knees to trembling. It is a sensation of overpowering terror and excitement which cannot be described. There in that great dark void, which is the fourth dimension of the stage world, crouches a hungry beast with only one set of staring eyes, one pair of wagging ears, one great red mouth which can roar with pleasure or eat you alive. There it sits, silently absorbing, devouring. An audience entirely composed of perfectly nice, considerate, and well-behaved people, becomes inevitably fused into the personality of this monster, promptly with the darkening of the house.

Shuddering, and meditating on these things, we hear Angelotti make his way into the open, and we wonder at the magnificent courage of the man actually to stand up and tread that stage. We look around with increasing respect at the crowding acolytes and police all about us, who await their entrances so unconcernedly. Suddenly there is a streak of black lightning through their ranks. A tall man clutching a score, and wearing the most worried and harassed expression ever seen upon a human countenance, dashes up the steps three at a time and arrives at the door of the tenor's room like a fury let loose. *"Signor, signor, pronto!"* he implores in fainting tones. "Three minutes—nineteen measures!" This poor man seems to have the least enviable life in the world, and yet when, after twenty-nine years of such stress and strain, he thought there was a chance of his losing his nerve-racking job, he wept like a baby.

His is the horrible responsibility of getting the principal singers on the scene in time. They are not required to stand in the wings like the minor characters, awaiting their cues, but remain in their dressing-rooms until summoned. If they are late, action and words cannot be extemporized to cover their tardiness, as in the spoken drama—no, the orchestra goes relentlessly on like time and tide, waiting for no man nor prima donna either. Sometimes singers, too much at ease in old rôles, try this poor creature to desperation by their delays. He is, in fact, the one person we have ever seen actually tear his hair. One night he seemed literally to uproot it in tufts and trample upon it in his endeavor to get Emmy Destinn on in time for the opening of *Tannhäuser's* last act. He sobbed, he implored, he raved, but nothing would hurry that amiable singer—she made maddening stops for a handkerchief, a jujube, a last word to her maid. Finally, when the poor man was sinking hopelessly upon the step, clutching his damp brow and calling upon his Maker to absolve him from blame, she came out and serenely plumped herself down at the foot of the cross at the identical moment the curtains parted. He may professs to like that sort of excitement, but we, who had been only a mute witness of his anguish, will never be quite the same again.

Now that all the necessary males are safely on the stage, we will pick our way around that narrow padded lane behind the back-drop and get across in time for Tosca's entrance. We must be very careful in this passage, for it is dark, and full of surprises, and should we stumble or collide, the transept wall of St. Andrea's would show alarming symptoms of an earthquake in Rome. We negotiate it in safety, only to perceive our prima donna pacing the small compass of her entrance *coulisse,* in a high state of agitation. She is hissing *sotto voce* words of despair to all within earshot. Sympathetic ladies of the chorus cluster and regard her; the stage-hand who is adjusting a cable near by grunts and perspires as he shares her distress; while shivering in the shadows is a wretched maid, sniffling helplessly and plucking at the leaves of the garland of roses and lilies which she is holding ready. We hover anxiously on the edge of things, and gather the information that Tosca's staff caught in the door on her way out and broke in two. She is now waiting for a selection from the property room which may, or may not, arrive in time. Such a cataclysmic horror as Tosca appearing without a staff paralyzes the imagination. Our own eyes dim with sympathy for the poor, distraught woman.

On and on goes the orchestra. Mario, out there, is excitedly arguing with Angelotti.

On a certain note Tosca ceases her pacing, seizes her flowers, and stiffens like a pointer. From nowhere in particular a dapper young Italian with an open score springs up, and confronting the prima donna, beats time with a forefinger . . . one—two —three . . . "Mario! Mario!" sings Tosca, then quickly adjusting her facial expression for the public, sweeps through the canvas door on the gracious strains of her familiar musical phrase. That is that.

People promptly fade away from there and go about their business, but we remain a moment to listen. That lovely first-act duet is in progress. When the singers turn in our direction, the air beats against our eardrums in waves of vibrating sound, as when there is too loud a needle on the phonograph, such is the power of their voices. The prompter, in his hot little hooded aperture, is rasping out every word in a singsong, piercing undertone, about one beat ahead of the singers; but they seem to ignore him, and he to be unconscious of their presence, as he bends over his brightly illumined page. He has to speak every word sung by every one in the entire opera, and the fact that his monologue seldom annoys the audience is one of the marvels of acoustics.

Another curious thing is that, although the most *pianissimo* of singing tones, be they faint as expiring sighs, carry to the uttermost parts of the house, the spoken word falls dead where it is uttered—which is fortunate for those artists who like to be conversational between their arias. Many and amusingly irrelevant are the remarks sometimes overheard from the wings. Even now we caught a murmur from Tosca which is not in the libretto, about a missing staff. There is, incidentally, one waiting for her now; in fact, a wide choice held in the arms of the wardrobe mistress, who stands chatting with the diva's maid, the latter carefully balancing a glass of water in one hand and in the other, held circumspectly by its exact center, an elaborate lace handkerchief into which her lady is to weep in the ensuing scene.

There is now a slight stir just below them. Our friend Scarpia—in all the panoply of his black magnificence, surrounded by his repellent sleuth-hounds, and Spoletto, a masterpiece of revolting make-up—is poised beside his entrance, his eyes fixed on the upraised finger of the indispensable individual with the score. *Boom—boom—boom*—and he, too, has sprung into the dragon's maw.

A few more minutes and the chorus is upon the stage. The wings are deserted, except for the carpenters and stage-hands who sit or stand about in apparent idleness, but in reality each is posted beside the particular bolt or screw he must negotiate at a given signal. It is their zero hour—they go over the top at the drop of the curtain.

And now suddenly the act is over, and the yellow curtains are held firmly closed in the pages' hands. A patter as of hail on a tin roof sounds from the other side. A yellow damask apron is lowered, and the artists who were not on at the close come quickly from their dressing-rooms and file out beyond it, bowing and smiling with that strained and gracious expression they keep for that special occasion. It has been a good act, so their smiles linger and become more natural as they exchange comments and squeeze each other's hands; they alter the order of their going, and cross and recross behind the apron. Anxiously they listen after each trip, to the now diminishing applause. "Seven," counts the faithful *fräulein,* who has approached with an enveloping white shawl ready for her mistress. They wait, carefully estimating the demand for a possible eighth. Perhaps, after all, it did not go so well as they thought—as they listen, their smiles turn wooden. But it comes, one more wave of staccato enthusiasm, before they rush off to that frantic and inadequate quarter-hour allowed them for transformation and rest.

Having once observed the terrible importance to them of an audience's too often casual expression of pleasure, let us never again adopt the pose of appreciative silence, or fail to bestir ourselves beyond a perfunctory pat or two; for this is our only point of contact with these fervid workers for our pleasure, and our applause is the only real reward which makes their vast expenditure of vital forces on our behalf at all worth while.

All the time these mutual salutations were progressing, the stage manager, and the technical director, with their various *aides-de-camp,* have been standing with backs indifferent to the demonstration, and have calmly and almost silently wrought a change in their domain—which is not the least of the miracles we may see. St. Andrea's is no more; chapels, grills, altars, easels, and fonts have apparently disappeared into vapor. There is no church there, but neither is there anything else, only a vast and extremely neat nothingness. Then a muffled whistle blows, and three walls and a window advance from their hiding-place and are at once firmly bolted into place while painters go about with brushes touching up joints and tears. We hop nimbly out of the way of a smoothly unrolling carpet; furniture gets placed in exactly the right spot by the most expert of movers. The property man and his assistant butlers set Scarpia's little supper-table carefully and bring in the fruit and wine. Mirrors are hung, and the important Crucifix is put just where it will be needed. Candles are lighted on the table and still others on the desk at the right.

These latter used to be left for Tosca to kindle for the funeral rites, an effective piece of business, but now abandoned ever since one famous and overwrought singer blew out the candelabra first, in a moment of dramatic miscalculation, and matches not being available nor in the picture, was forced to leave Scarpia in darkness. Straightway all Toscas lost their nerve, and now there are plenty of burning tapers for all purposes.

Officially sealed papers should be on the desk too. Their special guardian takes them from their special drawer and scatters them, places a quill pen in its stand, and fades away, just as that fatal buzzer sounds.

Moonlight springs into being through the window, and the sound-curtain slowly withdraws. The baton taps. Breathless silence, dodging pages, the yawning maw again—and the act is on!

We hurry over to the left rear, where something of interest seems to be happening. An assistant conductor of importance is perched somewhat precariously upon a tall ladder, and, with an eye glued to a very small hole in the palace decorations, watches the beat of the *Maestro's* wand in the remote pit, and duplicates it simultaneously with one of his own. Below him is assembled a curious group. The chorus, having strutted its brief hour, is on the way home in garments which, for once, conform somewhat to the current mode, but en route it must pause a while to take part (happily unseen) in a very elaborate ball and entertainment supposedly under way in Queen Caroline's salons. They gather around a little melodeon, where another assistant presides and keeps them upon the key so difficult to maintain thus remote from the big orchestra. The audience, picturing contentedly a brilliant gathering of satins and swords and red heels, might resent these overshoes, and derby hats, and umbrellas, but the vision of Tosca standing there among them looking like an angel on a Christmas tree could disappoint no one. Her diamond crown catches what light there is in these dim shadows, and the lamp which shines upon her score is reflected in her jewels and the gleaming folds of her silver dress. Her lips are parted in concentration, her eyes dark and dilated with excitement and eagerness. Her heavy velvet cloak is over her shoulders, but she shivers slightly and tries her voice in little, nervous "Hmm —hmm's." She pulls the rack upon which rests her music a little nearer her and examines the latter attentively as if it were new and she not quite confident. It is a remarkable fact that artists, no matter how often they have sung a rôle, nor how brief the phrase, always read their off-stage music from the notes.

So Tosca sings, and her voice soars above the surrounding murmurs like moonrise over a mountain lake. Snap! The conductor is down from his ladder, the derby hats fade away, something conveniently swallows the melodeon, and Floria Tosca, pausing a fluttering moment to step with her silver slippers in a tray of powdered rosin as insurance against slipping during the violence to come, springs tiger-like and aflame to the door which a soldier opens, and the most stirring scene of all opera has begun.

The act gathers dramatic force. Even the electricians and "hands" gather where they can see something of the proceedings. Poor Cavaradossi is dragged into the torture-chamber and now sits panting beside us in the wings, sketching nasty greasepaint bruises upon his temples by the aid of a mirror held by his dresser—and upon the advent of the assistant with the score, screams "Ouch!" upon the proper beat with heart-rending anguish in his tones. Then in a moment he is staggering back onto the stage, a mere wreck of his former self, in the hands of Spoletto's ruffians, who scuffle and whisper elaborate and extemporaneous threats to him for their own amusement.

At last, for the bloody finale, we crawl out as near the scene as we dare, in order to miss no murderous gleam from Tosca's eyes. As she leans against the table, her head thrown back, her soul almost out of her glorious panther-like body, we are devoutly thankful that the knife she holds has an innocent blade of silvered leather, and quite agree with Scarpia that it is the only safe thing, ever since she pierced his vest and drew blood one night in her realistic play with the tin one previously supplied her.

At the finish a great sigh seems to come from all over the house, from behind as well as in front. Tosca totters just a little as she shakes the mists from her eyes and struggles to control her trembling. That act, played at the pitch which all great interpreters establish, will reduce the most case-hardened artist to a state bordering hysteria. She gratefully twists a silken shawl about her warm throat and heaving shoulders, snatches a mirror from her maid, and with a little brush repairs the state of her complexion, then joining her late victim, whom some one has picked up and dusted off, and taking the hand of her faithful and sorely tried lover, she trails out before the yellow apron with them, and curtsies low. Still shaken and wide-eyed, she yet realizes the dramatic value of her failure to smile. This time the solicitous *fräulein* ticks off thirteen calls upon her fingers. One more is coaxed along for good luck, and already the palace is giving way to the parapet of Sant' Angelo, and a stage-hand is experimenting with an electric fan aimed at the limp folds of the gorgeous Roman banner just run up its staff.

The wait is shorter this time. No one has a change of costume, although Tosca sometimes insists on it, much to our annoyance. Fancy taking time to be comfortably and appropriately clad, with an execution to intercept, and dawn already on the back-drop! Some one has to remember to take Tosca another "Safe Conduct" in case the one she tore from Scarpia's claw became too damaged; but some one always does, and she has nothing to worry about except the firing-squad, which all women hate on either side of the footlights.

The act is on. *"E lucevan le stelle"* sobs its popular way into the standees' hearts, as always, and the applause swells and is suppressed. The shepherd, having sung her song in a tailored suit and hat, just as we prophesied, has blithely gone her way. Tosca goes down the back stairs to disappear in that under-stage labyrinth of steam-pipes and levers—to reappear in the hatchway, on the scene. The firing-squad follows suit. The shot is fired. In the dressing-rooms maids and valets are frantically packing up the litter of the evening. Scarpia's room is dark; he has long since departed, whether to the "beeg party" or home, we pause not to inquire, for we must be right on hand for the prima donna's spectacular leap from the ramparts. So we follow the *fräulein* with the shawl. We can have a very good view of it here in a rear *coulisse*. A thick mattress is spread between the braces of the wood and canvas structure, four feet below the edge.

As we gaze, Tosca springs into view, pauses a moment in an exultant, splendid pose, then jumps up and out into the air. She has to give this impetus in order to heighten the illusion of space, otherwise she might suffer dear Madame Eames' plight when her train lingered gracefully upon the wall in plain sight long after she was supposed to be in the Tiber, and had to be gently removed. But this more agile lady does it superbly, and landing on hands and knees rolls carefully over on her side and amiably blows a kiss up to Spoletto, gesticulating so effectively a foot or so above her face.

She can afford to be gay and amusing now. The

long strain is over. She embraces Cavaradossi fervently and jovially as they saunter to the curtain, and playfully attempt to leave each other alone before the footlights, to take the last applause. Even as their backs are turned, the whole castle is disappearing like Merlin's structure, and the great doors at the back are opening and admitting a blast of cold air. What a scampering of the *artisti* this brings about! Off they go to their warm dressing-rooms and their admiring friends, who now begin to swarm, in well-dressed and sated splendor, across the stage. Proud and happy husbands or wives stand to receive them, protecting yet exhibiting the wonderful helpmeet, who now sinks upon the divan, clutches the throat a little, and smiles up at the visitors, radiant, if exhausted, speaking in whispers only. Enviable gods and goddesses, who have done their titanic work and can rest because it was good! There is no earthly satisfaction so warm, not even the crisp crackle in their pockets of a newly drawn check.

Outside it is raining, and there are still actually such things in the world as crowds and subways and evening papers, and people talking the weird vernacular. We give one last look at the flowers and the lights, fill our ears with the echoes of the music, step reverently across the once more deserted and tranquil stage, and regretfully take the plunge back to earth.

CHAPTER IV

"AS HARDY AS THE NEMEAN LION'S NERVE"

In order to prosper and thrive in the musical back-stage, it is necessary to have the constitution of an ox and a nervous system adjusted like the finest of Swiss watch springs. The mere layman, sitting at ease in an orchestra chair, has no more idea of the endurance test a season of opera represents than he has of the movements of the astral bodies. How much brawn and muscle and brain fever, how many panics, crises, strategical maneuvers, and forced marches have been involved in the preparation of just one evening's entertainment for him may be a matter of complete ignorance, but cannot remain one of indifference for more than a moment after he has his first glimpse beyond the frontier represented by the stage-door.

No matter what hour of the day or night may be chosen for the invasion, work will be going on somewhere at high pressure, even if it be only a scrub-woman frantically trying to cover an enormous amount of square feet between a morning rehearsal and a matinée performance. The opera job is distinctly not a time job, and he who watches clocks is a rank pretender. Stop any one you meet and ask him what are his holidays and his hours off, and he will look at you with the same expression of pained astonishment and pity he might bestow upon a babbling madman. The woman who dresses the wigs for the chorus begins her day at noon and ends it long after midnight; a famous wardrobe mistress, Louisa Musaeus, who took her work very seriously indeed, always moved over, bag and baggage, to her workshop during the rush of a new production, and slept there upon her cutting table. As for the executives, the business officials, the clerks, and secretaries, one wonders what sort of meager life, if any, they are able to snatch away from their responsibilities in twenty-four such crowded hours.

William Guard, the best known and best loved of press representatives, makes his daily appearance at ten in the morning, and departs somewhere along toward the following dawn; and Signor Gatti, or any other great manager, practically never goes home. When, from time to time, his body is reluctantly led out to eat or sleep, his mind and heart still remain at work in his office. Then, there is the orchestra. When they are not playing one opera, they are rehearsing another, and on "off nights" they are traveling to Brooklyn or Philadelphia. They always have a Sunday concert; their mornings, afternoons, and evenings are solidly booked. One supposes them to eat occasionally, but quite certainly they scarcely know their wives and children by sight. Last, but by no means least, are the artists, big and little, who dare not go beyond call of the local telephone during an entire season; in fact, it is usually in the contract of all the important singers that they shall not absent themselves from their homes for more than two hours without notifying the management where and how they can be reached.

The chief trouble with the opera machine is that it has to be one hundred per cent perfect, and perfection is the most intolerant of masters. A play house can spend fabulous sums and weeks of feverish effort upon an elaborate production, but when it is at last complete it can settle down to a comfortable round of sameness. An opera house makes an equal exertion, with difficulties multiplied by the stringency of musical requirements, only to have the show run at the very most for seven performances—less than a stock company's week, all told. Seven is a generous allowance, the average is four or five. To the outsider, it would scarcely seem worth while.

Incidentally, cross-word puzzle enthusiasts might enjoy the herculean and brain-twisting problem to which the average impresario sits down daily. Every subscriber must, in a season, hear practically all the operas, but must by no chance have to hear any of them twice. That would seem simple enough, but wait a moment. Each week's repertoire must be varied and balanced so nicely that a visitor in town may attend every night, and feel that he has sampled a representative sector of the season. Six local performances and one outside, to say nothing of extras and benefits, involve at least seven changes of cast. No artist will sing twice on the same day, or two nights in succession, except in great emergency and they must all be given their contracted number of appearances. This is the first knot to be unraveled. Then consider that rehearsals for future performances must be going on all the while, and that all of the important singers strenuously object to rehearsing the day of an appearance, or even the day before or the day after—some even have the rule written into their contract—and we begin to see why the manager wears a slightly worried expression. The repertoire is worked out on great charts upon the wall of his office. It is very amusing, and keeps him and several other officials from ever getting bored. Perfection cracks the whip about their heels; for what would happen, for instance, if Scotti found himself rehearsing Iago in New York when he was supposed to be singing Scarpia in Brooklyn? No subway could bridge the gap, nor doctor repair the damages.

There is something definite, final, and relentless about music. In the theater, an absent-minded electrician may delay his moonbeam a second or two, but nothing dreadful happens. The actor, not seeing the silver light quite as soon as he expected, can cough, or yawn, or stroke his chin, can somehow fill in the time, but when the full orchestra demands "moon," or "wind," or "thunder," it means business. That natural phenomenon has got to put in its appearance, or several worthy people will have apoplexy. Wagner is particularly exacting, with all his *leitmotifs*. Why carefully educate our children to listen for and recognize *dragons, swords, birds, et cetera,* which may appear a moment later on motifs of *dwarfs, spears* and *rainbows?*

Then consider the singer. He is required, let us say, to cross a large stage and arrive at a window at a given moment. Incidentally he is parting from the lady of his heart. Let those actors who claim that their art is so inferior upon the operatic stage try to enact an unrestrained and passionate love scene while subconsciously counting 14—15—16, and realizing that by 19-and-a-half he must have finished with kisses and be seated upon the window-ledge! Here is perfection pulling two ways at once.

Even the laws of costume, make-up, and properties are uncompromising. When the stage is set, and the singers assembled—if a cushion, or a pin, or an eyebrow needs adjusting, it is now too late. Out beyond the footlights a *Vorspiel* is being played —on the proper note up will go that curtain whether everything is there or not.

Considering all this, and a thousand other instances equally upsetting, which make up the warp and woof of the tension which never lessens from November to April, and for some goes on all during the long summer months, is it any wonder that the opera is the conservatory *par excellence* for the cultivation of that exotic flower, Temperament?

Some witty juggler of words once insisted on leaving off the last two syllables, and unfortunately the average layman has seized fast upon the idea. If is meant the quality of fine, true, and flexible steel, that man is right, but otherwise we, and all who have been privileged to know and work among real artists, take violent exception to the theory. Temperament is as hard to define as charm. Webster calls it a preponderance of one or other internal characteristic humors, and he is right, if obtuse. A preponderance of the artistic sense, mixed with intelligence, keenness, alertness, and indefatigability—there is temperament for you, and the fact that nervousness more often than not creeps into this symposium is only a recognized result of all over-stimulation.

Many a play and story has depended for its humor and its sensational appeal upon the spectacular tantrums of a prima donna. These may be entertaining enough in fiction; but in real back-stage life they are rarer than popularly supposed, and when they do occur they are often justifiable, and almost never absurd. Of course a prima donna is excitable, and her nerves red-hot wires. If she were not, could she for one instant carry off the big job of the evening? Put one of your everyday friends, whose calm and poise you so much admire, on that stage, in all the light and heat and noise and tension, and she would probably swoon or fall groveling on her face with fright.

Prime donne vary greatly, however, in the way in which they take their work. Some, like Geraldine Farrar, are always at home between the acts, to their friends. They seem to need the stimulation afforded by personal admiration and that phenomenon which the Germans call *Schwärmerei* and for which we have no equivalent. Others make the evening of the performance into some sort of mystic rite, and remain unapproachable and aloof. For example, Emma Eames, one of the greatest singers who ever graced the Metropolitan, never received any one at all during or after her performance, and on the nights she sang, every call-bell was wrapped in cotton wool, and the signals had to be sent all over the vast house by messenger. But back-stage they adored her, and thought the more of her for taking her work so hard. They called her "the Queen." She was, although strikingly beautiful, extremely restrained, not to say frigid, in her dramatic interpretations; she was also, we believe, firmly convinced of the contrary, and fondly deluded herself to the hour of her farewell that she was the most passionate and emotional of actresses. Certain it is, anyway, that she endured a tension of nerves compatible with the most devastating fire.

There is probably no more enduringly popular artist than Louise Homer—a beautiful voice, a charming and amiable person, but one who seems to have no nerves. Many a time have we stood with her in the wings as she waited for her cue in an important rôle. It might have been an afternoon tea, for all the excitement she seemed to be feeling, and up until the very moment which released her to the footlights she would be deep in some anecdote of the "twins'" latest mischief. If, by chance, she had to interrupt the tale, she would say cheerfully, "I'll tell you the rest when I get back!" and after singing Fricka's marital hymn of hate, or Brangäne's unearthly and difficult "Warning" to the utmost satisfaction of every one present, would return serene and unperturbed, and continue, "Well, as I was saying,—"

Contrast with this the dynamic Olive Fremstad's attitude of complete immolation toward her work. One night *Götterdämmerung* was being sung. She had returned to her dressing-room after the first scene, so completely in her rôle that she was unable to endure the confines of the four walls. After a few moments' restlessness, it seemed to her that her next entrance must be at hand—the intervening scene in the Hall of the Gibichungs completely left her mind—so off she went with her great, free strides down the corridor toward the darkened stage. Her spirit was already æons away upon a peak above the Rhine. Blindly she opened the door, and promptly walked off into space, landing in a heap at the bottom of a short flight of steps—steps she must have gone familiarly up and down a thousand times. Stage-hands rushed to pick her up, but she was unable to stand; one ankle had been cruelly twisted beneath her. They carried her back to her dressing-room, where she lay in her long white robes like a quivering muse of despair. Her frightened attendants ripped off the high sandal, and already the ankle was twice its size.

What was to be done? A long and cruelly exacting rôle lay before her; a packed house was waiting, for this was one of her greatest interpretations; it was too late to get an understudy. Well, naturally the performance *must go on!* The house physician entered on the run, laden with his habitual throat-sprays and gargles, but seeing the unusual nature of the catastrophe, threw up his hands and called upon high Heaven in excitable Italian. Out in the audience, however, was the singer's brother, a skillful surgeon. Some one remembered the number of his seat. In a few moments he was there with compresses, plaster, and gauze. He bandaged that ankle so tightly that it became temporarily a club-foot, but it could be walked upon—with a dreadful limp and a stab of pain at each step, to be sure, but still possible. By this time the corridors were thronged with reporters and sympathetic fellow artists. In the room stood the manager, exhorting her with words of consolation and entreaty, and a dozen other panic-stricken officials.

The curtain was actually held only four minutes, and Fremstad, carried bodily to her entrance, went on and sang such an inspired and marvelous Brünn-hilde that the performance is marked with a white stone in musical annals. She strode about with dramatic abandon, or stood poised in majestic dignity; never a limp nor a slip throughout the long unfolding of the opera, while she was in character—but the very moment the curtain fell at the end of each scene, she dropped to the floor, utterly unable to stand alone. Never has there been a more striking example of the power of mind over matter.

Next to the prima donna, the tenor [1] probably holds the record in the popular mind for eccentricities; but the greatest of them all, Caruso, was noted for his bland and amiable behavior, especially during a performance. Perhaps he chose to mask any nervousness or strain he may have been suffering, under a cloak of droll and ingratiating buffoonery; certain it is that during the off moments of his appearances he conducted himself more like a frolicsome child at a party, than a high priest in the temple of Art.

On a certain first night of the season, always an occasion when even veteran nerves are apt to be strained to the breaking-point, Caruso had in the course of dressing somehow picked up the name— new to him—of Fairy Soap. It seemed to intrigue his fancy; he went about among singers and officials inquiring mischievously if they had "a little Fairy in their homes," and laughed immoderately all the evening. His antics when he had to sing off-stage always proved convulsing to his confrères, and his

[1] See reference on page 64 to Kurt Taucher's recent demonstration of a tenor's "temperament."

good humor was phenomenal. The only occasion upon which he was wont to show any irritation was during the two seasons when *Armide* was revived, and he, as Renaud, had so little to do. The long pauses in his dressing-room palled upon him greatly, although they proved the occasion on which were produced some of his best caricature sketches.

Riccardo Martin, the well-known American tenor, made a point of kissing his wife every time he stepped on the scene. In some operas where he must make many and varied exits and entrances, she was a most active lady indeed, making breakneck dashes from wing to wing in order to present her talismanic cheek at the crucial moment. He also indulged the obsession that to wear linen not laundered by the fair hands of this same patient Griselda would be to tempt Providence in regard to his career, so that, in addition to her osculatory duties, Mrs. Martin obligingly turned herself into a *blanchisseuse de fin,* and no Cavaradossi in the company wore more beautifully fluted ruffles than her Riccardo.

Contraltos, bassos, and baritones are supposed to be less temperamental, for some reason; but we know one of the latter who, when he finds himself unable to sleep at night, goes through the apartment waking up the entire family and corps of servants, because he finds it unbearable to think of them enjoying the sweet slumber denied to his own overwrought nerves.

Of course in the labyrinthian back-stage world,

where nothing at all is what it seems to be, the most absurd, terrifying, and amusing things are always happening. Probably the one and only emotion never, never experienced by any one there is *surprise*. Against such a possibility both the press representative and the impresario have little telephones with loud-speakers right over the desks in their offices, so that, no matter what they are about, they can keep one ear upon how matters are progressing on the stage. Sometimes they hear very startling things indeed, as upon that night when war was declared in 1917, in the midst of an act a sudden terrible silence came—Margarete Ober, the German mezzo, had fainted before the footlights.

Sitting at his desk one night recently, Mr. Gatti lent his attention to an unusual amount of applause conveyed to his ear over the wire. So insistent and clamorous did it become that he finally put down whatever puzzle was occupying him for the moment and went forth to seek the explanation. He met "Bill" Guard in the corridor, sniffing the air like a hound upon scent. Together they reached the stage breathlessly, to discover that all the commotion was about a certain young baritone, Lawrence Tibbett, who had been in the company a year or so without ever causing a ripple, but who to-night, in the character of Ford in *Falstaff*, had been suddenly "discovered" by a rapturous public. This modest individual, never having been greatly concerned with curtain calls before, had calmly retired to his dressing-room.

Mr. Gatti sent for him on the run, and in another moment the public had what it wanted, and another young man's fortune was made.

The one thing which the manager dreads with unbearable apprehension is the last-minute failure of an artist, and the consequent gymnastics involved for the entire staff. Herein lies the wisdom of the two-hours clause in the artists' contracts. Singers being, after all, human, are, in spite of the care they take of themselves, as liable to the ills of the flesh as the rest of us. However, they usually keep on hoping up to the last minute that they can appear, for they not only dislike disappointing their public, but they also relinquish very unwillingly the evening's stipend; so there are apt to be, several times a season, some eleventh hour crises. In this case, the distracted manager has to do some very quick thinking, and usually tries to substitute a singer just as good, if not better. He will go to any lengths to avoid the frightful necessity of changing the opera itself, with the appalling amount of detail and unpreparedness it is likely to involve. For a secondary singer to step into the star's shoes and grow famous in a night is a golden opportunity. It has been done—witness the occasion upon which the late Rita Fornia, hitherto almost unnoticed, took Emma Eames' place in the cast of *Trovatore,* without a rehearsal, and so successfully that not a person in the vast audience asked for a refund. Or the more recent occasion when the enterprising and courageous Karin Branzell began a performance of *Die Walküre* in a secondary contralto rôle, and because of the prima donna's sudden hoarseness, finished the evening as the soprano Brünnhilde. Such a *tour de force* takes consummate nerve and steadiness, but it has its golden reward. Incidentally it is one of those rare moments when the prompter comes to life and gets positively temperamental himself.

Then take the other side of the situation. A young friend of ours was secretary to a famous singer one winter, an artist of the very first rank. Madame had sung on Monday, she was billed for Friday, so Wednesday seemed a safe enough date for the secretary to dine out. At eight o'clock she was called from the dinner table to the telephone. The calm yet tense tones of her employer sounded over the wire.

"Come," said Madame; "I'm singing to-night!!!"

The young girl's hostess has never recovered from the hoarse cry of "My God!" which was uttered fervently, nor her precipitate rush from the house without a word of explanation. But the secretary remembers only that she ran out into the street minus hat or coat, and plunged into the subway. Vaguely she recollected that the opera was *Tales of Hoffmann*. The singer had Giulietta of ACT II in her past repertoire, but as a much lesser star had been announced, she was thus doing a very gracious thing by leaping into the sudden breach.

At home all was confusion. A maid was frantically taking the wig out of curl-papers, but the costumes were not pressed, there was the chauffeur to be found and summoned, and the make-up and other accessories to be collected and packed. Yet in forty minutes she must be upon the stage! Here was indeed a golden opportunity for the traditional prima donna to display a few fireworks, indulge in hysteria, hold up the management for an extra *cachet*, or otherwise conduct herself according to the usages of fiction. Even that secretary, inured to the crises of operatic existence, had her weather eye apprehensively open; but all was as calm as a May morning. Things went like clockwork. Giulietta arrived in plenty of time, and to the amazement of all, the whole thing put her in excellent spirits. The delighted audience, accepting this pleasant surprise vociferously when it was announced by a nervous gentleman before the curtain, left her in no doubt as to their appreciation; and above all she seemed impressed with the ease with which the whole thing had come off. "Never again will I take two hours to make up!" she exclaimed blithely, and thereby released herself from a large measure of slavery.

A conscientious artist receives unlimited consideration and understanding from the management, but there is one seemingly harsh rule which is never broken for star or super. No telegrams are ever delivered until after a performance. The reason for this is perfectly just from the executive's point of view, for with him the integrity of a performance takes first place above King, Country, Flag, or Mother. A telegram handed a singer as he is about to "go on" may contain news which will incapacitate him at one blow. Such a telegram once came for Carl Burrian, that dependable Wagnerian tenor of a decade ago, on a night in Boston. The opera was *Tristan,* with a famous Isolde, and the greatest of living conductors. Burrian had left his wife seriously ill in New York, and just before starting for the theater he received a message that she was suddenly worse, but that hourly bulletins would reach him there throughout the evening. The company was far from home; there was no other Tristan available; so of course it never occurred to him not to sing. He flung himself into the rôle with the most inspiring courage, and very naturally gave one of the greatest performances of his career; but all through those long hours he knew that the yellow envelopes were arriving, lying there waiting. We, behind the scenes, watched and listened with lumps in our throats. What must have been his thoughts as he sang the passionate second-act music of Death in Love! And later, what tortures of longing and memory was he able to express in the delirium of the last act! Isolde's tears were real that night; she knew, as did we all—for tragedy seems to burst physical bonds and stalk revealed in an atmosphere so tense—that the last telegram had come, and that he, like the stricken hero he so poignantly depicted, would reach out burning, empty arms.

The mishaps and emergencies are not all on the side of the singer, by any means, and accidents are bound to happen in spite of the most rigid discipline and care. One of the most precarious of operas is *Parsifal*. It is a dangerous thing to be caught napping in the wings that day. It is the most *moving* opera! Floor, wings and back-drop are never still. Dignified posts which one has learned to depend upon suddenly become whirling dervishes, and wind landscape around themselves like Salome and her seven veils. There are moments of darkness so profound that every last person not actually detailed to a certain task must stand frozen to the spot where he happens to be, scarcely daring to breathe until the perilous moment is past. Klingsor's entire castle has to go through the floor somehow, and one is more than apt to accompany it unless one is wary.

This very thing happened in another Wagnerian opera, *Siegfried*. Kurt Taucher, singing the hero, stepped incautiously around behind a shadowy rock and plunged through an open trap twenty-two feet into the cellar below, giving every one heart failure and himself several broken bones. With unparalleled pluck, he went back and finished the scene, not even missing his cue.

Kundry, or any other lady who, in the devious course of operatic libretti, is required to come out of the ground and utter cryptic sentiments, does not have an easy time of it. In her heavy veil she is led by a solicitous mechanician down under the stage among the steam-pipes and electric cables, bellows and what-nots, and eventually mounts a small elevator where she is strapped to a species of iron brace not unlike the devices which aid dolls to stand erect on toy counters. "Now, get your nerve, Madame!" cautions the mechanic, and gives her a few trial jouncings just to see if she has it. Then suddenly a trap above her head rolls back, a spotlight strikes through, the inevitable individual with the open score appears and says, "Now!"—and up goes the elevator, projecting her head and shoulders through the trap as neatly as a thread through a needle's eye.

In the old days Kundry used to stay down there and be raised to her Temptation Scene upon a flowery bed of ease; but ever since that appalling occasion upon which the big trap above her opened too soon and the flower-girls, dancing over her in darkness caused by an electrician's misunderstanding, were in momentary danger of being precipitated into the chasm on top of her, while hoarse cries of *"Attention!"* *"Pass' auf!"* "Look out!" wove themselves into the transformation music, it has been thought wiser to have Kundry securely established in the wings and trundled on behind a rosebush when the time comes.

Klingsor's garden has to undergo a sudden and blighting frost at the end of this act. Stage-hands with buckets of withered leaves sit above on flying bridges, ready to scatter these lightly through the air at a given signal. One memorable Thanksgiving Day something happened to the pulleys which held the bridge, and it descended with its human and shirt-sleeved freight into full view of the audience, and hung there for long and effective moments above the paralyzed Kundry's head, whose subsequent efforts at Parsifal's seduction were considerably distracted. The stage-hand, in uncontrolled panic, ran frantically from one side of the bridge to the other, seeking escape; and the audience committed a sacrilege—right in the middle of Richard Wagner's Consecrational Festival Music Drama they laughed out loud.

Our sympathies were with the stage-hand, for it is a devastating thing to be revealed unexpectedly to the audience in the rôle of yourself. It happened to us once in St. Louis. At the end of each act an apron or screen is dropped behind the curtain at the Metropolitan, so that when the artists acknowledge the applause, they may do so without exposing the stage. One forms the habit of hovering behind this, and forgets that it is not so everywhere. Thus, upon a painful occasion, a St. Louis audience was treated to the spectacle of a young girl in blue serge

and white collar, frozen with horror in the midst
of a group of prehistoric gods and goddesses.

Another operatic danger to be avoided is too
much emotion—the singing voice cannot stand it.
Once, when the Chicago Opera was playing in Min-
neapolis, an artist was cast for Brünnhilde who had
grown up there as a child, and had just visited the
near-by graves of her parents and family. Many of
her old friends were in the audience, and she felt
herself mystically surrounded by the sad and loving
ghosts of her girlhood. When her work was done,
and her pitiful pleading to her father Wotan was
still, she could no longer restrain her emotions, and
sobbed in his arms like a child. But poor Clarence
Whitehill, the god of the evening, was not yet
through his part of the performance; he had the
difficult and deeply moving "Farewell" to sing.
Looking down at the beautiful, sobbing goddess in
his arms, he felt his own throat constrict danger-
ously. Between phrases he alternately, *sotto voce,*
complained, scolded, petted, and comforted her.
He has probably never given a worse performance
vocally, but emotionally the whole thing was overwhelming. The audience caught the hysteria, and
when the curtain fell, there were audible sobs from
every part of the house.

This same Brünnhilde, a few nights later, playing
in a city where the regulations forbade the use of
colored fire, or any other lifelike conflagration,
found herself, on her rocky couch, suddenly smoth-

ered in a reek of chemical fumes which had been substituted. Choking and spluttering, she announced in a voice which, were it not for Wagner's orchestral enthusiasm at this point, could have been heard in the farthest reaches of the house, "If they don't turn off these fumes immediately, I shall get up and walk off just as I am!" The diverting picture thus conjured up so upset Whitehill, this time with merriment, that once more he had difficulty in finishing his rôle. But his summons to Loge availed nothing that evening; a terrified stage-hand had heard Brünnhilde's threat, and only the music caught fire from then on.

Against this very peril of emotion, a new rule lately has been brought to being. Now, posted in dressing-rooms and on call-boards, artists may read that under no circumstances are they allowed to address the public from the stage. The immediate reason for this was that a few years ago there was almost an epidemic of important retirements from among the ranks of the leading stars. It became the custom for the singer to speak a few words of valedictory, which usually proved so moving, not only to the audience, but to the singers themselves, and to their colleagues gathered around the curtain, that with difficulty was the disciplined mood of the performance restored. The drama of these occasions made such an appeal that other artists, not permanently retiring at all, began to seize upon all sorts of opportunities for a little chat with the audience, and a wise management suddenly foresaw the whole carefully reared structure of mystery and glamour about to be threatened by familiarity. The new ruling appeared forthwith.

At the same time he took occasion to abolish a practice which had been in vogue for many years and had of late undergone much abuse. That was the famous "Battle of the Flowers." It had been the custom for tributes sent by admirers to the singers, to be presented during the *entr' actes* by pages before the curtain. It was always a pretty scene, and the audience enjoyed it thoroughly, but very naturally it led to a good deal of heartburning. It is, on the whole, scarcely fair to judge of a singer's ability and standing by the number of floral pillows and gilded doves which she receives, but a large part of the audience was bound to make that mistake. It boiled down to the fact that the artist with the richest friends got the most applause; but eventually it boiled even further than that, down to the dregs, in fact, when the artists began sending flowers to *themselves!* It was discovered that one lady left a standing order at a leading florist's and charged it off as professional expenses, which was entirely her own business, of course, until she began so to contrive her position before the curtain that, no matter where she stood, the pages bearing gifts would always have to cross in front of a certain rival artist, to make the presentation. This other, having wearied of all this silly ostentation, had long since given orders that her flowers be sent direct to her dressing-room, so she never retaliated in kind, but when at last it came her time to say farewell, she had a little talk with the manager, and bequeathed to her successors relief from at least one harassment.

One more rule appeared about this time, and it seemed to many the most drastic of all. Prime donne dote upon small dogs, and always have one or two in attendance. A certain singer, a beautiful, untrammeled daughter of the Vikings, whom one would only associate with wolfhounds and great Danes as pets, if any, possessed and dearly loved a diminutive and yapping Pomeranian, which was her constant companion and shadow. One day at a dress rehearsal—which is, in its way, as important as any performance—another singer, making a friendly visit in the wings, perceived the little creature in the arms of the maid, and, taking it from her, began to pet it. Then a mischievous idea was born, and, without waiting to consider, she set the animal down and pointed its nose toward its mistress. Of course the inevitable happened, and a small, woolly dog immediately joined the procession of the gods to Valhalla. All the critics out front burst into unseemly mirth, and the mischief-maker in the wings clapped her hands in an excess of glee. She could take liberties, perhaps, where angels might shake with fear, for she was Madame Gatti-Casazza herself. Nothing terrible happened to her, but Mr. Gatti, after smiling one of his rare and enigmatical smiles, caused a sign to be tacked up in a prominent place:

ABSOLUTELY NO DOGS ALLOWED!

CHAPTER V

THE TOP OF THE LADDER

How many of us would like to be a beautiful, popular, and successful prima donna, poised in the full glory of her powers upon the hospitable, but certainly uncrowded and precarious ladder-top? A silly, fatuous question, perhaps, wherewith to begin a chapter, but one which is sure to bring such a thundering chorus of "I's" from vast hosts of the hopeful, the disappointed, and the romantic, that it has moved no less a person than the lovely Jeritza to answer it too. She, however, makes bold to think that none of us would really care about the thing at all if we knew the complete and ghastly details. Something about her statement, however, fails to carry a great deal of weight, for never in the world was a human being more obviously delighted with that state of life unto which it has pleased God to call her.

She is bubbling over with desire to prove her point, her eager words tumble out in a charming *mélange* of two languages; but she only succeeds in thoroughly convincing us in the end that she is quite wrong, that all the sacrifices one must make are the most delicious of agonies, that hard labor is an exhilarating pastime, that weariness is an utterly pleasurable satisfaction. But, of course, interviewing Jeritza in a mood of cold consistency and frigid fact is as delightfully impossible as conjugating verbs out of doors on a May morning when the early sun shines on a wind-blown field of wild narcissus.

Once in a blue moon the little gods, or the fairies if you like, take an interest in the making of a mortal, and when they do, amazing things may be expected. It hardly seems fair, however, for them to have done quite such a perfect job as in this case—it is so frightfully discouraging for the rest of us. Surely this woman should be satisfied with her voice, and her extreme youth which guarantees long golden years to come, and her intelligence, and her genius for the stage, and not persist in tempting writers to lose their heads and resort to obvious quotations such as "divinely tall and most divinely fair," or bewilder them with her ridiculously long eyelashes. What is more, romance and love have come early her way, and riches flow into her pockets in chinking cascades. But even this does not end it. It is a staggering fact that she actually has to worry about becoming too thin, when it is notoriously regrettable that her colleagues throughout the world's opera houses inevitably put on fat with every breath they draw.

No avid reader of musical romances, no ardent trailer amid star dust, can possibly suffer a twinge of disillusionment if privileged to meet this radiant lady, although scarcely any of the traditional trappings of the "diva" are in evidence. A hotel, and a clerk announcing one in tones of deference, a procession of commodious trunks almost blocking the passage outside a door, from the other side of which comes the sound of laughter, and a note or two on the piano—all this is the usual setting; but that door does not lead to a salon replete with flowers, small dogs, exotic dolls, and heavy perfume. Doubtless she has all of these she wants somewhere beyond our vision, but here is only a small room divested of everything but a chair or two, a broad and littered desk, a typewriter, a file cabinet, a chest of drawers, and an atmosphere of business. And right in the path of the invader stands a Dragon, a fearsome creature in the person of the Baron Popper, who is not only the husband of the fairy princess, but a very charming person in his own right, once he has convinced himself that your intentions are honorable and your credentials impeccable. This ordeal successfully negotiated, Jeritza appears, looking as childlike and bland as little Lord Fauntleroy, in velvet and wide lace collar, and grasping your hand with a pretty mixture of shyness and cordiality. She sits down quite informally, with the amiable, wistful expression of one really anxious to please. The fact that a brilliant lamp shines down upon her like an obliging spotlight seems not to disconcert her in the least. But why should it? It only turns her hair to a shimmering halo and proves that the flush upon her cheeks was not purchased in a shop. Besides, it is symbolic of the thousand-candle-power ray of public curiosity which illumines her daily existence and which she has had to accept with what grace she can.

"Now I will tell you," says she, confidentially, "what a terrible thing my life is. I cannot do anything that I want to do. . . . I must do all day things I don't want to do . . . and I am happy, happy, *happy!*"

Then she began by throwing her most sensational bomb. She gets up early! Eight o'clock every day except the days when she does not get up at all, which are those when she is to sing. Then she lies in bed throughout all those long hours, gathering up strength, only to express it to the last drop that evening in the comparatively brief duration of her performance. But even this is robbed of its terrors. . . . "I *like* to sleep, I can never seem to get enough!" she assures us.

Up at eight, however, amazing fact! Then a faithful perseverance with Swedish exercises, followed by breakfast, a modest one of coffee and rolls. After that there is the very formidable matter indeed of the mail. Even the trusty Dragon cannot spare her much of this arduous business, for letters meant for her must be sure of her personal attention, and the autograph of even the best of husbands upon a picture would not be acceptable to the hundreds—one might almost say thousands—of admirers who avidly clamor for this trite form of souvenir. So the diva herself and none other must set her hand and seal upon portraits by the dozens and tens of dozens daily, until the extraordinary long fingers ache with writer's cramp. This chore disposed of, there are scales to be sung, or a scene from the next opera to be gone over with piano, and then perhaps, along toward noon, she takes the air.

Even going down in the elevator has its terrors for her, the people stare so, and when she starts up the Avenue, it is very apt to become a triumphal march or a game of follow-the-leader; for no matter how urgent the business upon which they are bent, all the pedestrians she encounters will immediately renounce it, and decide forthwith to take a stroll in the direction she is going. This may sound delightful, and perhaps it was until the thrill wore off, but wear off it did and promptly became a matter of real annoyance. Stimulating as are the evidences of public adoration, they are a little too agile at leaping the bounds of propriety, and one's morning constitutional with banners waving and bands playing becomes tiresome. Hence she hit upon the relief of a disguise; and now, if you meet a tall lady wearing a hat pulled down to the very fringe of her phenomenal eyelashes, a hat which covers every spear of what might be conspicuous yellow hair, and a fur collar which is apparently suffocating her as it climbs up over her mouth and nose, a lady who looks furtively to right and left, and slinks hurriedly

around corners—let her go in peace; it is only a
poor hunted prima donna enjoying her daily walk.
Rejoice greatly, instead, that your own beauty usually fails to devastate the world at large, that you
can breathe unhampered, and see your way untroubled by tangled meshes of eyelash, and may even
develop a tiny rip in the back of your stocking without causing the public any serious shock of disillusionment.

Back then, from this freedom of the great outdoors, a walk which has been curtailed not only by
publicity but by that other haunt, the dread of getting thin ("It is extraordinary how *very* slim I become in no time at all! . . ." Oh, enviable Jeritza!)
some lunch is permitted. Ah, if she does not have
to count calories, here is a real joy awaiting her,
the—to a Viennese—not inconsiderable pleasures of
the table. But mark how she searches the menu
with troubled eye. This food is bad for the throat,
that other delicious but has a slight percentage of
digestive risk. Some fish then? But no, that might
harbor a stray little ptomaine. And so it goes.
The festivity of the dining-room is rarely hers either.
Eating through a fur collar and blinders is uncomfortable business; and besides, there is always, always a mysterious little draft lurking somewhere
about those big rooms, and the inevitable cloud of
tobacco smoke to set a sensitive throat to coughing.
So lunch, like most of her meals, appears upon little
tables in the aloofness of her ivory tower, after a

long and not always beneficial journey from remote kitchens.

"Then I sleep! . . . And then I study!"

"Study? But have you not arrived? What should you study?"

She laughed. "Do you not know that nothing is ever finished? And besides, there is always something else. Now it is English and Italian lessons, and my concert programs with Madame Sembrich, and on those three things I work, oh, terribly!" We really cannot shudder in sympathy, however, for she looks as if she were telling us she had been to a party.

But there are the evenings . . . surely the poor, beset lady must have a bit of diversion of an evening. Wrong again. She goes to bed early!

"And the thing I like best of all to do is to go to the theater," she wails. "I have been here in the city five months and I have not yet been to one single little play, not one. Two or three times to the movies, perhaps, or some friends in to tea or for bridge, but that is the most I can do in a season. Am I not dreadfully dissipated? And I have so many lovely invitations too! I tell you it is the life of a cloistered nun. And I cannot smoke; I cannot violate prohibition like other young women; I cannot have any fun at all! What an unenviable lot is mine! Only think, I know probably less about the opera than an outsider. I never can go to a performance; I rarely have the opportunity to observe the art of my colleagues unless I drop in by chance at a rehearsal." And the saddest part of all this seemed to us the fact that she is deprived also of seeing *Jeritza* in her famous rôles.

The pitiful recital of this downtrodden servant of the public continued. It seems that in a day so completely booked she must somehow manage to fit in appointments with dressmakers and photographers, and talking-machine studios, and she must give unlimited half-hours to this wretched business of being interviewed.

"I don't mind this so much," said she with gracious consideration, "but some stupid questions do upset me. For instance, just at first, every one demanded, 'How you like American man?' Now, what a question to ask me, a married woman! I do not think of other men!" She and the Dragon exchanged glances, but her naïve indignation was so refreshingly Old World that we all laughed together out of sheer delight.

"And rehearsals take a good deal of time," she offered tentatively, as if not quite sure that it would prove interesting. "I work very hard at them too," she assured us with great earnestness. "Although not every one does so. At the end I always look like a dirty little pig, because I throw myself on the floor, or whatever I have to do, just as I expect to before the public, sometimes even more, when I am trying something new. I often am so tired from it that I can scarcely walk.

"It is the same at a performance. I am so absolutely *kaput* (no word in English is quite so *collapsed*) that I cannot even speak, and going anywhere but straight to bed afterward is unthinkable. Some singers say, 'Spare yourself!' but I think they are wrong. How can you expect the audience to feel deeply unless you do yourself? The trouble is"—she explained it almost deprecatingly—"the trouble is that I have been *living* my rôle. From the time that I decided to sing the part I have been studying the woman, even the country and the times in which she lived, and the way the people of her world felt and behaved, ate, fought, loved, and died. I know her so well that I am sometimes bewildered to know who I am myself. When I sing the rôle, however, I am that woman during that opera, and no one else. When she is frightened, I am sick with fear, when she is happy I almost die of joy, and when she weeps, my tears are terribly real. I think the audience knows the difference, don't you?" She asked this quite simply and humbly, and was promptly assured with deserved warmth that they certainly do.

"Some friends of mine," she went on, "came here lately to tea after hearing a performance of a great Wagnerian opera, and laughed and talked. I had not been there, and they did not say it, but I knew then at once that that performance was not so good as it should be. Nobody should be *able* to go out anywhere to tea after that great music drama—if you see what I mean.   When I have sung, I like them to go out of the opera house somewhat stunned and dreamy, and feeling as if their feet had left the earth for just a little while."

This was all so stimulating to the imagination that it seemed a pity to drag her back to the matter in hand; but the clock was ticking relentlessly on toward the close of the interview.

"But, Madame Jeritza, all this strain, and stress, and self-denial, and hard labor is but one side.   Tell us a bit of the other."

She opened her distracting blue eyes very wide "But you are wrong!   It is all the sides there are . . . is it not so?"   She looked appealingly to the friendly Dragon for confirmation, and he—responding promptly with colloquial fluency, "It's a *helluva* life!"—laughed delightedly.

"Well, perhaps there *is* one thing," Jeritza amended.   "Of course I receive many, many flowers and presents, and much applause; but nothing is worth so much to me in all the world as that wonderful moment when I come on the stage, and something goes from my spirit out over the footlights to meet something from the hearts of the big audience, and with a spark like a strong electric current, a living contact is made.   It is for that, I suppose, that I am killing myself."   (If there is anything more radiantly alive than Maria Jeritza, it should be suppressed as dangerous.)   "And that is why I never disappoint an audience, no matter how bruised and battered I may be!"   She alluded by a sly grimace to some recent crucial moments when dramatic fervor upon the Metropolitan stage almost ended fatally for her.

"You do it, *Gnädige Frau,* because you are a true artist, and for no other reason."

"Perhaps—but give me no credit.   An artist is born, not made.   I . . . I think I have been kissed by the Muse!"

There was a gentle explosive snort from the Dragon.   "What are you calling me, a Muse?" They laughed together merrily.

The half-hour was up, but one thing had to be known.

"Do tell us that you rest sometimes; it would be so comforting and relaxing to think of you on an occasional holiday."

"Oh, but yes, for three long months in the summer I never open a score or sing a note.   I have a little house in the Austrian Alps where I live like a real person.   I take long, beautiful automobile tours.   Then I sing a few weeks in Vienna, old rôles—it is not hard there, it is like being at home."

We were moved to compassion.   "Poor Viennese, what do they do without you?   And—horrid thought—what will the Metropolitan be when you go off on your concert tour!"

"Oh!"   She disposed of this lightly.   "Nothing is so good as to be missed.   It is better, *nicht,* to

have people wish that you would stay than want
you to go?"

Just in case there might be a hint of personal ap-
plication in this remark, we rose hastily and gathered up wraps, relentlessly smothering a dozen questions yet unasked. The singer rose too, and shook
hands warmly, then had a sudden thought and van-
ished through an inner door, to return in a moment
with a bunch of great double white violets. "For
you—a present," she said. *"Auf wiedersehen!"*

Another handclasp, and the Dragon had ushered
us from the presence. We are out in the dull,
prosaic world again, but holding white flowers. Regarding them and inhaling their fragrance, it occurred to us that, could their loveliness only be
caught and imprisoned on a printed page, this article
could well be left unwritten.

However, it would scarcely seem fair to any
artist to let her portrait hang upon so frail a thread
as the scent of a white violet. Real achievements
in her brief past and her glowing present shoulder
their way into the foreground insistently, as one
sits down in the hotel writing-room to secure impressions safely on paper before they fade, after
their annoying habit, into generalities. The orchestra in the dining-room, with an uncanny and
very obliging instinct to be helpful, is beginning to
play something from *Tosca,* and recalls to mind that
astonishing evening three years ago when Maria

Jeritza, new to us and almost unheralded, gave such a startling performance of this well-worn rôle that a note of real tragedy suddenly struck sharply through the lurid melodrama. The audience, at the end of the second act, rose from their chairs in a wave of hysterical enthusiasm which the late Mr. Krehbiel, who never exaggerated, described as "not applause, but an emotional tumult, like an avalanche which swept thousands into a frenzied demonstration." So she awoke next morning to find herself famous, and before her first season was out, she was securely, if somewhat dizzily, established upon the throne so lately left vacant by the incomparable Caruso. Since then she has gone on steadily adding one shining portrait after another to our operatic gallery. Sieglinde, Elizabeth, and Elsa, those most tender and appealing women of Wagner's creation, and in apposition to their frail purity, Santuzza the swarthy and lachrymose, Thaïs, the Alexandrian courtesan, Sardou's imprudent Fedora, and only lately a newcomer, the lovely and sorrowful Jenufa of the entrancing Moravian costumes. It is Tosca, however, for which the public clamors. Charities have grown rich on benefit performances. There is never a vacant seat in the house an hour after the opera is placed on the bills.

And only fourteen years ago, a tall, slender girl, still in her teens, was making a humble but auspicious début as Elsa, in the remote and obscure little city of Olmütz, in Austria. Soon, however, the sound

of that strong, lovely young voice, the fame of her
beauty and vivid talent, reached the proper ears in
Vienna, and another year saw her a member of the
Volksoper in that enlivening city.   There she began,
with great earnestness and intelligence, to study
and master a quite overwhelming number of rôles,
in which her astonishing versatility and the flame of
her developing genius made her, before very long,
the absolute idol of her audiences.

Those were the gay, happy pre-war days, and
the old Emperor was alive and still taking his summer "refreshment" at Ischl in the Salzkammergut.
Jeritza was making a guest appearance there one
year when he dropped in for a performance.   He
was completely charmed with her, and lost no time
at all in suggesting to the proper authorities that
she be straightway annexed for the Court Opera,
inquiring plaintively, "Why do you only engage such
artists as are already beginning to grow old and
fat, when there is anything so youthful and lovely
as this about?"

So, at the Emperor's "suggestion," Jeritza went
to join the forces of what was then the Imperial
Opera, where she made her début, most suitably, as
Aphrodite.   And there she stayed, her art unfolding
year by year before the ravished eyes and ears of
her adoring public, reigning on securely even when
crowns and courts were swept away.

Nineteen-fourteen marked an important year for
her, as for the rest of the world.   In the first place,

at the Lido one day in early summer she decided to add to her stage romances a private one of her own, and promised to become the Baronin Popper; but that is, our national publicity to the contrary, her own affair. What concerns us more nearly is the fact that in that very same week she met and talked with our own Mr. Gatti-Casazza about coming to America. However, the wise and zealous young fiancé thought the time was not ripe, and she not yet in the fullest possession of her powers, and sternly exercised his prerogative to keep her at home. A few months later his instincts were justified by the cataclysm which shook the world, sent him to the trenches, and left Jeritza, one war bride among many, to her mission of cheering as best she could the people of her dear and stricken city.

Nevertheless, when peace conditions made it possible, Mr. Gatti showed his excellent memory and tenacious purpose by putting through his contract at last, so that now she is ours—at least by adoption and grace.

"I have lived for Art, I have lived for Love!" (The violin in the dining-room is sobbing, with Tosca) . . .

"Never have I hurt a living soul———"

CHAPTER VI

THE "CHORUS LADY"

IN order to hear the truth about a person, talk to his valet; to learn of his shortcomings, eavesdrop upon a group of his friends; but to know his virtues, those especial qualities which make him a picturesque and adorable figure above the rest of his fellows, go to his mother.

Therefore, really to appreciate the opera chorus, we must spend an hour with Mother Savage. Her title, of which she is exceedingly proud, does not necessarily imply age, but a rare endowment of understanding, sympathy, and authority, combined with wide experience. Jean de Reszke, twice her years, first called her "Maman"; and artists, chorus, ballet, and all the rest, have affectionately followed his example. Her two lovely daughters, and her son, a war cripple, have had to share her with the whole opera house ever since they can remember. She is "only" a member of the chorus, with no more privileges or opportunities than any of the other hundred and nineteen of her colleagues; but because she is, in her humble capacity, a true artist, with all of the sincerity, enthusiasm, intelligence, and spontaneity which the word implies, plus a striking stage presence, she has become quite as notable a figure in the local opera world as some of the soloists whose salaries delight the revenue officers.

Patrician ladies of advancing years are her specialty, although sometimes she slides down the social scale to become a beggar, a shopkeeper, or some one of those unpleasant old hags who populate the peasant operas. Lately, however, in *Jenufa* she blossomed forth so young and kittenish in her abbreviated skirts that they called her, in the dressing-room, Baby Peggy.

She is an adept at make-up, and has an appetite for realism, stopping at nothing. There is one thing, however, which has always given her pause, and that is her inability to smoke without immediate and embarrassing prostration. Thus you will not see her in the chorus of cigarette girls of *Carmen's* first act, but will discover her in the rear, engaged in selling *papier-mâché* pumpkins. In a certain opera, put on a few seasons ago, she was offered the character bit of an old gypsy addicted to her pipe. This might seem an insuperable obstacle, in view of her notorious weakness, but, true artist as she is, she was keen for the part and refused to be vanquished by physical qualms. One or two puffs found her inevitably stretched out in the wings, but she persevered, and every one watching her valiant behavior became greatly concerned. The property man offered her corn-silk, incense, and a variety of smoke-producing ingredients, all in vain; and Caruso sent her some of his finest tobacco, specially imported, with no better result. Finally she went in despair to a noted tobacconist with her problem, and he solved it once and for all by giving her a little bag of an extremely well-known and rather despised brand, which she smoked then and ever since without further distress. It seems incredible that she can have overlooked the advertising value of such a testimonial for the manufacturers; but such is the truth—tobacco and everything else in her life are interesting only in ratio to their usefulness at the opera, and no outside world exists at all for her. The utmost she will accord this gentle brand of the noxious weed is to keep a little sack of it—together with the historic pipe—on her living-room table as "Exhibit A," appropriately reposing in a pewter bowl, given her by a venerable and "real" gypsy.

Speaking of exhibits, she is a veritable walking museum when costumed as one of the aristocratic guests in *André Chenier*. She displays a photograph in this rôle with pardonable pride, and points out so many gifts and souvenirs upon her person that they are almost impossible to catalogue from memory. Geraldine Farrar's wig, a ring of Caruso's, pearls and a pin from Nellie Melba, and a fan given her by Sybil Sanderson, are a few of the treasures. The next time one attends this opera it would be quite worthwhile focusing the glasses upon that tall, bedizened Countess who stands out with much impressive dignity among the other guests, and study her decorations. The walls of her home are literally papered with portraits of all of the great stars who ever illumined musical skies. Geraldine Farrar and Caruso have corners all their own, and only the ingenuity of real friendship could have conceived the variety of affectionate sentiments which they have inscribed athwart their decorative diaphragms. In a painted wooden box of suspiciously "property" origin, are letters and cards of a flatteringly personal nature from many of those famous artists who are no longer with us because, as the sentimental balladist explains, "God needed more angels in heaven."

Mother Savage could talk all day about the stars who have crossed her path: they are her great enthusiasm; but even their luster does not dim the glamour of her own work. The opera is her world, won through blood and tears; for when, as a very young girl in Belgium, she manifested a talent and a desire for the lyric stage and pursued her avocation to the extent of obtaining an engagement, she came home from her first night's performance to find the parental door bolted against her, and herself an outcast in the streets. This did not daunt her, although it cut the first lines of sadness about her mouth. She stuck to her profession, against odds which exist nowhere to-day unless possibly in some parts of provincial France.

The reason for her family's vigorous action was that few opera singers at that time were able for very long to maintain their reputations inviolate. They were paid a minimum wage, out of which

all of them, down to the least member of the
company, were required to provide all their own
costumes. As this was an utter impossibility, most of
them, in order to continue their careers, resorted to
the Easiest Way. A young girl joining their ranks
was, according to popular belief, as good as damned.
But the little Marie was of sterner stuff, and when
she heard that even choristers were well paid and actually respected at a place called Covent Garden, in
London, she borrowed enough money for the journey, applied for a position, and because of her looks,
her enthusiasm, and her proficiency in languages, got
it Those were the days when Jean de Reszke had
just persuaded the management to introduce the
novelty of operas sung in the languages in which
they were written, so the girl very soon acquired a
varied and unusual repertoire. She remained there
twenty-five years, only leaving permanently for New
York with the beginning of the War, although she
had already sung here for seven winter seasons. She
married an Englishman, but her children have grown
up here, while she herself remains fiercely and
staunchly Belgian. In England she sang minor
rôles upon occasion, but as she says: "Once in the
chorus, always a chorister," and she has gone back
to her first love with unmitigated enthusiasm.

We have quoted her story at length, not only because it is hers and that of an interesting personality,
but because it is fairly typical of a majority of the
members of that admirable and hard-working body

without which opera would lose much of its vivid appeal. Of course they are not all such outstanding figures as Marie Savage, but they are a passionately earnest group, with a fine feeling for the importance of their work. Most of them have exceptionally good voices, with a prodigiously developed sense of pitch and rhythm, and their vocabularies are astonishing. They know so many words that they find it difficult to indulge in ordinary conversation without almost unconscious quotation from some libretto. As for repertoire, a group of them were trying, one night during a "pause," to count up, but grew tired and lost track after reaching one hundred and ten. Most of these are letter-perfect somewhere in the cubbyholes of their brains, with all the accompanying complexities of musical and dramatic directions. Forty or fifty of the current operas, however, are always "on tap," ready to produce at a moment's notice; for although there are a plentiful amount of rehearsals, once in a while some catastrophe requires a change of bill without warning, and woe to the chorister who does not rise serene and equipped for the emergency.

They do not, in spite of performances every night of the week including Sunday, and a liberal sprinkling of extra matinées, consider themselves overworked, and the daily two hours of rehearsing, both vocal, and dramatic, seems to them quite inconsiderable. The average salary is $50 a week, with time-and-a-half for overtime, a perfect bonanza which

"the Union" has obtained for them, as against the
$18 of a few years ago, and the unlimited working
hours. And yet some of them resent this benevolent organization, and consider that it discredits
their standing as "artists."

The majority are still foreigners, although, as the
result of much propaganda, Americans are increasing in the ranks. "They are fine, too," says Maman
Savage, "with lovely voices, but they will *not stick
at it*." Our national traits of impatience and restlessness have never been the stuff with which to foster
a passion for routine and grind; we do not love
work for work's sake, and this latter quality is essential for a good chorister. With them the chorus
must not be a stepping-stone, a means to an end,
but in itself an utterly desirable consummation; they
must, like Marie Savage, prefer being just what they
are over and above any other possible career which
life can offer. But unfortunately, even among the
Italians and Germans (of which the chorus is two-
thirds composed) this old-fashioned spirit of devotion is beginning lately to give place to a commercial
attitude.

It is a strange fact that, careful and thorough as
are the rehearsals, it never seems to occur to the directors to tell them the stories of the operas in which
they play such important parts. It is sufficient for
them to know what emotions to express during their
scenes, without knowing why. The serious artists
among them usually buy books and scores, to pro-

mote their own understanding, but the majority wait until the morning after the first performance and read the newspapers to discover just what it is all about. It is the same with their costumes. The average choristers take what is given them, adjusting it after their personal taste as becomingly as possible, but some few study the period and add interesting and picturesque touches when they can, never hesitating to sacrifice their comeliness, if necessary. They are carefully drilled by the stage manager and his assistants in every bit of action, both concerted and individual; it is so firmly hammered, riveted, and fixed in their minds that they could no more sit down upon a measure where they are supposed to stand up, than the earth could fly from its course. This would not seem to leave much scope for original or spontaneous "business," but it will quite repay one to observe them carefully during dramatic moments. Personality will not be downed, and often their pantomime is delightfully ingenious and amusing. One quality which they all have in abundance is vigor, and their stock emotions—overworked, tried and true—are indignation, wonder, pity, and jubilation. They can register any of these with the wink of an eye; but some, our Maman Savage conspicuous among them, achieve it all with a difference.

To resume the subject of nationality. Americans have a wonderful opportunity to take up this "so fascinating career." In connection with the

Metropolitan there is a chorus school where ambitious youth may learn the first steps along the road, and have a chance to practice them upon the greatest stage in the world. A gifted gentleman, who combines within himself the contradictory qualities of ardent zeal and fierce energy with infinite patience, Signor Eduardo Petri by name, carries this whole undertaking upon his capable shoulders. A visit to one of his evening classes is an enlivening experience.

Sitting languidly about on the wooden chairs, chewing gum, or exchanging the airy persiflage indigenous to this particular stratum of New York, they do not inspire one as a particularly promising group of serious thinkers. However, let Maestro Petri raise his baton, and they are transformed, galvanized. He beats his poor music-desk with such force that he has had it bound with zinc to save it from annihilation, but that metallic stroke accomplishes extraordinary feats. Any one who has had experience with young people's choruses, or any kind, for that matter, within the realms of the amateur, knows the difficulties attendant upon attack and conclusion. Three or four notes will be sung before half of the voices are sufficiently awake to take up their parts, and these same ones will inevitably murmur amiably on a full second or two after the final beat. But there is nothing like that here, and we realize with renewed conviction the vast gulf which separates the professional from the outsider.

When Petri raises his baton, every eye is upon it, every brain alert. The attack is as prompt and abrupt as the firing of a gun, and the finale stops when it stops. No laggards are here, no happy trailers. Crimson faced, and perspiring from his windmill exertions, the instructor alternately mops his brow and punishes his innocent desk. Blazing with rage at a wrong note, caustic in his personal comments, and rapacious in his appetite for "Going over it all again from the beginning," he nevertheless holds all those young people in the hollow of his hand, and the enthusiasm of their response is overwhelming. Their attitude of ennui and sophistication drops from them like a cloak, and they fling themselves so whole-heartedly into their musical efforts that faces become tense, and brows knitted in anxious concentration.

Occasionally a great day comes when Chorus Master Setti, of the opera, needs an augmented chorus, and then these pupils are allowed the joys of costumes and footlights; but, for the greater part, their education is a succession of grind and performance in the bare and dingy studio. They are mostly working girls and boys, and so the classes must be in the evening, but the attendance rarely falls off. They learn all the principal operas in the original languages, and after the first lesson or two are not allowed to use their books. When they graduate they have already an enviable repertoire; but, although the Metropolitan provides all this bounty gratis, it does not draw upon the school exclusively for its choristers. It may, in fact, have the pick of the whole world, for engagement there is the ultimate ambition of every one connected with opera, from impresario to scene-painter, and trained and seasoned choristers come clamoring in great profusion. However, when a vacancy does occur, the school is given the preference. Other graduates are adorning popular musical comedies or important choirs, and some pursue their ambitions to the ranks of soloists, but most of them have their hopes firmly fixed where they were from the beginning. To wear seven or eight different and colorful costumes per week, to mingle with the great, and breathe the intoxicating *Bühnenluft,* or stage-breath, to strut, and sway, and tunefully clamor—it is their one desire.

The members of the chorus are always greatly affected by the performances of the stars. One artist, singing with sincerity and inspiration, can lift a whole stageful of lesser folk, and change the atmosphere of an entire act. On the other hand, a second-rate or slovenly principal can deaden the efforts of every one singing with him. To appreciate this phenomenon fully, we must go back and listen to more of what Marie Savage has to tell us.

She is more keenly sensitive, perhaps, than most of them, being, as she is, "mother" to so many, but she insists that when an artist is nervous or uncertain, the feeling is instantly communicated to the

others on the stage. When Martinelli came back
for his first performance after a serious illness which
kept him away for most of the season, he was naturally keyed up to a high pitch. Perspiration poured
from his face, and his hands, as he grasped others
in greeting, were cold and shaking. When it came
time for him to sing the famous "Ridi, Pagliaccio,"
the anxious Marie, forbidden with the rest of the
chorus to stand in the wings, stole out unobserved
upon a lofty fly to hear him; and when it was all
over, and the big audience in a tumult of appreciation, she ran back to the dressing-room and burst
into a storm of tears from grateful relief.

There is another memory of hers connected with
this same tenor. When Caruso was first singing
Samson, he had, as always, some difficulty with his
French diction, and as Savage is, on the side, a
teacher of that language, one of his mistakes greatly
upset her. In the first act, just before the inspired
Samson rallies the discouraged Hebrews, he exclaims
that he sees a fiery sword in the hand of angels!
But he pronounced it thus, "Je vois dans les mains
des *inges!*" which, with the lyrical elision, sounded
very much like "des singes." Mother Savage at
last drew him aside and gently pointed out to him
the striking difference between "anges" (angels)
and "singes" (monkeys). Caruso was horror-
stricken, and implored her to help him. Every time
that the moment drew near, however, he grew pan-
icky and could not remember which pronunciation

was the right one. At last he formed the habit of maneuvering until he was just beside her, and in plausible gestures of exhortation, would grip her shoulder sharply just in time for her to prompt him with the right accent. It became one of her most valued duties.

Then he died, and for a while this opera which he had made so much his own, was not continued. Eventually, however, Martinelli was put in the rôle and, saddened with memories, a performance was given. All through the rehearsals every one's thoughts had been, not with the excellent artist on the stage, but with their departed idol; and the evening proved a very tremulous and difficult affair for every one concerned, for it began strangely enough. As the first act drew to a close, and the moment for the "angels hands" approached, Marie Savage felt that she could scarcely bear it. Martinelli, never having had difficulties with the famous phrase, was not near her, but as he sang the words, suddenly, standing alone as she was, she felt the quick, fiery grip upon her shoulder, just as it had always been. Illusion, or spirit, or overwrought nerves, whatever it was, she staggered into the wings white and shaken, trembling like a leaf, and relating the incident to her colleagues, injected into the performance an atmosphere of excitement and exaltation which has seldom been equaled.

Her psychic powers stood her in good stead at another time. After becoming accustomed to the ideal Lohengrin of Jean de Reszke, and the Elsa of Melba and Nordica, she found it very hard to bear when a second-rate, bleating tenor and a simpering soprano from nowhere were given the rôles one season in London. At the first performance she said to herself, "Now I am in for a horrible evening!" but as the music swept up to her over the footlights it wove a magic spell, and she heard, instead of the inferior performance on the stage, the voices of the old days, and felt the waves of that remarkable glamour which they created. She was quite happy, and, when the other members of the chorus complained at the end of the performance of the suffering they had undergone, she looked at them in amazement. "It has been the most wonderful evening of my life!" she exclaimed.

Such illusions are rare, however. Very different was a certain night when Adelina Patti was singing in *Traviata*. It was a gala performance, with the King and many of the royal family in their boxes, and Patti had loaded herself with the entire collection of her famous diamonds. She glittered like a pawnshop window, and detectives were placed in all the wings, while the chorus was warned not to go near her upon the stage. Quite naturally and rightly they resented this, as an implication that they might, in a moment of cupidity, attempt to rob her. Therefore they slyly contrived a way in which to retaliate in kind. Their first opportunity came at the end of the scene where she is supposed to swoon

in the arms of her friends. Instead of hastening
toward her and catching her, the chorus cleared a
semicircle about her and leaned the other way in
abhorrence. The stage manager protested vio-
lently, but they only answered that they were but
following instructions; and in the last act, Savage,
who was singing a minor rôle, and whose supporting
arms should have eased the heroine's demise, calmly
walked to a safe distance and in utmost aloofness
contemplated the end. So Patti's brilliant performance was ruined, and the audience, mystified although greatly entertained, laughed immoderately.
Patti does not seem to have been much loved by her
confrères, perhaps because she had an endearing
little habit of spitting in the face of any one she
happened to dislike.

Melba, however, was the darling of all her associates. It seems that she was extremely generous,
but in a modest way. There never was a relief
fund of any kind raised behind the scenes that she
did not augment to a prodigious amount, but not
in the ostentatious manner of some stars. "How
much more do you need, Marie?" she would ask
quietly.

"About fifty pounds, Madame."

"Well, then put me down for *two*." It was her
idea that the small amount opposite her name might
encourage others to give who could not afford more.
"Then, when you have been to every one, come back
to me, and I will make up the difference."

Her charity extended farther than that, however, even to the giving of herself. Upon a certain occasion a young soprano was to make her début in Covent Garden in the same cast with Melba. To celebrate the event, she had, in her inexperience, allowed her friends to fête her *before* the performance, and came upon the stage shockingly the worse for much festive champagne. It was a horrible evening, the sufferings of her fellow-artists as they watched her staggering and stumbling through her part were indescribable. Somehow she managed to finish and leave the house; but Melba, realizing that if something were not done, that girl's career had ended then and there, sent for all the representatives of the press to come to her dressing-room. There she explained to them, slowly and distinctly, that Mademoiselle X had been *taken suddenly ill before the performance* and had only just managed to get through with admirable courage and fortitude. Fixing them all with a determined eye, the great diva then said, "If you gentlemen will agree to say nothing whatever in your columns about this wretched affair, I will promise to sing you a benefit performance of anything you may choose for your pet charity!"

They accepted her terms to a man, and the story never leaked out officially. The young singer, ashamed and remorseful, came back with devoted determination, and has had an honored career, while the Endowment Fund for Indigent Reporters, or some such noble cause, was the pleased and surprised beneficiary of a goodly sum, the result of a most brilliant concert which Nellie Melba gave, unexplained, in the midst of her most strenuous season.

"I have one special distinction," interpolates Mrs. Savage. "I am the only person who ever dared tell Melba when she sang badly. To be sure, I didn't have to do it often, for never was there a voice or technique like hers, but sometimes when she asked me, 'Marie, how was it?' I would say 'R-r-rotten!'"

The chorus loves an artist who flings himself whole-souled into his work, dying a thousand deaths, or riding on wings of mad exultation, as the case may be, making mistakes perhaps, but making them in the exuberance of complete immolation. When this dramatic fervor is wedded to musicianship and a God-given voice, that artist becomes for them an adored favorite whose cause they will uphold and whose battles they will fight, against all comers. Thus when Geraldine Farrar, the ebullient delight of their hearts, took herself away from the Metropolitan for reasons best known to herself, there was weeping and gnashing of teeth; and Maria Jeritza, her successor and so-called rival, did not have an easy time of it with the loyal retainers behind the scenes. Trying very hard to be gracious and friendly to every one, it was an uphill fight. The public swarmed and clamored long before the indifference of her associates was conquered. But the second year her sweetness and friendliness had their reward. Marie Savage impersonated Jeritza's "corpse" in *Tannhäuser,* a distinct mark of favor, and at her farewell for the season there were fond embraces.

Another singer who is regrettably no longer upon the stage was regarded by the chorus with a deep affection which amounted almost to reverence. This was Olive Fremstad, the beautiful Scandinavian who made Wagner's goddesses plausible and his humans almost divine. Toscanini said she was the finest musician who had ever trod the local boards, and "Props" states freely that in all his thirty-five years' experience he has never seen so true an artist; so the chorus would seem to be justified. Her operatic farewell was made as Elsa, and after the Bridal scene all the company stood about to watch her acknowledge the thunderous tributes of her audience, and listen to her deeply moving and rather extraordinary little valedictory. At the beginning of the act, Marie Savage had presented her, in the name of the chorus, with a heavy rope of large Roman pearls, which she received with emotion and wore upon the scene under her wedding veil. Now, as she waved farewell again and again, one of her impulsive gestures caught and snapped the chain and a shower of pearls rained upon the stage. It was a disturbing omen for any one who might be superstitious. "Pearls are tears!" breathed the singer in dismay, clutching at the broken strand. But Maman Savage saved the day, as usual, with the most delicate tact and appeal. "Dear Madame, do not be distressed; they are but the tears of the chorus falling, because you go away!"

Another farewell, in another Wagnerian opera, was marked by no such charming sentiment, and was as spirited an encounter as one may read of in all the annals of the late War. Things were becoming more or less strained in the polyglot world of opera, as the big struggle swept country after country into havoc. Italians gave Austrians cold shoulders and black looks where once had been jovial *camaraderie,* while French and Germans spoke not as they passed by. Lorn and lone representative of valiant Belgium stood Marie Savage. She never went anywhere, even upon the stage, without wearing a little brooch made in the image of her country's flag.

One night *Tannhäuser* was being sung, and just before the opening of the second act the singer who was the Wolfram of the evening and a radical Teuton chanced upon La Savage in the wings. He had just read and gloated over the latest *communiqué* from the front.

"Aha, my good Marie, your country is now Germany!" he boasted.

Maman turned upon him, for perhaps the only time in her life justifying her family name.

"Never!" she cried. "We shall yet live to see the day when all the world will bow in respect to little Belgium!"

In her vehemence she turned about and beheld the Elizabeth, a famous prima donna from Berlin, regarding her with eyes of steel. But the incident was not finished. For many years Maman Savage has always impersonated that elderly and dignified Countess whose arrival at the Song Festival, Elizabeth (according to traditional stage directions) honors by leaving her place at her uncle's side and personally escorting to her seat. Savage advanced as usual, but Elizabeth budged not an inch. Bewildered for a moment, the chorister looked for advice to the director in the wings. "Go on!" he motioned; and she obeyed, but not to her place among the others. Suddenly she knew what to do. The hostess of the Wartburg was required to bow her acknowledgment of each guest's greeting. The aged Countess therefore walked straight toward the footlights, and pausing just in front of Elizabeth, lifted high her hand in what seemed but an exaggerated gesture of salutation. In her fingers, however, she held tightly her little Belgian flag, and the proud Teuton, all unknowing, bent her head before it.

"A silly thing to do, of which I have been ashamed," says Maman Savage; but her eyes do not look conciliatory.

Added to the charms of adventure and excitement and hard work, the chorus has its moments of companionable relaxation. Remembering, perhaps, that *Tannhäuser* experience, but more poignantly her own and other women's sons who still suffer from the effects of the War, Maman's latest motherly act has been to institute, during the progress of the longest and most difficult of the operas, a sort of tea-party in the big dressing-room, where the chorus provide for each other, and all the workers behind the scenes who wish to avail themselves of refreshment—cakes, hot tea, coffee, and sandwiches—all for a price, whatever you choose to give, for the Blinded Soldiers. It promotes not only the relief of these sufferers, but good fellowship, unselfishness, and smoothed-out nerves for her large and obstreperous "family." Certainly the first obligation of a mother.

CHAPTER VII

RAGS AND TAGS AND VELVET GOWNS

EVERY little girl who delights in the process of dressing her dolls should pray the dear Lord to make her a Wardrobe Mistress when she grows up, for here is either the most imaginative and beguiling of occupations, or else the most colossal and nerve-racking of "jobs."

To hold this position with an institution like the Metropolitan or the Chicago Opera Company is much more important than it sounds. The Europeans, especially in the great municipal houses of Germany and Austria, consider necessary a special research department, under a "Professor-of-the-Arts-in-charge-of-Costumes," but in America the burden is calmly placed upon one woman. The qualities necessary for such a responsibility are varied. She must be a bundle of nerves without being nervous; she must be systematic and orderly, yet capable of leading her daily existence amid apparent confusion; she must be a skilled dressmaker, yet too clever to wield a needle often herself; she must speak three or four languages; must have originality, yet absorb the ideas of others with readiness and submission; must possess a passion for detail, yet see things only as a whole; and above all must be able to be in two places at once.   As you may perhaps deduce, the applicants do not come in hordes.   One should really arrange to be born in the opera house if possible, in order to begin the necessary training early enough in life.

And the women who have arrived—what are they like, and what do they do?   The best way to find out is to stalk them in the fastnesses of the great storehouses where they hide.

It is five-thirty, and the end of a busy day, yet Madame Castel-Bert of the Metropolitan is as calm and unruffled, as neat and serene, as if she were just starting for church on a spring morning.   She leads us through a forest of racks upon which hang garments of every tribe and nation, and sits down on a bench beside the window.   She is rather deprecatory.   It seems odd to her that there should be anything that people might like to read about in her work-a-day world.   She is utterly unconscious of the romance hanging on a hook just over her head, where the cloak of a bygone Delilah is waiting to be made over for a super.

"I am *not* a designer!" she proclaims at once, just in case one might think her too clever, but then she proceeds to explain that when a new opera is put on or an old one re-costumed, sketches in color are sent in by the artist who has been engaged for the production.   There is a separate plan for each soloist and for some character parts in the chorus, but for the remainder, and for the ballet and supers, there is only one for each type; for example, man-at-arms, page, lady-in-waiting, or peasant—perhaps twenty all told. The chorus numbers one hundred and twenty, and the ballet almost as many more. What then does this wardrobe mistress who is *not a designer* do for the rest? Why only this—it is simple enough. She goes to her historical albums, or even to the public library, and from what she discovers of the period, she devises variations of the original plates sufficient for all her needs. All the color combinations, the choice of materials, the patterns of embroideries and brocade, are hers. That, however, is only the beginning. Once everything is gathered together, the fun starts.

All the artists are permitted to have their costumes made upon the premises if they wish, but they are not required to do so, and several of them, particularly the more prominent of the female stars—as we shall see later on—bring theirs from abroad. This is all very well; it makes less work for the Wardrobe Mistress. But does it? Recently, at the dress rehearsal of *Tannhäuser,* Jeritza, gowned in all her appropriate finery for the Tournament of Song, came face to face with one of the chief choristers costumed almost identically. Quite naturally the star saw no occasion for making any changes in her own dress, but the wardrobe department had to make a forced march and supply that chorister with a complete new outfit before the day after to-morrow. When a novelty is to be produced, Madame

Castel-Bert very prudently, before she even begins work, gets in touch with those soloists who have private costumes, and ascertains, if possible, the general color and pattern, so that she will not, for example, clothe Brangäne in the same, or a conflicting, shade to that which Isolde has elected to wear.

Another harassment is the horrible thing that the footlights do to her most carefully thought-out color schemes. She used to lose much sleep, and agonize greatly over the problem. Bales of material were taken over to the stage for their own little rehearsal, but now she calmly lets the matter alone. If the lights change one color, they change all that are on the stage at the same time, and their relations to each other remain so nearly the same that she has given up worrying—although the public may mistake her roses for violets.

Contrary to the opinion of most laymen, every costume used in an opera is fitted and made for the individual who wears it, excepting always the supers —who are the lowest form of operatic life. Think of the number of fittings you require for an ordinary gown, then multiply them by the number of the opera personnel, by the number of operas produced, and again by the number of scenes in those operas, and you will have a fair idea of what the Wardrobe Mistress and her twenty-two seamstresses are up against in this respect alone. And she cannot say, either, "Come at ten!" or "Half-past two!" She must adapt her time and opportunities to such moments as those fiercely zealous and jealous conductors, stage managers, ballet masters, chorus directors, and so forth, do not claim.

Everything the soloists and important choristers wear is real, with the exception of their jewelry. Velvet is of silk, satin is of the heaviest quality, and not all the fur by any means is pussy-cat. Embroidery and spangling is done as carefully as if the garment were to be worn in a parterre box, and all stitches are stronger and hooks and eyes more durable than any to be met with in the outside world these days. And that is another problem. A garment must be so fashioned that it can be hurriedly and easily donned by a prima donna in a state of nerves, and also, when once on, it must stay on and show no makeshifts. Recently the dignity of a fine individual performance was marred by the inadequate fastening of the contralto's bodice; and one performance of *Tristan* was threatened because the Brangäne, Margarete Ober, was too nervous for the intricacies of her costume, and gave the signal that she was ready long before she actually was. The final fastening of her gown took place upon the stage as the overture was playing its relentless way toward "Curtain," with Ober actually jumping up and down in distress, which symptom was not calculated to help the distracted dresser. Nevertheless, it got done, and nothing terrible happened; but that was because the Wardrobe Mistress, who was herself officiating in this crisis, had *steady* nerves instead of no nerves.

Certain singers, notably one famous Venus, practically construct their costumes each time they sing a rôle. It is then that Castel-Bert, or her understudy, stands apprehensively in the wings, loaded with safety-pins and anxiety, and desperately tries to fix in her mind the way the yards of chiffon or silk "go," against the hour when this costume has again to be designed upon the spot.

In any big production even some of the chorus and ballet wear the "real thing." If the sketches call for, let us say, some brightly colored shawls, the Wardrobe Mistress will sally forth to obscure little shops she knows about and poke around until she finds what she wants. She will then buy perhaps a dozen, but not more, for all such importations are expensive. Armed with these, she returns to her warehouse, and seeks her painters and stencilers. For every real shawl there will be six imitations or even ten, at one-half the cost, and the audience never knows the difference, although there are some heart-burnings among the choristers. These painters are very clever and can copy almost anything. The only difficulty with paint and the sparkling glue, which is sometimes used instead of real spangles, is that they defeat their own economical purpose in the end, and rot the material beyond repair. A costume will last, fresh and presentable, for about five years. This may seem a long life, but we are reminded that this is less than fifty performances all told.   Rarely are they used for two operas, with the possible exception of a few where period and setting are almost identical as in *Lohengrin* and *Tannhäuser,* or *Rigoletto* and *Les Huguenots.*

With enough garments to clothe the population of a fair-sized town, and accessories to stagger the adding-machine, one wonders how they are catalogued and filed.   All costumes not in actual use are kept in the warehouse, where is also everything pertaining to productions in preparation.   This includes shoes, for there is a complete cobbler's shop on the premises, where two hard-working little men may indulge their fancy in soaring flights.   There is small monotony at a bench which mends red Russian boots one day, and constructs Japanese sandals the next.

The costumes for all the current productions, about forty or fifty, are kept at the theater itself in great closets marked with the name of the opera and the number of changes.   Each hangs upon its own particular hook, complete in every detail down to hosiery and gloves, and that hook is numbered to correspond with a certain chorister's hook in the big dressing-rooms.   On the day of the performance the dressers merely take them out and transfer them from the hook in the closet to the hook in the dressing-room.

Nothing complicated about that at all, it would seem.   But there are a dozen hateful mishaps which may occur on the other end.   There is many a slip, alas, between the time a chorister or dancer takes off the dress, tights, ruff, and so forth—to be gathered up, mended, sent to the laundry or cleaner—and the serene hour when all goes back complete again and in order into the closet.

The artists' costumes are not hung in the general cupboards, but each has appropriately an exclusive compartment of its own, with the names of the various rôles, instead of mere numbers, over the hooks. When a singer has his or her own costumes, they are usually given over at the beginning of the season to the Wardrobe to care for, although some stars give themselves and their maids a great deal of exertion by taking everything home with them each time.   One explanation of this strenuous measure is that some of them have been at great pains and trouble to find original ideas and designs, and so elated are they that they wish to keep them all to themselves, and are fancifully apprehensive that the Wardrobe Mistress, *having nothing much to do,* will, in some of her *spare time,* take off a paper pattern of their property.   Others just naturally like to have their possessions about them.

Laundry and dry-cleaning are about the only activities that are not performed upon the premises. The dressers, of whom there are two for every type of performer to be dressed, have learned the intricacies of every one's individual foibles, and rarely make a mistake with even a stick of grease paint they

lay out. Prime donne having maids are the least of
their worries; but they are in the minority, and the
dresser's life would seem to be a harried one at best.
She must know and remember just which goes on
before what, and the exact angle of a feather. She
must have flying fingers—there are quick changes
even on the lyric stage—and patience, and calm, and
still more patience. She must be resourceful to a
degree, and very spry on her toes, and she must be
as reliable as the Bank of England. An artist's
dresser can usually be spotted as a short woman in
a black apron, a little dusty, and wearing magnificent jewels. The singers give their watches, bracelets, and rings into her keeping while on the stage,
and she strings them upon her person like scalps.
She is usually placid and good-natured, the result of
deep philosophy, but if there is one thing above another she detests, it is toe-tights. To get a nervous
artist into these garments without either a rupture of
tights or temperament is a task for superwomen.

Thus, approximately, is the general clothing of
an opera accomplished; but, as the Wardrobe Mistress admitted a while ago, with a puzzled frown, as
if in her opinion there was no accounting for the
vagaries of opera singers, some artists do actually
prefer to discover, study, select, and, alas, in con-
sequence, pay for, their own costumes! In fact most
of them, especially the women, take a vast and wholly
natural delight in this branch of their art. They
go about it in various ways. Some of them start with

themselves as a premise (it gets to be a habit, this state of mind in your average prima donna) and select first what is becoming, and as a secondary consideration, adapt it to period correctness. Others, especially those trained in Central Europe, go at it the other way around. Jeritza, for instance, talks very seriously and learnedly about the way she attires her characters, and is surprised that we do not give the matter deeper study in this country. In Vienna the apparel of the prima donna is *never* left to individual caprice. . . .

"We wear what we are told to wear, down to the smallest ring upon our fingers—but one does not mind, it is always *right*. Professor Roller is one of the most important men in the opera and a real genius, a great artist, and extremely cultured. His studio in the theater is lined with books rare and valuable. He spends hours in the national galleries. He is insistent that every minutest detail must be absolutely exact. I should no more think of disputing what he told me to wear than arguing with the Almighty about the color of my eyes. When I first sang in Janacek's *Jenufa*, we made together a great study of national dress, and old embroideries and accessories in the museums. Finally the costumes were actually woven and embellished for me by the Moravian peasants themselves, and were presented to me as a gift. They are extremely rich, quaint, and perfect, and are among my greatest treasures. But often, for the sake of accuracy, I am very un-

comfortable. For instance, Elsa's wedding cloak
and crown are so heavy that it exhausts me terribly
to wear them even for an act, but I do so uncom-
plainingly because I know that they are exactly what
a Brabantine noble woman wore in that period and
nothing else would do."

Jeritza is a very beautiful woman, far above the
average in height, and of an arresting blondness.
She can carry off successfully almost any sort of
striking costume, and hers are usually very effective.
However, she and a number of other well-known
artists fail occasionally in a certain subtlety which
comes only from a consideration of what the *character's own taste* would be in the matter. In other
words, few singing actresses say to themselves,
"What would Thaïs, or Tosca, or Isolde, as the
case may be, have selected, knowing her as I do?"
They are far more apt to say, "What did a woman
of her day and locality wear?" and then proceed
to consult, in accordance with this surmise, their
own personal tastes. So we are shown, for instance,
the very illuminating spectacle of how Maria Jeritza
would have dressed had she lived in ancient Alexandria. She falls into this trap less often than most,
however, for no one in the world but the provincial
and sanctimonious medieval Elizabeth would ever
have chosen the virginal satin basque she wears in
Tannhäuser, ACT II. The saints on the portals of
Chartres had just such frocks in their wardrobes.

One famous Wagnerian singer spends her time in

art galleries looking at the smallest details of portraits and statues which can be combined effectively for her rôles. Her secretary accompanies her with pencil and sketch-book. A girdle, a clasp, a sandal, an arrangement of the cloak, even a pose, are copied and adapted. Her beautiful posture as Venus is a replica of a very famous statue in a Florentine gallery, and one of her classic attitudes, assumed only for a lovely fleeting moment, and then gone before the audience has grasped any detail save its grace and "rightness," is copied from a huge canvas in Rome. This singer has now retired, but so strong is her interest, so alive the various women she has created, that she never goes into a gallery or a museum that she does not instinctively seek new clothes and ornaments for them, as if she were a fond mother buying Christmas presents for her daughters: "There is a lovely staff for Tosca!" she will cry eagerly to her companion. Or, "See, those are just the bracelets Kundry should have—or perhaps after all they would suit Salome better!"

And what becomes of all these dolls' clothes when their years of service are ended? The chorus and the ballet waste very little—bits are made over into other bits, discards and misfits are kept for the lowly super, rented to other companies, or sold to the movies. As for those of the artists, one can only imagine. What a glorious attic for grandchildren would be the trunkroom of a venerable prima donna! Mother's and auntie's funny clothes would never be noticed among the intoxications of grand-mother's treasure-chest. Perhaps that is what happens to old costumes on rainy afternoons—it is a whimsically pleasing notion. Little Gloria Caruso, with dear Papa's ruff and sword, and red-heeled boots, could give the nicest kind of a party. But, unfortunately, few but contraltos go in for large families, so much of the proud finery which once trailed in glory or bowed before princes is now peacefully asleep in dark, forgotten storerooms.

It is rumored that in Emma Calvé's little feudal castle of Provence the great singer's costumes were brought to a sort of still-life again. One of the vaulted rooms was peopled by a distinguished gathering of wax figures resplendent in the gay apparel of her great days. They were seldom visited, however, for it made the famous Emma sad to contemplate the irretrievable past; and except for an occasional guest, and sporadic activities of the housekeeper with a feather-duster, they remained undisturbed to enjoy what secret waxen revels they would. Now a recent visitor reports that this engaging *musée* no longer exists.

Geraldine Farrar proved herself a true Yankee when she put her theatrical effects up for auction. She thus accomplished several things at once—she obtained a desirable amount of novel publicity; she gave her numerous admirers an opportunity to acquire mementos of her operatic career; and she did not have to pocket a dead loss when she brought that chapter of her diverting life to a close. But also, before ever the auction took place, she distributed much among her professional colleagues and intimate friends, and kept the most precious bits for her own little chest of souvenirs.

Then there is the matter of the wig, a very important subject we have not touched upon at all. For the men it is an article which comes distinctly under the heading of make-up, but for the women it is really a form of head-dress, and belongs in the realm of costume almost entirely. The audience seems constantly fascinated by the possibility that "it is her own hair," but, sorry as we are to disillusion them, it almost never is. Farrar once tried the experiment of singing Marguerite in her own dark curls, but it so upset tradition and shocked conventional sensibilities that even her bold spirit capitulated and back came the golden plaits. Jeritza, who boasts among her lavish personal endowments as lovely a head of corn-silk hair as one could find among the angels, nevertheless rarely displays it upon the scene; and with the exception of *Tosca*, when in a dramatic moment of ACT II, she "allows" it to tumble down in charming disarray, it is usually hidden away beneath the bleached, dyed and transfigured hirsute product of some Chinaman.

It is a fact, and a slightly distasteful one, that the hair for most theatrical wigs has this oriental origin. It is coarse, more durable, and capable of holding shape and dressing for a longer time. Needless to say, it goes through a process of purification and transformation which satisfies even the prima donna's cautious nature. The average wig is a wonderful piece of workmanship, a system of minute knots and interwoven strands which does credit to unknown, patient fingers; but its arrangement and adjustment have not kept pace with the forward-stepping art of costuming. If you doubt this statement, take up any album of musical celebrities of ten, twenty, thirty years ago, and observe that the hair looks as familiar as the operatic coiffures of 1925, while the clothes, although conforming in detail to historical accuracy almost as carefully as those of to-day (for example, the beautiful things which Emma Eames' first husband, Story, the painter, used to design for her), they are nevertheless remarkably "old-fashioned." Could it be that seamstresses, used to the tight corset and peplum, could not restrain themselves from putting the contemporary cut into everything they touched? Or was it due to the wearers, with their figures "curved in loveliness," and their fixed ideas concerning the waistline which unconsciously affected everything they did? All of which makes us wonder, in the midst of our modern artistic complacency, what a woman's flair may really have been back in the remote centuries; and also—if we are as accurate as we think we are.

The wigs, then, have not changed, and Vienna, the home of the most skilled workmen, is guilty of popularizing the little frizzes and bangs about the temples of every one, from prehistoric Sieglinde to Fedora. And oh! those hateful, precise *ondulations* which cover the back of every one who walks in a Wagner opera! It never seems to occur to either artist or *perruquier* that even if some of these ladies of old were blessed with natural waves, their facilities for combing and brilliantining the same were limited indeed. One longs for an Isolde with the courage and enterprise to wear her famous auburn hair simply parted and falling in heavy strands of an utter straightness; and the remarkable wig of Mélisande, a real masterpiece of the craft, would be so much more plausible if it had not obviously just visited the coiffeur. One well-known singer caused a perfect uproar in Munich because she dared make of the *Walküre* Brünnhilde a vivid young creature whose hair was a wind-blown tangle coming only to her shoulders, and which, after her protracted sleep upon the rock, she represented as having grown long and heavily soft like a cloak. It was a subtly indicated delineation of the transformation in Brünnhilde herself; but the Germans, who deify tradition, rose up and excitedly pawed the air.

The bob is proving a boon to prime donne, for the operatic wig is a warm and uncomfortable affair at best, and when drawn over the tightly braided and bound hair upon the head, it is responsible for many a *migraine*. Contrary to the general impression, however, they rarely worry about its coming off, for they wear beneath it, tight about their brows and pinned to their own hair, a band of coarse net. Into this, in turn, they insert the hairpins which hold the wig; so it is practically immovable, and accidents like the famous one when Scotti, "dead" upon the floor, groped in his agony for a recalcitrant periwig, are quite avoidable. When there are crowns or helmets, or other stiff and uncompromising headgear, to go on top of it, many are the sufferings endured and the wounds inflicted while the things are securely fastened. Long pins are put through holes and out again, and bent much in the manner of a mechanic's cotter-pin, the while the poor artist, bowing the head, tries not to be irritable at the dresser's frantic efforts.

Every opera company has a wig department, in charge of an expert with two or three helpers. He makes, fits, and adjusts all wigs, beards, and whiskers, and sometimes assists in the actual dressing of the male principals. The assistants are detailed to the various classes of artists—one for chorus women, one for men, and another for the *corps de ballet*—and one of these may double on taking care of the stars, who, nevertheless, fondly believe that no one but the *perruquier-in-chief* ever touches their special property.

The room where the work is done is gruesomely reminiscent of an Inquisitional torture chamber. All about are clamps, vises, and horrid instruments of clustered steel spikes quite suitable for scratching a Dissenter. In a corner, irons are heating, while, like an exhibit at the Traitors' Gate, a long row of heads on poles ornaments the foreground.

Most of the stars have their own wigs, selected with the same care and by much the same process as their costumes. A patently blonde Tosca, never at her best in brunette locks, is overjoyed to contemplate the portraits of Titian's Italian ladies, and henceforth wears with a clear artistic conscience an auburn coiffure. Mary Garden explored and experimented a long time before she adopted the cropped wig which makes her Salome unusual. The interpreters of Aïda and Selika wrestle with the problem of a nice compromise between wool and beauty; and Kundry, ACT I, gives up all such ideas and takes to horsehair, remembering the compensations of ACT II and the value of contrasts. Some of the singers' maids take care of their mistresses' wigs, but usually they lack the necessary technique, and most of the wigs are sent to the dresser. One singer, however, has a secretary who, for sheer delight in silky strands and golden curls, has voluntarily taken that duty upon herself. Incidentally she once left one of Isolde's braids on the wrong side of the Atlantic Ocean, and never discovered the omission until two days before an important première. Confronted with a strange city, a strange language, and the complicated necessity for "a braid of a certain color and weight, containing a pliable wire in each strand" to be *secretly* ordered, made, and brought to the dressing-room, she somehow accomplished the impossible. The moment at last arrived when the prima donna was ready to adjust the thing upon her brow. Feeling her own hair rising and probably turning white with anxiety, the secretary watched her doom approach. Finally. . . .

"What have you done to this?" asked Isolde, in what seemed a ferocious manner, through a mouthful of hairpins.

"Absolutely n-n-nothing!" whispered the culprit hoarsely, and with truth, for the strand had only just arrived. "W-w-why?"

"Well, only that it seems better than usual!" announced Isolde.

The secretary swooned.

CHAPTER VIII

IN MARGUERITE'S DRESSING-ROOM

Cast: An opera singer.
　　　 An inquiring visitor.
　　　 A call-boy.
　　　 Another opera singer.
Time: Just before the first act of *Faust.*
Place: An opera house in New York.

The Scene is the most romantic spot in the world,
the dressing-room of Marguerite! It is a charming
apartment, not large, but certainly not small, and
the dingy doorway, marked simply "10" and noth
ing more, gives not the slightest hint of what it hides
behind it. On entering, to L. are mirrors bordered
with electric bulbs, to R. more mirrors, and in C.
again mirrors. The place is alive with them, a
chamber of horrors for any shrinking, self-conscious
individual who might suffer embarrassment at beholding himself thus multiplied and illumined in a
dozen startling and unfamiliar aspects. However,
diffidence is a rare bird in this aviary; stage-folk
learn early to bear with fortitude the sight of their
own reflections, however insistent. C., L. and R.
we have also an easy-chair, a couch, a silken screen,
and two dressing-tables littered with a fascinating
array of bottles, jars, trays, and curious little sticks
of various hues.

These things are to be studied later at leisure, for just at first all details are lost count of in a misty springtime haze which engulfs one with a strange subconscious insistence that we "come down to Kew in lilac-time." May skies, flowering shrubs, and pale hyacinths. But as the vision clears understanding comes. One perceives that the effect is obtained thus: Upon the walls, the furniture, over the window, and upon the floor are coverings, hangings, and drapery profusely and subtly blue—dainty, shimmering, candid, innocent, dangerous baby-blue. Along the molding, tiny organdy ruffles bound with blue ribbon, naïve as a débutante. If Marguerite were to do over her little house in Frankfort, would we not say, knowing her as we do through the kind offices of MM. Barbier, Carré and Gounod, that she would indeed choose only curtains of this identical shade, that her chaise-longue could be of nothing but this very azure taffeta? Absolutely.

Blinding mirrors, blue vapors—and a smell. This last is very important and must never be left out of the set, or ignored, for it is the very essence of intrinsic glamour; a pleasing, whimsical, teasing smell, unforgettable, yet impossible to remember. Dust, grease-paint, powders, mascara, brilliantine, cleaning fluid, hot coffee, oranges, lozenges, and reminiscent ghosts of banished perfumes and flowers. But why dissect it? It is steam from a witch's cauldron, if you like, but prime donne breathe it as their natural element; no dressing-room is complete with-

out it, and it exists nowhere else.   Mirrors, blue
haze, and a pleasing smell.——We are now ready for
the dramatis personæ.

Enter Marguerite: (She is already there, of
course, but she appears suddenly from behind blue
silken screen, L.)   It is she, and it is not.   It is
also Frances Alda, and it is not.   That is the worst
of dressing-rooms: they are a sort of borderland or
Purgatory, if you will, a half-way stop between the
real and the unreal.   Marguerite, gentle village
maiden, would never have been guilty of beading
her lashes to this exuberant length; nor for that matter would Madame Alda, although *she* might use
a lip-stick.   Marguerite is innocently abhorrent of
cosmetics, but inordinately proud of her long plaits;
while Frances Alda would never, never go in for
demure flaxen braids.   Dressed for medieval Germany, looking and behaving like twentieth century
New York.   Who is she?   Which, both or neither?
At any rate, she is strangely fantastic and beguiling.

INQUIRING VISITOR (*Who is quite the reverse*):
How delightful!

MARGUERITE: What is?   Who is?

I. V.: You, of course, and your room.   The whole
thing is exactly as it should be.   Every soprano in a
Main Street choir sees just this in her dreams.

MARGUERITE: There is a lot that she doesn't see,
thank God!   I could tell her a few things.

I. V.: Oh, don't!   Why not let her dream?
Don't you know that a prima donna about to sing

Marguerite to an enormous, waiting audience is the most romantic and lovely figure—nothing can equal her appeal to the imagination. When the girl tries it for herself, it will be time to wake up. Let us enjoy our illusions!

MARGUERITE (*Who is rapidly resolving into* MADAME ALDA): I'll try not to be too upsetting. So you like the room? It is a magic room—it won't be here to-morrow!

I. V.: No?

MADAME ALDA: No. I have this transformation made every time I sing, and for one other artist, who is my very good pal. But between times, *presto,* it disappears! I'm afraid you would not be tempted to rhapsodize about blue hyacinths if you saw the place undressed. I've taken a good deal of trouble about it, on the whole.

I. V.: Just why have you done it? I'm interested. Do you sing better, coming from a pretty room?

MME. A.: Perhaps; but to tell you the truth (she laughs and adjusts the line of her right eyebrow) I'm afraid I'm like the Main Street choir-singer, after all. I think this is the sort of dressing-room a prima donna ought to have. I think so to such an extent that next year I'm going to have the place permanently done over. Panels—pastel coloring— you know. (This is now a third personality speaking, MRS. GATTI, wife of the Director, a lady whom MADAME ALDA and MARGUERITE are both very reticent about exploiting. "Why should I?" she demands with disarming frankness. "What earthly difference does it make in an opera house whose wife I am? I'm here to sing, and that's the only thing that counts. If I sing badly, it isn't going to make it sound any better, being married to Gatti— worse, if anything. If I sing well, it is myself personally who does it. Singing is one of the many things a husband can't do for you.")

I. V.: (*Who is unmarried, brightly*) : How true!

MME. A. (*Studying the position of a curl against her cheek*) : And this is my farewell for the season, too. You didn't know it? No one does, but last week the Press was worked overtime with another singer's good-bys. You see I'm not exactly an *enfant gaté*. I suppose—

(*A knock is heard on "10." "Curtain, Madame!" calls a solicitous voice. Clattering footsteps depart outside.*)

MME. A. (*Opening door and calling*) : How long have I?

ADMONITORY VOICE: Fifteen minutes!

MME. A.: (*Turning to* I. V. *politely*) : Will that be enough?

I. V. (*Effusively*) : Fancy any other singer letting me hang about here at all just before she goes on! I *do* appreciate it. Be sure to turn me out whenever you want to.

MME. A.: Five last minutes for the voice, my

dear, will be enough. Well, I suppose you want me to *talk* about something. What?

I. V.: Well, you've sung for a great many kinds of audiences. That is an interesting subject. And you have been listened to by more thousands at once than any other prima donna except Mademoiselle Bori. Tell me, was it very terrifying—singing on the air?

MME. A.: Dreadful! But not as bad as I expected. I had been thoroughly frightened beforehand, so the reality was less alarming. I did not like the padded, hermetically sealed room, however, in which I was shut up with the microphone. They say they change the air every six minutes, but it didn't seem so. I felt trapped, a sort of submarine feeling. And I had the strangest sensation when I began to sing. I tried to picture all the people listening: farmhouses with little groups around the sitting-room lamp—lighthouse keepers on lonely headlands—sick people in hospitals—and my own family having a party at home and hearing me as if I were right beside them. Then the dead silence at the end, which was so striking because I *felt* the most deafening applause without hearing a sound. It is, of course, a miracle, this radio, and it is very moving to have a part in it. Then the telegrams and letters arriving so soon, and all the new friends! Probably that audience is the most marvelous one in existence. Still, that big, friendly one out there . . . (*Faint applause is heard in the distance as the*

conductor takes up his baton.)   That audience is
my favorite.   It is so unexacting.   No continental
hisses and boos here when we fail, but bravos and
thunder when we please—and applause all the time.
Of course, it probably isn't good for us.   There is
nothing like a little wholesome discrimination and
rebuke to jack one up to new heights.   With so
much kindness we have to watch ourselves for fear
we will just sit down and relax somewhere around
par.

I'm off for a concert tour now, which I don't enjoy so much because I have the uncomfortable conviction that the audience is bored to death.   It is a
very chill and clammy feeling.   They would really
so much enjoy something quite different, but they
must not let themselves demand it, and I must not
let myself give it to them.   A *Lieder-Abend* is the
ultimate in vocal art—so the public has been told.
They listen politely and patter perfunctorily for
Schumann and Schubert and Brahms, or my lovely
Russian things; but how they do warm to the popular group at the end of the program.   I am to give
several concerts in private houses, and this I quite
like, although many artists hate it.   It is really great
fun, for it is all so *intime* and informal and they
don't mind at all asking for what they want.   So I
sing them "Mighty Lak a Rose" and "What'll I
do?" . . . could anything be easier? . . . *Come
in!*

(*It is* MARTHA, MARGUERITE'S *neighbor, in a*

make-up so convincing that it seems impossible that a really charming face hides beneath. She wants to borrow a bit of ochre powder, but beholding the I. V., scents an "interview" and backs out in confusion. "Apologies!" she offers, in two languages, and trails her woolen petticoats rapidly away.)

I. V.: Do you know, *she* has written a book—and most amusing, too!

MME. A.: Oh, dear, everybody's doing it, from you to the property man. I'm going to write some memoirs myself one of these days, and they will be worth reading, too. But not from here, my dear, not by Mrs. Gatti, wife of the Director! It wouldn't do at all. Wait until we've said our good-bys, then I will give something to a waiting world! Twenty years at the Metropolitan, and Nothing but the Truth. What do you think of that?

I. V. (*Thinking hard*): W-well . . . (For Marguerite-Alda-Gatti-Casazza is famous for her directness and candor. Only to-night an important person in the opera said about her: "People like her because she always says when she doesn't like them." Incidentally, this same individual went on to expound, "She is so thoroughly honest, that woman. When she says she'll do a thing, she'll do it, by Jove, and you can depend upon her to the last ditch! Likewise, when she says she won't, she *won't*. But that's a good deal more than can be said of every prima donna.")

MME. A.: But I'll not hurt any one's feelings. I'll not express opinions, just state facts. There *are* a few facts lurking around this opera house from time to time, even if it is the land of make-believe. I've seen some comedies in my day and some tragedies too. It is quite a life, on the whole.

I. V.: Yes . . . yes. . . .

MME. A. (*Now beginning rapidly to fade out to* MARGUERITE, *as she listens to distant notes*): But I love it, even when I plaintively lament. And now run along, for I've got to make sure that I'm in as good voice as I think I am.

(I. V. *scurries away, grateful and somewhat inarticulate. Blue mists close in again over blinding mirrors, and the smell grows pungent.* MARGUERITE *has come,* ALDA *gone, and a strong, happy voice climbs up and down a scale.*)

Epilogue.   Heard in the Lobby.

GENTLEMAN - WHOSE - GLASSES - HAVE - A - BLACK - RIBBON: You know, *there's* a talented, clever woman! She has steered her ship pretty safely through troubled waters—and operatic seas are not easy to navigate, by any means. But her family has always been mixed up in musical diplomacy; it is in her blood. Her grandfather took the first Italian Grand Opera Company out to Australia; and her aunt was—well, a worthy aunt to such a niece—no less a person than Frances Saville, who, some people will remember, was one of the first to sing the rôle of Manon in New York.

GENTLE LISTENER: Heredity is *so* interesting. . . .

GENTLEMAN-W-G-H-A-B-R: A lovely voice and a lovely woman, who does her job without jumping through hoops, that's what!

CHAPTER IX

MAKING FACES

At no time does enchantment owe a greater debt to distance than in the opera house, and fastidious folk who believe that beauty is skin deep had best keep right on sitting in their comfortable orchestra chairs, and not come poking about behind the scenes where they will quickly discover that its depth is a thick and sticky layer of grease-paint.

Encountering Faust in the wings after adoring him from beyond the footlights will be a distinct shock. He may be a handsome man to begin with, but in order to project that beauty to the remotest corner of the house, he must certainly forego the privilege of fascinating those close at hand. His face, strangely stiff, the flesh scaly, and of a sunburned hue, is covered with little shining beads of perspiration, signals of distress from the grease-filled pores. A white line runs down the bridge of a nose which seems to be separating from his face at intervals. His wavy hair is seen to spring not from an Adonis-like forehead, but from a cloth band which very obviously joins his eyebrows with an ugly puttied crack. His little beard has an uninviting look, as though long innocent of the comb; and in the corners of his eyes are oily daubs of carmine.

Strolling beside him is Mephistopheles, who, we must confess, strongly attracted us from the front, but whose face on close inspection is such a lumpy, lined mass of disfigurement that we turn from him in strong distaste, and seek out Marguerite with a hope of better things. But even she is a sorry sight, as blatant as a cheap chromo, a caricature of a masquerading hussy.

This will never do. We perceive that we must approach this matter from quite a different angle if we wish to realize its true values. The artists do not find each other repellent. You, the outsider, with your pale, featureless face, are the misfit. These are painters and sculptors at work, and the wart upon Martha's chin, the subtle pouching of her eyes, are admired by the initiated at their true worth. The make-up box is the keystone of existence here, the trademark of the Guild.

Kathleen Howard, who is young and pleasing to the eye, in spite of most people's conviction to the contrary, explains away your surprise by declaring that as half her life is spent impersonating ugly old women, quite naturally the public identifies her with them. It is a sort of compliment, if one chooses so to regard it. Being a contralto, in the first place, dooms one to a long sentence of nurses, witches, mothers, grandmothers, and a general assortment of more or less disreputable old hags. It never seems to interest a composer to make his heroines ladies with chest tones. Delilah and Carmen are the only possible exceptions, and thus many an ambitious singer has raised her voice by its boot-straps, so to speak, in order to fulfill what she considers her artistic destiny. Happy, however, the opera house which possesses a Howard, or her masculine counterpart, an Angelo Bada, who has so many interchangeable parts that he is called the "operatic Ford."

Miss Howard boasts a collection of at least fifty faces, and almost as many souls, we should judge, considering the ardor with which she flings herself into each of these characterizations. Her moments upon the stage are frequently brief, but no matter what may be the hodge-podge impressions of the evening which we carry home, we are not apt to forget the significant and often mordant bits which she contributes. The critics fasten their delighted eyes upon her at every new production, and she is rarely lumped with "other adequate performances were . . ." but appears much higher up their column, with "outstanding figures. . . ." She has a voice, too, of so rich a quality that it sometimes astonishes when it unexpectedly strikes through a disguise; but many have voices, and few have all her talents, so we have chosen her to initiate us into the mysteries of rabbit's-foot and nose-putty.

She claims that she was born knowing how, and that a painter and a famous sculptor in the family are an asset. Be that as it may (the helpfulness of clever relations is always a debatable question), to one of her statements we thoroughly take exception, namely, that she has a blank canvas to paint upon. When she modifies this, however, to mean that there is nothing particularly striking in the way of inordinate protuberance or eccentricity, such as a beaknose, a receding chin, or prominent teeth, that her eyes do not pop nor cross, and that she is neither fat nor too thin, we concede that she is fortunately right. "Therefore," says she, with some satisfaction, "I can make myself into almost anything, without people saying, 'Well, she's *Kathleen Howard,* no matter what she does!' I regard my nose merely as a stump upon which I can and do rear the most astonishing edifices, and my chin is hardly ever itself. It is probably lucky that few of my characters inspire much affection, for even the most reliable putty is apt to become disarranged during the ardor of lyric embraces. Powder on the tenor's shoulder can be overlooked, but never an eyebrow nor the bridge of one's nose."

Having mostly to interpret the very aged, Miss Howard spends much of her time studying the various types to be found upon the streetcars and the subways. She made one important discovery—that almost all old people are colorless, and that the shadows in their faces are gray, while with those who obviously have not the advantages of ladies' maids and facial treatments the appearance is inevitably slightly soiled. Most of them look either sad or slyly malevolent, and on the faces of some

foreign types there is a woodenly patient bewilderment and resignation. These latter, instead of being
pale, are a sort of thickened reddish brown. These
are her models, yet she never examines them closely,
but rather gazes at them from the most distant point
available, or through squinted lashes. She wants effects only, and her mediums are very different from
those used by time and the hand of God. If she
has industrial or racial types to portray, she goes
boldly where they are to be found, in the factories
and mills, and when she fails to hunt down exactly
what she seeks, she has recourse to libraries and
picture-galleries. She and Franz Hals reach hands
across the centuries and meet upon the stage of the
Metropolitan.

Faces, however interesting, are by no means all
of the picture. She never forgets, as do so many
artists, the significance of the *hands*. If aged coun-
tenances are not apt to give the impression of complete cleanliness, aged hands are gnarled and positively dirty. The joints and knuckles come in for
their black shadows and red highlights, but color
does not do it all. Holding them like claws, or
rheumatically knotted, gives more illusion to a whole
personality than was ever obtained with a hoary
wig and spectacles. As the witch in *Königskinder*
she gave the creepy illusion of fingers a foot long,
by a neat use of lines, and a manner of holding them
so they seemed to drip. The secrets of optical illusion are among the most important pigments in the

make-up box. The human eye is always docile about
following a line and reaching its own conclusions.

Especially is this true when it comes to height.
The clever character actor can practically shrink or
grow at will, like Alice in Wonderland, but without
her cakes. He uses brains. A straight carriage,
high shoulders, a head slightly thrown back, a noble
tread, free sweeping gestures—and we have an illusion of tall and slender stature. On the other hand,
relaxed shoulders, a drooping head, a slight collapse of the spine, a minute bend at the knee—and a
little person confronts us, and not necessarily an
unattractive one either. If some of the Junos
among the dramatic soprani would only experiment
in this manner, how much more moving might some
of their love scenes with the diminutive tenori prove
to be. These latter gentlemen are very addicted to
a strange sort of foot-gear which have inner soles
of sometimes two or more inches in thickness, and
do indeed add cubits, but also rather a club-footed
appearance which is far from romantic.

When it comes to a matter of age, the good old
overworked stoop is the actor's stock-in-trade, although for the singer it is an attitude not particularly conducive to the best in vocal expression.
Mime, the smallest dwarf in *Siegfried,* is a striking
example of what can be done with the body almost
bent double, a hump, thick hairy legs, scrawny arms,
and a bushy head. It would doubtless surprise the
average opera-goer intensely to meet this singer the

next day face to face and discover him to be an up-standing gentleman of average stature. But it is a back-breaking process, the holding of such an un-natural position throughout a long act, and any arti-ficial relief is welcomed.

During the preparation for the local première of *Jenufa,* the peasant opera, when Miss Howard im-personated one of the oldest of all her rogues' gal-lery, she decided to be wracked and bent with rheu-matism; and consulting with Herr von Wymetal, the stage director, who is almost a wizard in the matter of make-up, they decided that one shoulder should be drawn up and distorted. This seemed to Miss Howard a little too much to ask in the way of physical torture, and she meekly requested that a hump be sewn into the right half of the costume. Von Wymetal was adamant, however.

"Then when you sit down, that shoulder would stay up just the same, eh? And *you* an *artist!*"

Quailing before his righteous indignation, she meekly accepted the decision. Up went her shoul-der, aching muscles were ignored, and another ar-resting characterization was added to her repertoire.

Many parts, however, do permit a little help from the costumer; and some of her trunks are full of what might easily be discards from the check-room of the Hospital for Ruptured and Crippled, or fan-tastic souvenirs from the famous Court of Miracles.

If called upon to act a boy's rôle Miss Howard is particularly successful, for she fills out hollows rather than vainly attempting to suppress curves, according to the usual practice.

And speaking of help from the costumer, when Antonio Scotti, who has as neat and svelte a figure as a baritone could desire, divests himself of the *Falstaff* garments, he is like a sleek butterfly emerging from a cocoon. His recent body lies like a shell upon the floor, a nut with the kernel removed. Legs, forehead, whiskers, and chin, not to mention the most conspicuous corporosity, were put on with his doublet and hose, and augmented his weight sixteen pounds.

In character acting the stage manager always has a great deal to say to the beginner; and wise is the artist who listens and profits thereby. What they learn in this way will be mostly tradition, the alphabet of the art, but a reliable framework upon which they can later hang their original ideas without anxiety. Miss Howard to this day declares that she always begins in a totally conventional manner, when a new part is put into rehearsal, and then patiently anticipates that moment, which is sure to come, when the whole thing clarifies and "sets" in her mind. This does not mean that she does no work, and sits about waiting for inspiration, but that, when she has learned to know the groundwork of a part, and has conscientiously studied it from this point of departure only, the highlights which will eventually bring it into strong relief will burst upon her at the least-expected moment. Perhaps at the end of a long rehearsal, perhaps in the middle of the night. But the revelation never fails her before the opening performance.

Making much of a small part, yet never in any sense obtruding beyond the importance of that character to the whole, is a delicate matter to negotiate. When the Russian opera *Snegourotchka* was given a few seasons ago, to Miss Howard's lot fell the part of an old peasant woman who, in all four acts, has but seven phrases to sing, but is almost constantly upon the stage. She was convinced that the old creature should be doing something, but what? She early exhausted all the conventional things allowable to such "atmosphere"; so in desperation she sought the public library and a collection of Russian prints and illustrations which she had heard existed there. Here she soon found the answer to her problem. Almost every Russian group seemed to contain an ancient supernumerary such as she, and their postures, their expressions, their trivial occupations were without delay transferred to 39th Street and Broadway. Reviewing the first performance, the late Mr. Krehbiel ventured to opine that the part of the old woman was so marvelously and completely limned by the composer and librettist that it was practically fool-proof, which remark Kathleen Howard wisely decided to take as one of the finest compliments she had ever received, albeit a left-handed one.

The actual process of making-up is, as this particular artist regards it, "a great deal of fun," but to some it is an arduous process indeed. *Parsifal* requires of the prima donna who sings Kundry, that she, in the brief course of an evening, portray three of the most widely different women who ever walked the mimic earth. For ACT I she is the wild witch, the savage but tender-hearted creature who is condemned to wander upon the winds and storms, unlovely and unloved. Her skin is dark, her hair tangled and flying, her costume uncouth, her personality repellent. ACT II finds her the most ravishingly beautiful of pale, golden-haired seductresses—jeweled, curled, perfumed, wrapped in a thousand wicked allurements; while the third act shows her the sorrowing, repentant, nun-like Magdalen.

The make-up for the wild creature of the first act is done with broad strokes. Bushy eyebrows, staring eyes obtained by giving them no frame of any kind, a complete smearing of the face, neck, and arms with brown grease-paint and powder, the rough horsehair wig, the dress of rags, and fur, and ropes—and she is complete. But getting it off and reconstructing from it the dazzling white beauty of Kundry II is a frantic procedure, in what seems like a very small allowance of time. Before her exit, everything in the dressing-room is covered with paper, and three dressers stand ready with cotton, olive-oil and towels. The costume and wig are ripped off, and the poor woman, still quivering from the drama of her performance, is literally soaked in oil and wiped as clean as possible. Many a laundress has given notice on beholding those towels the following Monday. When finally every trace of the witch's swarthiness has been removed, Kundry has to begin again from the very beginning and construct the most perfect make-up within the power of her artistry, a process which under ordinary conditions requires anywhere from forty minutes to an hour and a quarter. For the last act she has, however, a simple expedient—merely wiping all the make-up whatsoever from her face, darkening her eyes, and going on the scene looking as ravished, weary, and spent as only the footlights can make the unpainted.

The first secret of any character make-up is to assume as far as possible the likeness and expression of the part without any artificial aids at all; in other words, see what your possibilities are. Having discovered this, calmly proceed to rub everything which you cannot use right off the slate. Most women of the stage have soft and clear complexions, and no wonder, when one considers the bath of cold cream which they constantly receive. It is the beginning and the end of all cosmetic things. The grease-paint chosen for the foundation color is next applied with a generous thoroughness, and then one's canvas is ready. Upon a face which looks curiously blank and featureless, the sketching now begins. No make-up tray is complete without quantities of those little paper draughtsman's stubs. These are the brushes, although a giant hairpin is another useful tool.

Every veteran possesses a hundred odds and ends which are more precious to him than fine gold. Candle stubs, tiny frying pans, bottles, jars, creams, and, more than all else, lumps of old and tractable nose-putty, and infinitesimal scraps of colors obtained long ago in some forgotten shop or theater, and irreplaceable. Chalk or white paint is used for highlights, such as the aristocratic bridge of Faust's before-mentioned nose, and also the rolling edges of wrinkles, and puffs, and pouches. Red is placed traditionally in the corner of each eye, in the nostrils, and on the ear-lobes for beauty, but Kathleen Howard, in her galaxy of scarecrows, often rims the entire lid with it, and once even obtained a *succès fou* with two crimson sacks beneath the eyes which gave to her face such a dissipated and wicked appearance that she could hardly bear her own reflection in the mirror.

Speaking of mirrors, here is a point which is very apt to lead the beginner astray. In the excitement and interest of self-transformation, he is very prone to forget the enormous distances for which he must plan, and to do a little too minute and careful etching. Hence is one treated to the odd spectacle of an artist, who knows his trade, busy making himself up at the opposite end of the room from the mirror into which he peers so anxiously. Almost all singers have a relative or friend "planted" out somewhere in the front at dress rehearsals or first performances to report results and suggest changes; but lacking that, there is nothing to do but to retreat to the farthest end of the dressing-room, and there with squinted eyes criticize the effect oneself.

Wrinkles are a pitfall for most beginners, and their first efforts are apt to look as if they had run amuck with a piece of charcoal. The wise painter never uses black or brown, but a deeper shade of the skin color; for, after all, what are these wrinkles but sharp shadows? "It is all a question of shadows, anyway," declares Miss Howard, disposing of the subject with a gesture. That may be all very well for a sculptor's sister, but the average reader athirst for advice clamors for details.

High rouge and a light forehead for youth, low rouge, and highlights on the sags and bags for age —and always follow your own lines when sketching them into prominence. If one is so blessed as to arrive upon the lyric stage unlined and without visible marks of wear and tear, then one may obtain a prophetic vision of oneself a few years hence, and also a fair working basis for the necessary delineations, by puckering up whatever portion of that interesting countenance is under consideration, and noting where the pleats lie. Singers and actors sometimes make collections of types, culled from magazines and illustrated journals, which they keep with their make-up box, and use for details of which they are not entirely certain; but the technique is soon acquired, and they learn the value of angles and strokes as accurately as a sign-painter.

The men are more fortunate than the women, for they have the added and invaluable assistance of wig, mustache and beard. The former is designed and cut to carry out the personality of the character according to both tradition and the individual taste. High foreheads, low brows, peaked heads, square-heads, flat-heads—all are legitimate means to the desired end, and all within the wig-maker's realm of possibilities. As for the supreme assistance of crêpe-hair, in other words the fuzz which adheres to the face through the kind offices of spirit gum, and is clipped and adjusted into semblance of any desired hirsute adornment, it covers a multitude of shortcomings. Occasionally the women resort to it. Miss Howard augments her brows thereby upon occasion, and does not even hesitate to fasten a little tuft unpleasantly to a wart if realism requires; but ordinarily it is the perquisite and the exclusive salvation of the men.

As for the full beard, one might as well wear a complete mask. Wigs are very accommodating too. The red spikes of Loge lend his face an elfin, fantastic look which even the most hesitating pencil could follow, and for the wig of Wotan, with the ingenious bang which veils the question of whether he has an eye or not, he scarcely needs any other make-up.

The male stars rarely take the same delight and satisfaction in the ornamentation of their persons as do the feminine contingent. One is very apt to notice a distinct disparity in hue between Aïda and her parent, the latter slathering on his burnt cork with complete indifference to anything but "local color," while his daughter is torn to shreds by the strain of deciding just how écru an Ethiopian can be and get away with it.   Tenors, however, are prone to be a trifle vain.   Doubtless the continued impersonation of godlike heroes, and perfect young gentlemen of every period, eventually gets under their skins and they begin to think a little more about the reflection in the mirror.   And who can blame them?   The life would be a perfect landslide for a man with the slightest of effeminate tendencies; in fact only a prize-fighter or a Yale half-back could permanently withstand the subtle influence of all the ribbons and furbelows and perfumed curls.

CHAPTER X

REHEARSING

ONLY just the other day a little slip in a rehearsal of *Götterdämmerung* postponed an important début, upset the management's careful schedule for a week or more, disappointed a large subscription audience, and gave the first-line critics an unexpected night off. None of the artists were responsible, nor any of the directors, stage-hands, electricians, or musicians. The slip was made by an important member of the cast, however—Grane, the horse, who did a neat and surprising *glissando* upon an iron binding in the floor, and leaned a trifle too heavily upon the foot of Madame Larsen-Todsen, pinned beneath him. It happened three days before the much-heralded Scandinavian was to make her initial bow in her greatest rôle, Isolde. With her foot badly crushed and bruised, this was, of course, out of the question; so by a quick shifting of casts one of the adequate routine singers was put into the part and the début was put forward over a week and into another and less sympathetic rôle. Disastrous enough, one would say, but in the meantime the culprit, in disgrace, nervously munched his oats and favored a bruised rib or two. His was the real tragedy in the case.

Consider for a moment that horse, and his anguish should this mean that he must permanently step aside for an understudy. His social leadership in the stable would be undermined, his life a barren thing. All through the weary round of his daily tasks, which vary from delivering laundry to pulling the humble hearses of the poor across the Queensboro Bridge, he is sustained and quickened by the thought of his real career, that brilliant night life of his, when, caparisoned in purple, he bears kings upon his stiff old back. He takes enormous pride, also, in escorting Carmen to the bull-fight, or marching in Rhadames' victory parade; but his greatest artistic triumph is this very opera with the long name, when he, an accredited unit in the dramatis personæ, is privileged to walk with gods and heroes. One can imagine the prestige it gives him with the other horses, who look up to him tremendously, and never suspect that he is not the fiery Pegasus of his glowing tales, but is chosen instead for his poor, half-blinded eyes, and his docile spirit.

The audience must perhaps stretch its imagination considerably when the Valkyr leads out so proudly her *haute-école* Luft-Ross in the person of this broken old hack; but the artists, not apt to have been reared in the saddle, so to speak, always regard him with the same wholesome respect they would accord a prancing and snorting young stallion. To them he is a potential calamity. Brünnhilde's gingerly grip upon his halter and her long-distance caresses are as nothing to the relief with which, at the end of her rhapsody, she presents him to Siegfried. Never was giver more enthusiastic or gift less welcome. Siegfried hurries out with him at the earliest possible moment. For the finale, Wagner, himself safely in the conductor's stand or still farther away, in Paradise, directs that Brünnhilde leap lightly upon Grane's back and dash headlong into the blazing funeral pyre—but this is one of the few of his meticulous stage directions which has been blatantly disregarded from the first, although in Germany a daring super, in red wig and cloak, has been known to attempt some such equestrian stunt.

Rehearsals are not, however, principally rodeos, although they are often in the nature of nerve-tests, to establish an easy familiarity with the exciting mechanical contrivances used in the production of the more fantastic of the operas, as we shall see shortly, when we look in at *Rheingold* in the making.

Every opera produced during a season has at least one full stage rehearsal with orchestra. If all the principals are veterans in their parts, if the settings are familiar, and the ensemble perfected from season to season, one complete rendition usually suffices; but the chorus, ballet, and orchestra are drilled separately and often, before that date arrives, and the electricians and scene-shifters have gone through their duties a dozen times under the supervision of minor conductors with piano and annotated scores.

This general rehearsal, as it is called, is rarely in costume or make-up, unless some innovation in properties or investiture makes it advisable for the chorus to be partially in character. The medley of incongruities thus revealed to the wondering layman is intensely amusing, but the accustomed artist will see nothing mirth-provoking in a company of men in sack suits and yellow shoes brandishing spears; Faust, if it is draughty on the stage, may wear a brown derby; Elsa may practice with her heavy wedding-cloak over a modish *tailleur*. Most of the female stars, however, have designed for themselves some sort of rehearsal costume, a simple, comfortable garment which, while it is not unbecoming— you may be sure of that—is also practical and permits great freedom of gesture and stride, as well as offering the maximum resistance to the inevitable stage grime. As the scenes progress, the amateur watcher will, little by little, be so drawn within the magic atmosphere that he, too, will cease to be amused, and will become indifferent to everything but the music and the drama.

Such perfection, however, is seldom attained. Twenty times the stage manager will cross before the footlights with flying coat-tails and hastily revise some bit of action. Sunlight, moonbeams, and lightning will be snapped off and on in bewildering confusion; singers will step out of their parts and come down to argue heatedly with the prompter; while the conductor will sing in the funny, unmusical voice he usually possesses, and go back patiently over and over a passage with a recalcitrant oboe or harp.

The rehearsal progresses by installments, and during orchestral discussions the singers usually gather in little groups to chat. Let the music begin again, however, and they will snap back to their original positions and suspended gestures, for all the world like marionettes suddenly jerked upon their wires.

So inseparable must action and music become, in an opera-singer's mind, that on a certain note he will subconsciously take a certain step or assume another pose. A certain veteran and incomparable Scarpia, was, during a particular musical phrase of *Tosca,* ACT I, accustomed to stoop and pick up, with a courtly flourish, the prima donna's fallen staff. A new singer ignored the conventions and carried no staff in this scene; but before he knew it, one evening the baritone found himself, to his own amazement, bending over to pick up nothing at all, upon the familiar note.

Some singers use almost the full voice in rehearsing, but usually they spare themselves all they can, and adopt a sort of *mezzo-voce* which is louder than a whisper, and something like singing speech. From the back of the auditorium, the effect thus produced is extremely interesting. The orchestra plays on at full blast, the singers go through all the motions and contortions incident to the production of mighty volumes of sound, whereas little can be heard beyond the proscenium arch, save a sort of sibilant murmur. The chorus may take no such liberties, however, and chant with their usual enthusiasm; but the leading ballerina is almost sure to dance at "half-voice," if the expression may be permitted, indicating rather than performing some of her more intricate steps.

To gain admission to one of these general rehearsals is almost an impossibility. Wire pulling is useless. Only those who "belong," in their own right or by close and famous relationship, can hope to pass muster with the calm and all-seeing eye of that official—often the mighty director himself—who strolls with apparent indifference up and down the aisles, but lets nothing escape him. The dress-rehearsal is easier to attain, being a sort of semi-public occasion, especially in the case of an entire novelty, when critics and other accredited journalists are habitually admitted. It differs very little from a performance, although of course the various directors have the right to, and sometimes do, make remarks and corrections. Every one is in costume and complete make-up, and there is the same atmosphere of concentration and strain behind the curtain; for the critics often write the major part of their reviews after this preliminary glimpse.

In this connection there is that famous and lamented case of the Metropolitan's first *Salome*, which, at a dress rehearsal, so shocked the sensibilities of a certain shareholder that only one actual performance could be given before wheels were set in motion which effectively drove it from the boards.

The house is darkened, the curtain rises and falls

—there is nothing missing but the public and the applause, which one would suppose to be the least of the ingredients of a performance, but the supposition is incorrect. It is like a boat race on the rowing racks of the gymnasium, the movements are identical, but the water is lacking; and he who sees only dress rehearsals, be they never so perfect, may be said never to have seen opera at all.

There is, however, a more pleasing aspect for the privileged beholder, in that he may here enjoy some taste of the luxury which mad Ludwig of Bavaria found so beguiling, when he commanded whole representations for himself alone and sat in solitary state to savor them. When one is part of a little group of perhaps four-score scattered throughout a vast auditorium made to hold many thousands, and can roam or sit down at will, unrestricted by a number on a bit of pasteboard, one can snap fingers at all princes and their perquisites.

The dress-rehearsal and the "general" are, however, the culminating point of much previous effort. In the preparation of a new opera, it is inaugurated with a piano, and the principals with scores are seated comfortably about in the Ladies' Parlor, where at night the youth and beauty of society come to powder their noses. Little do they know, as they peer into the mirror at their handiwork, what a scene of earnest endeavor that same glass has reflected a few hours earlier. From the parlor the rehearsal advances to the "roof-stage," which is separate from the ballet's quarters, and contains adequate equipment for elementary practice of the action. And after a time they move downstairs to the big stage, and each act is gone over a dozen times, by itself, with the real conductor at the piano. Many rehearsals are always going on at the same time in a great house like the Metropolitan, and time is nothing—the luncheon hour is anywhere from eleven to four, if at all.

When companies go traveling, the work of actual preparation is supposed to be practically complete; but if, in the case of a guest artist or any other innovation, a rehearsal is required, all sorts of odd places are made use of. Once a cast of famous stars went through *La Bohème* in a "Hall for weddings and social gatherings" up over a saloon on Eighth Avenue, New York—so delighting the proprietor, who happened to be musical, that he had the whole place redecorated, and added to the price of its hire from then on.

Most artists are eager for rehearsals; but some dread them and others are bored by them. It is amusing to observe the difference in their attitude toward this phase of their work. Some walk through their parts, and others put all the fire and abandon they possess into it, insisting on every smallest detail. We have seen a famous Tosca, in tears of rage, go to the management and offer to relinquish her contract because a certain Russian baritone simply refused to exert himself during a rehearsal of ACT II. She was in the right, for the effectiveness of that particular scene is quite as dependent upon the drama as upon the music; but it was pitiful to see her, as he sat stolidly in his chair mumbling over his score, chase herself frantically about the room pretending that he was after her, and shaking herself loose from his imaginary embraces, flinging him, the while, withering glances of such scorn and distaste as had probably never been equaled in all her public appearances. As a rule, however, be they never so punctilious in the actual performance of their rôles, a rehearsal is the one time when the artists slacken their pace and let down their tension. There is a delightful informality about the occasion which is the more piquant because of its austere and grandiose setting, and often there intrudes, in ripples of captivating relief, a flickering of humor—that useful sixth sense which was buried beneath the foundations of the first opera stage. Its ghost, however, does walk from time to time, and is the most welcome of specters. When Tristan and Isolde, upon their solemn garden bench, burst out laughing over a mangled phrasing, the world grows young again.

If we really wish to know all about rehearsals, the best way is to watch that quintessence of phantasy and mechanical despair—*Rheingold*—upon a day just before it has attained the dignity of the "General." Most of the leading artists are present because some important members of the cast are new, never having sung the rôles in this country, and the scenery is unfamiliar; so we shall have the benefit of every possible aspect before we have been very long in our seats.

The telephone girl by the stage entrance presses her magic button and the door into the house swings open at our touch, admitting us at once into the now deserted and gloomily lighted corridor where to-night will bloom forth again the city's finest gowns and furs and jewels. Through the swinging doors we pass into the half-darkened auditorium, where here and there are to be observed small knots of people whose faces are pale, featureless blots. The curtain is up and the stage is set for the first scene, although the lighting is not the green and submarine dimness we are accustomed to, but a bright and re-vealing glare which cruelly exposes the shortcomings of the aquatic flora which adorn the bottom of the Rhine. Quite plainly we can see the prosaic, dirty-looking lump on top of its rock, which, when il-luminated in the depths of its properly surrounding gloom, becomes the magic and romantic Gold. Its present guardians are not sinuous and graceful mer-maids, but stage-hands with ladders, hammers, and nails, who go about, unconcerned and apparently amphibious, in pursuit of their duties. An anxious and white-faced individual leans over the footlights, advancing an ear carefully in vain effort to hear, above the tuning and scraping and conversation of the orchestra, remarks being made at the top of leather lungs by some invisible authority in the rear of the house.

Then suddenly to our astonished vision is introduced the diverting spectacle of a young and delighted scene-shifter swinging rapidly up and down and across the entire proscenium space, and making free and noisy comment during his travels. We rub our bewildered eyes, then realize that they are merely trying out the swimming apparatus for the Rhine Daughters—which reminds us that if we wish to see this in all its mystery, we had better rush back-stage immediately. Some one has already sounded an imperative whistle, and the conductor has arrived at his desk and is wiping his glasses preparatory to the business of the day. In another moment the mighty river will begin to flow in stirring chords through the orchestra.

We slip through the doors unchallenged, and in another instant are threading our way behind the great circular back-drop which so competently confines the current of the fabled waters, toward a little group of people surrounding a tangle of wires and cables. We are not a moment too soon. Even now Woglinde is climbing into her little saddle and being strapped in place like a child on a merry-go-round. Her sisters, Flosshilde and Wellgunde, are already astride, and obviously getting a grip upon their nerves while pretending to struggle with the inadequacies of their far-from-flowing modern skirts. One of them wears a smart little hat. The last one

now being firmly and inescapably chained to her instrument of torture, produces a purse from her
bosom and extracts a soda mint. "This always
makes me so seasick!" she explains to us, with a
wry face. They are all young and slender, however,
so they need have no fear of repeating that famous
catastrophe, when Schumann-Heink's somewhat
superfluous pounds are said to have snapped a rope
and precipitated her to the bottom with a thud instead of a splash.

The mounting musical bubbles of the river's flow
now reach our ears. Cables are unloosed, three
répétiteurs with their noses in open scores take their
positions beside the three stage-hands controlling
the aerial trolleys upon which depend the swimming
proficiency of the mermaids. *"Los!"* cries Number
One . . . (we had forgotten, but of course the
language of the whole scene is German to-day) . . .
and off goes Woglinde. *"Auf! . . . Still! . . .
Vorwaerts! . . . Zurück! . . ."* directs the little
conductor, and the "hand" must be more of a lin-
guist than he looks, for he obeys with straining
muscles and perspiring anxiety, in some degree of
accuracy. In a pretty but sickening swoop Wellgunde makes her entrance, her hat already a trifle
awry. Flosshilde soon follows her and we gaze in
rapture. Surely Peter Pan never gave the Darling
children a treat like this.

We soon hasten back, however, to the auditorium
to observe from the front the effect of these very

strange fish at their maneuvers, and arrive just as Alberich, the dwarf, who is bald and wears a mauve necktie, is adjusting his pince-nez in order to be able to place his feet more securely upon the treacherous rocks of the bottom. His pursuit of the modish maidens is further impeded by an experiment of the electricians, toying with blue and green rays, and stereopticon waves. The illumination is reduced just in time, however, for the gold to begin to glow; and, taking advantage of a pause, Woglinde is heard begging in a pitiful voice to be allowed a moment to alight, and is brought a glass of water—an extremely redundant need, one would say, for a submerged lady.

The moment of darkness following Alberich's theft does not take place to-day, and we hope to see the mechanics of the transformation; but no—the veils and cloud-curtains are having their own rehearsal and so hide from us, as usual, the path to Wotan's arcadian camping-place. He lies upon his rock, or rather he sits this time, not considering it necessary to endure his habitual discomfort. He wears a brown suit, and for some reason looks at his wrist-watch just as the scene is revealed. Fricka, his faithful spouse, is not with him to-day, the impersonating artist being practiced in the rôle, and furthermore, billed to sing to-night; but her place is occupied by a sub-director with a score, who looks as he doubtless feels, very foolish indeed. When the goddess has to declaim, the conductor hums and

the prompter raises his modest voice. All progresses smoothly, even to the appearance of Walhalla upon the back-drop. The rest of the royal
family now arrives. Freia comes at once to the
footlights and, shading her eyes with outstretched
palm, peers over to see if her husband is in the
house, but springs back to position on the notes of
her *Stichwort* or cue.

Presently the Giants enter, and although they
clutch their young pine-trees as lustily as ever, they
are not nearly as big and imposing as usual, even
with their overcoats which they have retained to
heighten the illusion. Loge, however, provides the
greatest merriment, even moving the austere celes-
tials to a titter of amusement. It is very difficult
indeed for him to "flicker like tongues of flame,"
in his conventional apparel of the modern male, but
he does the best he can, with great earnestness holding out his coat-tails and pirouetting upon his pol-
ished tan oxfords with admirable abandon. When
he and Wotan start for Nibelheim we observe that
it is the day when the steam rehearses too, for the
pipes belch forth with such enthusiastic hissing that
they earn a sharp rebuke from the conductor, who
is now heart and soul in his work, with his collar
and tie depending from a corner of his rack.

The poor little Nibelungen slaves are revealed as
children—the smallest of the ballet babies, and the
sons and daughters, nieces and nephews of the
chorus, who earn their pocket money populating the

usual operatic street scenes, and indulging languidly in youthful capers. Just now they seem to be really enjoying themselves as they bend their cropped or beribboned heads and scramble off to the crack of Mime's whip. When Alberich and Wotan appear it is time for the first of the Tarnhelm tricks. The dwarf's vanishing act is at last understood. Backing up against a screen of black velvet in the rear of the cave, he steps quickly to the right and rear, and the screen revolves, presenting its blank side to the audience. By a similar step forward and left, he reappears as if by magic.

Wagner has, by his aptly descriptive musical phrase, saved the management the annoyance of introducing a real toad upon the scene, but the "loathely dragon" is another matter. This is a difficult moment. Unlike the *Siegfried* dragon, which only rears its ugly head and shoulders, this *"Wurm"* must actually slither and writhe across the stage. Six "hands" have carried the fearsome reptile to his entrance *coulisse;* the guide wire has been located and attached; and the man who impersonates the front legs and jaws has squirmed into his tight quarters—the tail will be worked from behind in the wings. *"Los!"* cries the individual with the score and to orchestral undulations the monster begins its progress before the footlights.

But it is not going well—it is three beats too slow! The conductor taps with his baton and says something bitter. The stage manager leans deprecatingly over the apron, then retires precipitately in search of the technical director. Everything stops but the *"Wurm,"* who continues his blind march. Then suddenly the director makes one of his rare appearances. In shirt-sleeved haste he pursues the creature, and remembering, although an Englishman, that this is Wagner, trumpets through his hands, "Bring back that *worm!*" The "worm" being some eight feet long and covered with horny excrescences, is not easily turned about, so he backs in a graceless and ignominious manner; and after some discussion the march begins again.

The last scene is uneventful. Freia, having by this time located her husband safely in the audience, throws herself into her part. Fasolt expires without even losing his footing, and walks straight off the stage and into a waiting taxi-cab which takes him home to lunch. We, although giving a thought or two to nourishment, wait to see the finals. Donner takes off his coat to wield his hammer, and, finding that the latter has somehow become mislaid, seizes his rejected garment and swings it about his head, producing just as satisfactory peals of thunder as with the proper tool. There are no mists around Walhalla anyway to-day, but the rainbow bridge has been there waiting for some time, and now the hungry gods and goddesses approach it. But the first one to mount its arc tests it carefully with his toe before trusting it with the not inconsiderable weight of his lyric family—remembering an unfortunate incident in the history of the scene. Now the Rhine Daughters, swathed in furs, hatted and gloved, wave to them saucily and sing their plaintive lament; Wotan brandishes an imaginary sword; and the curtain falls. Before one can say "knife," everything and everybody has faded away. The artists stand not on the order of their going, the orchestra exits as one man, with a parting shout or two the directors leave the stage. It is one-thirty. At two-fifteen there is a dress rehearsal of *Gioconda!*

In Europe things are much the same, even if slightly more formal. Firemen who, it is to be hoped, like music, occupy every wing during performances and full rehearsals; and for any outsider whatever to sit in the auditorium a signed permit is required. A certain popular tenor, Herr Bary, who was engaged just before the War for some of the important "Munich Festivals," was so blind that in darkened scenes a wire was always stretched across the stage to guide him, and other singers had to avoid it as best they could or risk decapitation. Once, when rehearsing *Lohengrin,* at that famous moment when the Silver Knight invites every one to witness his psychic and discriminating powers in recognizing Elsa without an introduction, Bary made his tuneful boast, then strode firmly over to a fat and tittering lady of the chorus and honored her with his salute. After that Elsa always took a necessary if unmaidenly step to meet him.

Bavaria had its democratic moods even under the

monarchy, and a certain prince of the blood, being
a skilled musician, amused himself and at the same
time made a popular gesture by playing first violin in the orchestra at special performances. His
democracy did not extend, however, to abolishing
the strict regulation that any one meeting a member of the royal family was required straightway to
salute or curtsy, according to sex. As he was, during rehearsals, often to be encountered in the back-
stage corridors, the peace of mind of a young American girl attached to the entourage of a visiting
prima donna became considerably disturbed. She
cherished a consuming dread of having to make such
a curtsy herself and managed successfully to avoid
the contingency until one day, being dispatched to
the hotel for a missing score, she returned with it
on the run, and flew up to the prima donna, who was
standing in a group of people at the top of a short
flight of steps. "Here it is!" she cried gayly, then
stopped, frozen with horror—for the center of that
group was His Royal Highness! The singer, with
twinkling eyes and unctuous utterance, made the
ceremonious introduction, and the girl, caught in the
relentless grip of circumstance, made the curtsy.
. . . But she made it backward down the steps, and
fell in an absurd and humiliating heap. Princely
laughter ensued, followed by gracious concern and a
royal hand to pick her up. As that girl was the
present writer, this incident must promptly close the
chapter in order to avoid much embarrassment.

CHAPTER XI

SPANISH GOLD

THERE is a Borgia in our midst, a descendant and a namesake of that famous and infamous Lucrezia who made a great many people very nervous in Renaissance Rome. Our own Lucrezia lives and has her being in an atmosphere as picturesque and, it must be admitted, sometimes as full of intrigue as that in which her ancestor pursued her devious ways. To the date of writing, however, she has shown no evidence of an inherited passion for doing away with an opposing colleague or otherwise upholding the family traditions in any way save that of distinction, grace, and accomplishment. What scope might she have for her family talents, did she choose to develop them! One's imagination quickens at the possibilities. A poisoned lip-stick, and presto! a powerful rival sinks lifeless in her dressing-room; a subsidized stage-hand, and another disappears mysteriously in full sight of the audience! No medieval palace could boast the number of trap-doors and oubliettes that honeycomb the average opera house; yet her personal reputation continues one of extreme and winning gentleness. In fact, there exists no prima donna to-day whose publicity files contain so few anecdotes of temperamental outbursts or any sort of spectacular behavior. It would not be fair, however, to deny her temperament, for she has it to a degree only possible, perhaps, to a Spaniard who is at once young, beautiful, and a real artist; only she reserves it for her actual performances, rather than her *entre-actes*.

Her *dossier* does contain, however, to make up for the lack of sensational maliciousness, one of the most moving romances in the history of opera, and one which should be read by every one who is discouraged, hopeless, and desperate, as a life-giving stimulant, and give pause to every girl who is preparing for a career.

Few prime donne have come to the Metropolitan at the tender age when Mademoiselle Bori made her auspicious début. She was barely twenty-two, although she had been on the stage already for four years, and more or less before the public since she was six. She also came during the declining years of what was known as the "Golden Age" of opera in New York, when audiences had become so spoiled by routine casts which gave in one evening such singers as Nordica, Eames and De Reszke, that they were clinging with a sense of desperation to a few survivors like Fremstad, Farrar, Caruso, and Scotti, and looked with doubt which amounted almost to antipathy upon all newcomers. However, from the first note sung by "La petite Bori" as Manon Lescaut, every one knew that here was promise indeed that the traditions of the house were not to die.

For two seasons she went her quiet and successful way, adding rôles to her repertoire, skill to her
acting, and beauty and charm to her rapidly developing personality. Everything she did had an engaging quality of freshness, crispness, and delicacy
which was entirely her own. Her star certainly was
in the ascendancy, and very lustrous, when—crash!
went all her beautiful edifice of hopes and ambitions
—her life itself—in a horrid mess of wreckage
which all but buried her alive. She had been singing
that season the rôle of Antonia in *Tales of Hoffmann,* a plaintive little sufferer whose chief trouble
comes from a desire to sing when her health forbids
it, and whose frantic efforts in that direction at last
prove fatal. There had been something strangely
moving and real about the little Bori's performance,
hardened opera-goers were startled and ashamed to
discover lumps in their cynical throats, and before
another season had swung around the newspapers
one morning revealed the reason why. The fact
was that she had been enacting her own tragedy before their eyes; for something had begun to be
wrong with the delicate throat, one of those
wretched little things, which the *cognoscenti* call
nodes, had appeared on her vocal chords. "Off
with its head!" said the first, and each succeeding
specialist who peered at the intruder. So the young
singer meekly laid herself down and some one's
knife flashed industriously. The node departed
forthwith, but so, alas, did the golden voice!

Of this tragedy she was not aware for some time, for until the throat was healed, she could not put it to the test. For agonizing weeks she sat about, speaking in whispers only, torn to quivering shreds between hope and fear. At last came the great day when she was allowed to sing. White and trembling, but with a brave confidence in the happy result of all her suffering, she opened her mouth, threw back her head—and nothing happened! No silvery, rippling notes such as she could in the old days match against the most ostentatious nightingale; not even a complete scale. A gasp, a squeak, a husky little sob, that was all. "Too soon!" said the wise doctors. "Wait another month!" But she waited two, three, and four, and each time the heartbreaking scene was repeated. "Never do I wish that any one will be as unhappy as I was then," she says solemnly in her pretty French—she refuses to struggle with English at all. "If I could not sing, what was I to do? I did not know how to be anything else but an opera singer. It was all that I had ever thought of in my whole life. It was the end of the world for me."

But she was young, and hope dies hard at twenty-four. At the beginning of the Metropolitan season she was back in New York ready to take her place upon the stage should the miracle for which she prayed with all the ardor of her devout Spanish Catholic soul, come to pass. But it did not. The season opened, gathered momentum, and drew to a close without the little Bori. In the meanwhile she tried, with ever-increasing desperation, everything that could be found in the resources of American medicine. She still croaked like a forlorn little crow.

At last she screwed up courage for another operation; at least nothing could be any worse, and there was just a chance. Once more she had to pass through the agony of uncertainty, and again face the crushing disappointment. This time even youth and Latin optimism lay down under the blow, and hope flew out of the window. Throughout the dark-purple weeks which followed she drew little consolation from the contemplation of the tragic ends of all her favorite heroines. Not one of their fates was a circumstance to hers; death in any one of the operatic varieties was sweet compared to complete frustration and despair in one's early twenties.

The public had been quite moved by her troubles, had read of her brave struggle and defeat, and had said very feelingly, "Too bad!" It had missed her for a while at the opera, and then, after its comfortable way, was beginning to forget, just as she knew they would, which was not the least of her woes. To its everlasting credit, however, the Metropolitan did not cancel nor void her contract. All through her illness she was still a member of the company. And the many personal friends she had made in her first seasons stood by her, and moved heaven and earth to comfort and console her. One day one of them was lunching with Madame Melba, who was then making one of her farewell tours, and happened to mention the tragedy of the little Spanish Borgia. "But take me to her at once!" cried the sympathetic diva. "I have something to tell her!" The friend, who was ready to clutch at any straw, came with the news to Bori, who received it apathetically. It was very kind of the good Melba, and it would be a pleasure to be visited by a great artist, but what was the use? She could not even talk to her in a whisper (she was strictly mute for many months), and besides, there was no hope now.

"Just see her, anyway!" urged the friend, in her cheeriest bedside manner; and at last with a patient, weary sigh the girl consented. So Melba came, in her breezy, robust exuberance, and with her, all unsuspected by her pitiful young hostess, she brought the most precious gift that one artist ever gave to another. The ultimate answer to the why of all suffering would seem to be the ability to offer the consolation of "My dear, I know just how it feels; I've been all through it myself!" And that is exactly what Nellie Melba, veteran of even more successful musical seasons than she cares to record, said to little Lucrezia Bori, and thereby opened the shutters just wide enough to let that fugitive, Hope, come hopping in again on the windowsill. Melba declared that after the first two seasons of her career, she had suffered the identical blow, and had staggered about in helpless despair, but that eventually the voice had come back, stronger and lovelier than ever, and had endured beyond her fondest hopes. "For here I am, my dear, singing still, and I'm a much older woman than anybody knows." Before she left she gave more sound advice from her vast fund of experience, and an hour after she had gone the light had come back for the first time in weeks to the dark melancholy eyes of the unhappy Bori.

Then, acting on the great prima donna's instructions, she began what she describes as "the most difficult thing I ever had to do." She took up the normal, healthful life of a young woman of her age, and completely "forgot" all about her voice. She declares that she rode horseback, swam, played tennis, went motoring, and otherwise behaved like a "regular" person; that she read novels instead of operatic scores, went to the theater, and took a walking tour in Switzerland, and never gave a single thought to such a stupid thing as music, or to such folly as wanting to be an opera singer. But the imagination balks, and refuses quite such a difficult hurdle, insisting on at least an occasional picture of a lovely, dark young Spanish girl slipping quietly away from a gay group of friends at tea-time, and hastening around the corner to some humble, dim little parish church, or vast cathedral; there to startle the good sisters with the number of candles she would buy, and sinking to her knees, bend an anguished brow upon her clenched hands, and *remember!*

Incense, and candlelight, and faith, and youth;

sunshine, and courage, and common sense—whatever it was, the miracle was wrought. Not all at once, by any means, but little by little; careful, tremulous, brief experiments which grew slowly but surely into beautiful certainty. That autumn she did not attempt the triumphant return which doubtless could have been carried through, but gave her new-found strength time to increase, and threw herself, instead, into the glorious oblivion of caring for the wounded in the war hospitals of Italy. That gracious year of hard work finished the healing begun in the difficult days of pleasure, and eventually the happy ending to the story arrived. She did come back to the Metropolitan, and, just as Melba prophesied, she did sing even more beautifully than before her dreadful ordeal. The shadowy valley through which she had walked had left its mark upon her too, in that her acting gained in poignancy and eloquence, and her whole art ripened, mellowed, and matured. Not only was a place waiting for her, but a very specific need for what she had to give. And in this land of publicity "stunts" she found, to her surprise, that there was a very definite "cash value" to her brief tragedy, and that her fame had grown as it might have been longer in doing under normal conditions. All over the country people wanted to hear and see "the girl who lost her voice and found it"; and she is almost as much in demand for concerts as for operas, although she wisely does not entirely forsake her best medium, and sings many of her songs in the most entertaining and exquisite of costumes.

This was, of course, a few years ago, but when she talks about it, it might have been yesterday, for the pain which comes over her face. Not that there is any fear now of another disaster; she has put it to too long and grueling tests; but the horror of remembrance walks with her wherever she goes.

That is the story of Lucrezia Bori, whose name is really Borgia, but who prefers the one which she was forced to choose when the Romans declared that a little upstart singer was making a bid for fame by annexing past glories. "I've as good a right to it, however, as that first Lucrezia, but I'll let her have it. It will interest me to see if I can build a little better reputation for the new name than she did for the old."

This tale seems to point a moral, but it should come best from her own lips, although when urged to pronounce it she only looked unutterably pathetic, and said, *"Je suis morte!"* The fact was that she had been rehearsing all day without lunch and it was then four-thirty, so it seemed cruel to persist in questions. However, her looks so denied her fatal words that no pity was shown. "This is the worst possible day for me to give advice to young singers. I tell them all never, under any circumstances whatsoever, to even think of becoming an opera singer. It is an inhuman existence, it has no alleviations!" With which statement she burst into merry laughter.

"Of course I don't mean a word of it, but I am so tired that I can scarcely be polite. I have never sung Mélisande, and am rehearsing it every day, besides singing twice a week, and it is the end of the season. However, I rather think you may have discerned that I am just a little enthusiastic about the career, after all. So I say really, to young students, go ahead and be a prima donna, if you can't imagine life without being one. It is like the correct attitude toward matrimony. Not 'Can I do it?' but 'Can I resist it?'"

In other words, begin at the age of six, and do nothing else the rest of your days. Play tennis, swim, motor, and dance as a penance only. Be prepared to give up life itself rather than your voice, and if that goes, have the courage to hang on like grim death until it comes back. For it probably will—have not both Melba and La petite Bori gone through it for the very express purpose of saving you from despair?

And if you are not, and do not want to, and could not if you would, be an opera singer, you may find large crumbs of comfort in this tale, too, for whatever your woes may be. It is not a fairy story, but it has a moral, which you may adapt for yourself, saying the while, to Miss Lucrezia Bori, *"Merci beaucoup!"*

CHAPTER XII

STARS IN ECLIPSE

THE name of the Property Man of every great opera company should be billed on the programs in display type, for his importance is actually greater to the ensemble than any prima donna on the whole roster. As he himself succinctly observes: "A singer can make a dozen mistakes and no one knows it—if I make one it stops the show." He knows a good deal more about Art and a number of other things than the average tenor, but he is not technically one of the "Artists," hence he must pursue the course of his feverish existence beyond the reach of the spotlight. He receives no bouquets.

Philip Crispano has been at the Metropolitan Opera House for twenty-seven years, and his father for untold years before him, so perhaps it is the heritage of time which makes the complications of his daily routine so clear and simple to him; to the average layman the mere mental review of a few of his duties brings on a *crise de nerfs*. When one considers that this man is responsible for every bit of material used in a performance which has form and shape, everything from the enormous wicker elephant of the *Magic Flute,* to the small gold ring of the *Nibelungen;* that trees, flowers, food, furniture, and live-stock, as well as the mysterious instruments for producing the angry elements, the flow of rivers, and the quiver of forest leaves, are under his personal supervision, one regards him with nothing short of bewildered awe. Let it also be said, with the proper amount of modesty, that the writer who succeeds in getting an interview with such a man must have a certain amount of perseverance. His usual time for knocking off work and calling it a day is in the neighborhood of one A.M., and he returns from his suburban home about six hours later in order to be right on hand, living up to his personal slogan: "A cool head and a clear brain," and ready for the next day's job. He takes a half-hour off for lunch—perhaps.

It might be interesting to view a cross-section of that "clear brain" of his under the biologist's microscope. Without a doubt, it would bear a striking resemblance to the storeroom and cupboards and lofts of his domain, where everything is apparently in hopeless confusion, but which in reality are as orderly as a file cabinet—to those who know the system. There's the rub! If one dread day a flying rope-end should carry off this omniscient Crispano— no further than the hospital let us hope—who would remember, for instance, that a solitary cocoanut, very much needed in *Petruschka,* is sitting all by itself waiting for a coat of brown upon the vast paint bridge? Yet he claims that even you or I, armed with his elaborate and meticulous "plot book," could successfully see through a performance of *Parsifal* and *Butterfly* on the same day.   The fact is that that book is somewhere gathering dust upon a shelf.   He can find anything at all in less time than it would take him to turn over a page.

Properties are not like costumes, in that they are repeatedly used for two or sometimes a half-dozen different operas.   This naturally does not simplify things; but he has his own methods.   For example: In the cubby-hole devoted to *Meistersinger* is *one* stuffed stick.   Now in ACT II a great many of these are needed, when poor Beckmesser is belabored so thoroughly by the merry apprentices, but these sticks are "busy" in another opera this week, and this lonely sentinel stays behind as a reminder.

A tour through the storeroom is not overimpressive as to the beauty of the *objets d'art* revealed. "Pretty junky!" admits their guardian.   "But the good old footlights do wonders for 'em."   He takes up a goblet which, as seen from an orchestra chair, might have been from the hand of Benvenuto Cellini, but which on close inspection proves to be a bit of silvered pasteboard, cracked and chipped at that. The dummy of the murdered Siegfried gazes down upon us from a hook on the wall, looking far sicker than this hero could ever have felt even in his last agony.   Fricka's rams, which once trotted with such diverting docility upon the stage, are here, but pronounced "dead," for their contribution to the scene is no longer considered up to date, and now we have them trussed for sacrifice to some heathen god —two very dejected animals indeed. Neither a perfect banquet of desiccated fruit, nor many garlands of crushed and dusty flowers, contrive to lure us further here. So we cross the corridor and inspect the armory.

Very few of the properties used upon the operatic stage are real, but probably the swords, shields, and daggers, the spears, and helmets come nearer perfection than anything else which appears. In event of a mutiny of the scene-shifters, or any such interesting upheaval, these weapons would be capable of much bloody work. Only the "fancy" oriental equipment for *Aïda* and kindred operas are made of wood and pasteboard, but the tip of the spear with which Hagen dispatches Siegfried the Hero, is made of silvered rubber, and Scarpia's carving-knife has a leather blade. Artists may take spectacular plunges through trapdoors, horses may tread upon them, or colleagues fling them among the footlights, but, if Philip Crispano can prevent it, there will be no gore spilled upon his tidy stage.

In reference to trapdoors, when in a recent season Mr. Taucher descended twenty-two feet most unexpectedly and nearly brought to a sudden end his own career as well as that particular performance, he lost his sword somewhere in the abyss. So trained, however, are the property assistants to every sort of emergency, that before he had reached the stage-level there were actually four swords waiting for him to choose from.

In the matter of assignments and responsibilities, this particular Master of Properties does not believe in always giving one article to the same man to look after. He wants no specialists on his staff; only the versatile and resourceful have long careers. At a final rehearsal, A and B sometimes find out just what their particular duty is to be, but oftener it is not settled until the evening of the performance, and occasionally only from act to act.

"When I tell them things, they remember them, though. And just in case they don't, I go around and make sure myself, just before the curtain rises."

He carries no lists, but he seems to appear serene and untroubled wherever and whenever anything is happening. He remembers, at one and the same moment, to have a bit of solder put on the sharp end of Romeo's masque wire; to order a special traveling box made for Lohengrin's crown; to give directions for a mirror and a couch, with sundry odd appurtenances, to be sent to the Ladies' Parlor where a rehearsal of *Hoffmann* is in progress; and all the time the requirements of the three one-act operas of the evening are running through his mind in tranquil array.

If a bell is to be rung off-stage, and must be pitched in A-flat, he refers to a scribbled chart upon

a board, calls to an assistant, "Number nine, Jim!"
and in a moment Jim appears holding a long pol-
ished tube which he gives to the under-conductor.
As soon as the note is struck it is immediately trans-
ported back to its special hook. Likewise can he
with the same dispatch produce F-sharp or any other
key in the scale. All the strange and outlandish
musical instruments used in the endless processions
of opera come under his jurisdiction, although once
delivered to the players, his responsibility ends.
The same with torches, lamps, stoves, and candelabra. Every one of these has taken form and
shape in his workshop, but the Union steps in and
sternly insists that once these have accommodated a
wire or a bulb in their anatomy, they become the
wards of the electrical department.

As a caterer, Crispano does himself proud. Many
are the meals consumed in the course of the varied
libretti. *Tosca, Bohème, Zaza, La Juive,* and various others call for quite a menu. Ginger cake is usually the *pièce de résistance.* Garnished with sprigs
of parsley, it adapts itself obligingly to the rôle of
fish or meat. The principal advantage is, however,
that the artists are partial to its flavor, and it is important never to serve them anything unpalatable.
When possible, the personal tastes of the singers are
consulted. Geraldine Farrar always liked something
with chocolate icing which she could cut off and
really enjoy. In *La Juive* real *matzoths* are passed,
but *Zaza* has, instead of fried eggs, some appetizing

halves of canned apricot in a saucer. Drinkables are a problem, now that prohibition does away with the real wine which so delighted the Italians upon occasion. Grape-juice, coca-cola, ginger-ale, are all popular substitutes, but never the traditional burnt-sugar water or cold tea. They lack the necessary temperament for the opera.

Speaking of temperament, the live properties are one of the thorns in the flesh. *Götterdämmerung* assumes terrors proportionate to the length of its name when Grane, the horse, balks, objects to his rubber boots, or refuses to go sailing on his four-wheeled boat up the Rhine. The hunting dogs in *Tannhäuser* are so susceptible to the general excitement that they add fervid voices to the concluding chorus of ACT I. Even birds feel the impetus to be up and doing. When putting on the opera of *Versiegelt,* Crispano received orders from the stage director to produce a caged bird which under no circumstances would lift its voice. A visit to the dealer who specializes in live-stock with dramatic leanings ensued.

"I want a cheap bird this time, Bill," said Crispano. "A big fat one that is too lazy to sing!" And so an ancient and overgrown canary was forthwith engaged to join the Metropolitan Opera Company. It had preserved a golden silence for its entire and sluggish life, but when it appeared before the footlights in its *chic* new cage, and heard the orchestra making such an enticing appeal to its musicianship, it lifted up its head and gave tongue to a perfect flood of beautiful melody, carefully adjusted to the proper tempo and key. That bird was an artist; nothing could ever tempt it to deviate from the true pitch, and it could never be induced to remain silent when it had a public.

Nothing delights the property man so much as a puzzle—one of those neat, super-intelligence tests which accompany the specifications for every new opera, or elaborate revival. The librettist stops at nothing in the realm of the fantastic; the scenic artist ably seconds his demands—and then the Master of Properties invents a way to do it. There are almost enough tricks in his storehouse to satisfy Houdini. There is the clothes hamper, for instance—which has to contain removable laundry, yet admit the entire bulk of an overstuffed Falstaff. It must also allow him to make an inconspicuous egress through a stage trap, before it is lifted and thrown out of a window. This is managed by a sliding canvas shelf upon which the clothes rest, and which is pushed aside to allow the fat knight to enter. The real bottom of the basket consists of two doors which are already open when it is brought on the stage. As soon as it is carefully placed over a "trap," Falstaff gets in, and sitting with his feet through the stage, sings his final words. He then calmly descends all the way, and a stage-hand reaches up and snaps shut the bottom of the basket. The trap closes, the linen is put back in the hamper, and it is borne to the window looking as innocent as your own at home.

The cutting of William Tell's apple upon the head of his son is accomplished by a surprising mechanism which took Crispano months to evolve. An arrow comes up out of a hollow post against which the boy stands, and to which a chorusman has affixed a real apple. When a spring is released the arrow falls out from its groove on a hinge, but it is made of heavy metal, with a sharpened side, and the force of its fall to position severs the apple as neatly as a fruit knife. The whole thing happens so quickly that the audience actually persuades itself that it sees the shaft in flight.

Then there is the mighty riddle of how to make a dragon *(Rheingold)* on a wire turn a corner, but it is accomplished by means of a sliding ring, and a deft release of one wire as an assistant pulls at another. The curtains in *Walküre* seem to be blown down by a spring tempest, but it is only the property man hastily withdrawing the unknotted cord which held them in place instead of a pole. Later in the same scene, bushes quiver in the moonlit forest because Crispano's men are agitating little wires attached to their branches.

To have a raven fly away with a hat, and then drop it neatly down on a post is one riddle to which he found the answer. Raven and hat number one were simple enough. The bird flew off on the end of a wire which described a graceful curve, propelled by a long and unseen bamboo handle. It was not the same hat, however, but its twin brother, which later slid down another wire attached to the waiting post.

Most of these tricks are done with duplicates, as for instance the dove which takes the place of Lohengrin's swan. At the moment that the swan is snatched from sight, dove number one descends on a wire and rests just long enough behind the reeds on the river-bank to allow its understudy to be released upon a tall spring.

The most difficult of all operas, perhaps, in the matter of properties is *Freischütz,* for the various phenomena accompanying the casting of the magic bullets in ACT II are a perfect nightmare of complications. Skeletons on horseback, flapping owls, crawling snakes, shots, rumblings and a hundred spirit manifestations keep the property man and his assistants in a state of frantic activity. Permitted to watch it from close quarters, it becomes more wonderful than when viewed from the comparative safety of the audience. Shots which go off upon the stage are often really fired by a man in a trap below, but there is always some one with a second gun in the wings prepared to fire without an instant's hesitation if the first one fails. Wind is made by a revolving drum of silk, thunder by the delightful privilege of rolling iron balls down a long metal shoot, and shipwreck, and any other noisy disaster, is enhanced by what is known as a "crash"— a number of boards and chains and metal slabs loosely tied together and dropped from a height. It would not be fair, however, to this star's ingenuity, to give away all his secrets.

When he is not figuring out these diverting problems, or dressing dolls, or setting dinner-tables, he is often to be found reading and looking at pictures in the technical director's library. Somehow or other he gets wind of a new production before even the impresario himself has made up his mind, and manages to read up on the period and customs so completely that when the designs and specifications come in he is in possession of such a vast store of information that he can give points to the astonished director himself.

Another star which the public sees at almost every performance, but does not know it sees, is the Leader of the Stage Band. This gentleman must be so versatile that he can play a dozen instruments of which the average musician does not even know the name, and can invent, upon demand, a dozen others. He must also be a competent conductor, and an experienced actor. Added to these qualifications, he must be a practical business man, for in his hands is placed the responsibility of hiring, governing, and if necessary discharging, every musician employed in the house. This branch of his activities may not be as picturesque as some others, but it certainly assumes an importance of alarming proportions when one considers the problems that face him on the road. He naturally cannot carry with him

the full quota of "the band" used at home, so in
most cases he depends upon local players to fill out.
These must be by devious ways at least "spotted"
before the company arrives, and assiduously rehearsed as soon as possible afterward. A man who
has played a cornet peacefully and competently for
many years with home organizations in Cleveland,
Ohio, when confronted with the necessity of wearing
grease-paint upon his face, a wig, and a coat of mail,
will suddenly forget the C-major scale. Even the
veterans of the stage band at the Metropolitan will
upon occasion lose their nerve. Their leader,
"Tony" Abarno, almost always goes on with them
in costume and make-up, to give them confidence, and
when there is a ticklish bit of individual business,
as the black trumpeter of *L'Elisir d'Amore,* or the
gong-player in the marriage scene of *Butterfly,* he
assumes the rôle with ease and grace, although his
name does not appear in the cast.

The trumpets seem to be the largest family of
"queer" instruments used on the stage, for the
stringed lutes, violins, harps, or guitars are usually
dummies, and their music imitated in orchestra, or
by a soloist in the wings. There are the long brass
tubas of the *Aïda* procession, which have to be
specially made for this one scene, according to the
composer's directions; there are the countless "steer-
horns" used in the prehistoric Wagnerian operas,
which when "wound" will give forth a note in the
proper tone and key—accomplished by the insertion

of genuine musical insides under their rough exterior; and there are the dozen variations of bugles used by heralds and soldiers and medieval bands. These the audience sees; but how many stop to think of the labor involved in adapting, fitting, and learning to play these instruments, not to mention the countless stage rehearsals with those modest performers who have little or no dramatic proclivities?

The perfection of all this is entirely upon the shoulders of Mr. Abarno, or his counterpart in every company, as well as that of the "unseen music" which occurs in the course of almost every performance. Sheep-bells must ring in *Tannhäuser* and *Tosca,* and whole orchestras must play for dancing and other entertainment off-stage in a great many: *Tosca* again, *Traviata, Thaïs, La Gioconda, Romeo and Juliet,* to mention only a few. These must be in perfect accord with the big orchestra in the pit, or fearful will be the result; but Abarno, having provided them with the proper instruments and gotten them there on time and in the right place, hands over the responsibility for their actual performance, in this case, to an assistant conductor.

One of the most difficult effects to obtain is that of distance. The horns of King Mark's hunt in *Tristan und Isolde* gradually recede to the corridor outside the prima donna's dressing-room, and she, making a hurried departure to face the extremities of her great second act, is very apt to get tangled up in a maze of music racks. The *Siegfried* Bird is first a conscientious little man with a flute, and later, after Fafner's death, a young lady in street clothes. Many and varied are the instrumental soli from the shelter of the wings; and wherever the chorus is to enter singing, there will somehow spring up a small melodeon to set them right upon their first pitch. Other strange instruments, mongrel horns with piano keys, are stationed in adjacent *coulisses* as sympathetic aids to the perfect lyric exit.

Mr. Setti, the chorus master, when there is a difficult scene about which he feels particular anxiety, is very apt to assume costume and make-up; and even the property man has become an actor in emergency; Abarno, as we have observed, rarely lets an evening go by without doing his bit before the footlights; but the Stage Carpenter, or "grip," never distinguishes himself in public. Probably his nearest approach to a début is in *Rheingold*, when, dressed completely in black like a Chinese "props," with hood and veil over his face, he runs back and forth among the shadows in the depths of the river, guiding the navigation of a Rhine Daughter on a wire.

The Scene Shifter's life, if not a merry one, is at least seldom dull. A visit to his back-stage haunts will reveal a maze of ropes and pulleys which would stagger the most seasoned mate of a four-masted schooner. The approach of the end of any act will find the "grips" in silent, strained groups, resembling nothing so much as shock-troops in the trenches,

awaiting the signal to go over the top.   During the
operas in which changes must be made behind steam
screens, or during the playing of the orchestra, they
are all required to wear rubber soles, and in *Pelléas
and Mélisande* the entire back-stage has a sound-
proof mat.   There is never the slightest confusion,
although why a dozen of these infantrymen are not
killed at every performance is a mystery to an innocent bystander looking for a sheltering hole into
which to crawl.   The stage opens and shuts its hungry jaws, swallowing houses and landscapes, while
from the limitless loft above descend in obedient
composure exactly that portion of forest, sky, wall,
or mountain desired.   There is little or no shouting,
and "hands" running about with pieces of staircases
or bay-windows on their shoulders never seem to
collide.   It is a traffic system perfected without the
aid of one-way streets; but exactly how it is done,
no one seems able to explain.   Having watched over
two hundred performances from behind, we are still
completely mystified, and can only hazard the theory
that the scenery is trained to take care of itself.   To
be sure, men are often seen screwing down braces, or
touching up worn-spots with a paint-brush; some one
always sprinkles the inclined surfaces with sand;
some one else tacks down a carpet; but the actual
big transformation, the progression from "a room
in the palace" to "a wild rocky height" is done by
magic.   One minute it is there, and the next one—
where?

Not the least of the unseen stars is the Electrician, who is actually responsible for a universe of astral bodies. He makes sunshine and shadow, moonlight and Stygian darkness. He causes the thunder to roll and the lightning to flare. He lights torches, he makes sparks fly from the swords and pens of devils, and he controls the uncertain deviations of the spotlight. He is a deity who broods over a switchboard of deadly possibilities, and who talks into a little telephone steadily all through a performance to unseen angels in the flies.

The Engineer who controls those mysterious openings and closings beneath the unwary feet of the actor, who sends up clouds of steam upon demand, and performs any amount of other mechanical wonders, rules over *Nibelheim* below stairs, and rarely comes to the surface. Nevertheless, he is a star, for without him even the curtain would not go up and down.

A formidable profession indeed it is to be Librarian of a large opera company, which achieves a repertoire such as the Metropolitan augments from season to season. The mere thought of all the sheets of music in circulation during one day is overwhelming. Every member of the orchestra has the right partition, the stage band has theirs, four different piano scores are sent to rehearsals in parlors, foyer, and to the ballet on the roof-stage. An orchestration must be made for a song which a tenor wishes to introduce at a Sunday night concert; others must be shipped to the director's wife on tour, and finally all these must be gathered up again, mended, put away, and redistributed to-morrow. The star of this firmament must have his wits about him, and be the most methodical man in the world.

Other stars who might be mentioned are the Man in the Box Office, and "Clarence," the Head Usher; but these two would tell us mostly tales about *ourselves*. They are the scouts just over the border of our own familiar territory.

Wherever we wander, however, in the Music Theater, we find *coöperation*. Not always harmony—usually excitement—certainly nerves—but inevitably, above all, and through all, a long, strong pull together for the good of the whole. Without that other things may be accomplished but certainly not Grand Opera!

CHAPTER XIII

I. CHRISTMAS IN THE OPERA HOUSE

(Vignette)

IT may be Christmas, but there is not much festivity apparent. Holidays and holy days make little variety in this busy back-stage existence, and are usually distinguished principally by a little more work—an extra matinée. Nevertheless, the spirit of Christmas is very persistent, it will come creeping in despite the rush and the strain and the confusion.

A few short years ago there was a beloved Santa Claus who used to go all through the house on this day, his pack not large, but very, very heavy, for it was filled with gold pieces. Everybody got one, from the call-boy to the last stage "grip"; scrub-women, chorus, and members of the orchestra—no one was forgotten. Many of the coins were cashed at once, perhaps proving a happy alleviation of some pressing need, for the salaries of the stars are the only ones which soar phenomenally hereabouts, and there are big families behind most of the acolytes of the Music Temple. Others, however, kept their gold as souvenirs and heirlooms, and proud and happy they are now in their possession, for that Santa Claus was none other than the great Caruso,

197

gone now, alas, to celebrate Christmases with the celestial choir.   Beniamino Gigli, one of the successors in line for the mantle of this lamented tenor, is nobly and expensively carrying on this tradition, among others, so that when the humblest servant of the house is asked about Christmas he now says, with apparent irrelevance, "Gilly's all right!"   "And Alda too!" may be gallantly added, for the director's wife has also a sweeping hand with largesse.   Most of the singers remember the heads of the departments, and some special servitors, with gold and checks, and a few make it a practice to choose individual gifts, usually of jewelry, which are highly valued as mementos.   Although it was not Christmas when Geraldine Farrar left the opera, she gave every man a watch-chain or cuff-links, every woman a bracelet, marked with her initials, and money could not buy one of these from their sentimental owners.   Probably the opera is the one and only place in existence where axioms and proverbs about "familiarity and contempt" or "prophets without honor" are set at naught.   The great artists seem perpetually preserved in a syrup of glamour for their humbler associates, no matter what unfavorable revelations daily contact may bring about, and the least of the stage-hands has his souvenir collection.   The man concerned with rehearsal notices was recently speaking of a famous singer of other days who had not numbered a prodigal generosity among her many charms.   "I never thought anything of not getting presents from her, but I hate not having a *single souvenir!*" Some artists go farther afield. For instance, Antonio Scotti has a pleasing custom of sending some little remembrance to the critics and musical reporters on all the big papers; he discovered that A. S., of the *World,* was a "Miss," only after he had dispatched her a Bond Street cravat.

The day is advancing, however, and we have scarcely begun to look about. Upstairs in the big costume room, where the day's accouterments hang ready or in preparation upon the long racks and tables, sit four women under a shaded lamp. They are sewing with feverishly hurrying fingers and anxious eyes. Another bends an aching back over a pile of ruffs on an ironing board. The clock above them ticks alarmingly on toward the hour of the next performance—they dare not stop a minute. And yet, from time to time, their tired eyes look up to rest hungrily upon a gorgeous basket tied with splashing red ribbon there among the shoes and tights. Grapes and oranges and chocolates—it makes them feel as if they were going to sail off on some wonderful journey instead of working overtime on a holiday afternoon—Madame Alda was truly inspired when she thought of sending it to them.

The mail clerk has more to do than usual to-day, for admirers, anonymous and otherwise, have flooded the mails with greetings, poems, cards, gifts, every conceivable tribute. But the clerk is smiling broadly. In his tie is a stickpin from Brünnhilde, in his button-hole a red rose tossed to him by Carmen. And the telephone operator, a trifle distracted with the complications of her board incidental to the holiday matinée, has nevertheless an expression of intense well-being. Gigli's gold piece is only the keystone in her arch of appreciative gifts from a long list of the great ones, and when asked to describe the most satisfactory Christmas present she ever received, she promptly replies, "This job!"

On the other side of the cavernous stage the dressing-rooms are a blaze of light and industry. The time-keeper, wearing his Stetson with dignity, and a sprig of mistletoe in his buttonhole, strolls in to chat and compare notes with the dresser who is getting the room ready for the night's prima donna. He sentimentally recalls the Christmas when Farrar gave the Butterfly Baby a little squirrel coat and hat. That baby is tall and gangling now, but the small garments are packed away like precious gold.

Suddenly a chauffeur laden with heavy costume bags staggers in, grumbling at his spoiled holiday, and quickly upon his heels comes the secretary, her arms full of holly and small packages. These latter, labeled in her neat hand and meticulously tied with ribbon, are placed in a convenient mound for the prima donna to distribute. Then she and the maid festoon the mirrors and tables with the shining leaves and berries; the Pomeranian receives a bouffant scarlet necktie. The secretary looks down from time to time at an antique ring newly gracing her little finger and smiles happily. Through the open door she observes the contralto arriving: a large, motherly person, complaining bitterly to the dresser of how she has been forced to leave her darling children clustered about their tree, and go thus forth to labor.

The call-boy comes around with programs and tries to kiss the prima donna's maid. A flutist, strolling through the corridor, softly tries a bar of "Holy Night," a homesick look in his pale eyes. A member of the chorus, in pilfered wig and beard, comes strutting through as Santa, a stuffed property rock on his back for a pack, but he scuttles hastily through the door—for the diva is arriving.

"Merry Christmas, Madame, Merry Christmas!" mumble the loiterers around the stage-door. She nods and smiles, holding a white woolen scarf carefully over her mouth. At the door of her dressing-room she pauses. The secretary holds her frightened breath—suppose Madame does not like the decorations! As a matter of fact Madame does not. The leaves will prick her flying fingers at the make-up table, the gleaming berries will mock the sadness of her heart . . . for Christmas persists in awakening memories of gay, lost days better forgotten . . . but she will hide her irritation because of the look in the girl's eyes. "It is beautiful, dear!" she whispers.

And so to work. The great machinery of the

imminent performance stirs and creaks and gathers momentum. Violins and nerves tighten to concert pitch. The stage is cleared, the "grips" stand ready at their ropes, the pages are motionless behind the curtain.

"Do-re-mi-mi-mi!" essays the prima donna . . . "Oh—ah—oh—ah!" laments the contralto. Rap-tap goes the conductor's baton. This may be Christmas or Fourth of July for all it matters now . . . the play's the thing!

2. MAKING PHONOGRAPH RECORDS

(An incident)

Recording one's voice for posterity is an appalling thing and not to be undertaken lightly. On the concert platform, and most particularly in the opera, a dozen subterfuges are at a singer's command with which to cloak and veil a temporary shortcoming in pitch or phrasing. Personality covers a multitude of sins; but in the recording room costume, make-up, gestures, and temperament go for nothing; it is voice and voice alone which counts, and the slightest mistake is down for all time. No matter what the size of the royalty check, the artist takes very cold comfort in later sitting down beside the machine and detecting with futile heartburnings his musical peccadillos thus blatantly exposed to every one that hath an ear. Methods of reproduction are constantly improving, singers are slowly becoming inured, but certain essential conditions remain the same and always will.

We are permitted to be flies upon the wall of a studio on a certain day when a very famous singer indeed is engaged upon her first series of records.

It is ten o'clock in the morning, and the prima donna is due. Suspense reigns in the recording department. On one side of a curtained partition an anxious little man is carefully inspecting and brushing the dust from wax disks. Two well-dressed individuals are standing beside the arm of an enormous horn protruding from the partition, nervously consulting their watches, and absent-mindedly pricking their fingers to test the needles lying in neat boxes on a shelf behind them. A girl seated at a typewriter clicks away furiously. Out in front, seated on stools of various heights, tuning mongrel instruments which seem to have been bred from a violin and a tin horn, a dozen musicians intermittently practice a dozen different bars from seven different songs. Over in a corner reading his notes which are suspended from the ceiling sits the trombonist, making horrid noises.

Suddenly, outside, the elevator comes up and halts. The iron doors rumble open. The secretary emerges, bearing a music case under one arm, a tiny dog under the other. She stands quickly aside in order not to spoil the prima donna's entrance. The great lady wears chinchilla to-day, and a hat with a long plume.   There is not a sentimental office boy in all the building whose dream need suffer when he sees her.   Radiant with health, beauty, and professional well-being, the prima donna advances. The manager, having welcomed her effusively, walks and talks cordially at her side.

All the musicians scramble to their absurd roosts and tap their bows against their instruments in perfunctory greeting.   The prima donna smiles graciously upon them all and gayly salutes the nervous gentlemen who cease pricking their fingers to welcome her.   The music boy tries to recover his fallen sheets unobserved, while the secretary cleverly catches the prima donna's coat as she flings it off with a magnificent, free gesture.

The conductor appears and kisses the singer's finger-tips. . . . A great silence falls as she approaches the horn and balances herself nicely on her toes, advancing and retreating before it in rhythmical swaying, close for the low notes, away for the high. The music begins.   It gathers strength and volume and proceeds to a triumphal close.   The prima donna raises a white-gloved hand.

"This is terrible!" she laments.   "I can't hear anything.   It sounds like a cat-fight!"

She catches sight of the trombonist alone on his perch in the corner.   He seems to upset her.

"What is the matter with that man?   Why doesn't he sit where he belongs?"

"He has to sit there," explains the manager sweetly. "We have to keep all the loud instruments at a distance; you see the drum is outside the door."

The prima donna sings over some phrases of her first record. She sways the wrong way in a dramatic moment when she forgets herself. The record is tried out and produces a horrid shriek. Madame clutches her throat; she sends a despairing glance toward heaven, as if to say to the Almighty, "What would You?" Then to the manager, with an icy smile, she suggests that the next time it would perhaps be better to have things ready—rehearsed, as it were—before asking her to undergo this unnecessary fatigue. Only the secretary smiles readily at the prima donna's piquant sense of humor.

"Now let us all start over once more again!" says the conductor, with admirable courage and geniality, washing his hands with imaginary soap. He mounts his throne. Madame clutches her support handles. The music begins.

The manager smiles, the conductor beams as he waves his baton, the assistants finger the cigarettes in their vest-pockets. This promises well; things are going nicely. What a gorgeous voice that woman has! The lilt of the song swells and dies, the singer's last beautiful note is being spun out like a strand of silver gauze and . . . then the secretary *sneezes!*

There is a moment of black and scarlet, a tense-ness of white faces and dead silence. Frightened eyes are fixed on the wretched girl with dread fascination.

But replete as ever with charming surprises, the prima donna does not commit murder; on the contrary, she produces her most bewildering smile for the emergency.

"My dear Miss Simpson, go home at once and to bed!" says she to the quivering secretary, full of tender concern. "What is a small thing like one of my records, if you are catching cold? We will, in fact, call off my work entirely for the day. The fates seem to be against me, *Messieurs!*" With a fascinating shrug she turns toward the door, bowing graciously to the astonished gentlemen of the orchestra.

"But, Madame, your other numbers, what of them?" almost screams the perturbed manager.

"My dear man, I wouldn't go through this again to-day for a million dollars. They say you can do wonders, you modern wizards, so just cut the sneeze out; it is a good record!"

What can the man do? He bends over her hand in an excellent imitation of the Metropolitan's best manners. As suavely as possible he smilingly accompanies the little cortège to the elevator.

"Do not worry, the sneeze shall be blurred, cut out . . . never be noticed. Superb voice to-day, Madame, superb! Your *pianissimo* . . . Ah, nothing like it! Next week, then?"

But the elevator boy, scarcely sensible of his august passenger, slams the gates.

Some time later a harassed fat woman with many bundles and two small children in hand, stops at the phonograph department of a large store.

"Give me that new lullaby record of Madame Filligree's—the one with the lovely *sob* at the end. It's so sad and soothing.   Makes you feel peaceful and rested, now don't it, just to hear it!"

3.   FROM OPERA TO MOVIES

(An Interlude)

It is a cold February morning on a cliff above the Hudson River; not at all the sort of weather or scene best suited to the comfort of Thaïs, who never wore any superfluous garments.

Without preparation or any mitigating preliminaries, we are led from the frosty world outside into a cavernous cement, iron, and glass structure which houses many wonders, of which central heating is obviously not one.   We know at once, by countless signs and omens, that we are again in the mimic world, but there is an absence of tension, of the palpitating devotion to which we have become accustomed behind the scenes at the opera.   On the vast floor we pass many "sets," complete and deserted, or in the casual process of construction, but all real

activity is concentrated to-day in a special and remote corner, which has, for the moment, become a
boudoir in a villa of ancient Alexandria.   As we approach, a discussion is going on as to the exact loca-
tion of this venerable city.   A lady whom we take
to be Miss Mary Garden, although we cannot be
certain because of many enveloping veils and extra
wraps, has just made a humble suggestion, which
has met with disapproval from some gentlemen in
apparent authority.   It has been a question of de-
portment.   Miss Garden protests that thus and thus
is thoroughly *Egyptian*.   "But," cry the amazed and
indignant directors, "this ain't Egypt, Madame; this
here is Alexandria!"   Miss Garden opens wide, in-
credulous eyes.   "How very extraordinary!" she
murmurs, with just a mere *soupçon* of acerbity.

However, a whistle having blown, she indulges in
one of her special little shrugs, and with utmost
hardihood, flings off her consoling wraps and
strides forth, the complete Thaïs.   A one-layer
garment of pink chiffon, a golden girdle, sandals,
and a fillet in her hair—very beguiling indeed, but
scarcely adequate for that February morning in the
Alexandria which never was on sea or land or anywhere else but in a studio at Fort Lee, N. J.   She
is ready; she stands poised and shivering at the
entrance to her two-sided apartment.   No one else
is ready, however; for a slight commotion has been
caused by one of the youthfully pretty slaves having,
in an attempt at enhancing her beauty, slightly cut

her ankle. Blood films well, bandages even better. Therefore five minutes for coagulation!

Miss Garden, observing for the first time that she is observed, turns her charms full upon us, and we, although inured to the eccentricities of the grease-painted, stagger a little just for a moment, for she is the bilious hue of a ripe lemon, touched up with mauve, the pigment forming a coat far more sturdy and thick than anything with which she has protected her limbs. With us is another prima donna who has come to mark, learn, and inwardly digest any possibilities there may be in this branch of the arts for her own future, but her suffering colleague settles the question in a few well-chosen words. "M-m-my dear!" she advises through chattering teeth. "Don't d-d-d-do it if they offer you a m-m-m-million dollars! I n-n-never expect to sing ag-g-g-gain after this!"

Once more the whistle. The small slave's wounds are assuaged, and the scene may go forward. So, after one or two trial trips, Thaïs and her little court are eventually filmed in a two-minute progress across a corridor; and just in case it shouldn't be a success, they are filmed again, doing it three times more. This dramatic moment over, Miss Garden departs on the run for her dressing-room, looking, as she flees in frost-bitten haste, more like the Victory of Samothrace than any of the people there have the slightest idea. In five minutes she is back again. After all, it is not an involved process, this substituting of one wisp of chiffon for another, and this time she is all in smoky blue, and has added a serpent bracelet to her apparel, which makes her look almost overdressed.

Nicias, in a nice warm toga, advances from somewhere, and together they inspect the leopard-skin couch upon which they are to enact a few emotional close-ups. As they discuss the potentialities of the affair, they experiment with a tentative embrace or two, to the evident displeasure of a Levantine youth who calls himself Acting Manager.

"Look-a-here, Miss Garden, that stuff won't go very big, see? Movies is something else again from opera; you gotta just *hand* it to 'em good and plenty. Here, get the idea? I'll show you how to do it." He throws himself into the astonished arms of Nicias with what he fondly believes to be excessive and beautiful abandon. Miss Garden stands enthralled. "Oh, do it again!" she implores, as if she can scarcely look her fill, and when he has gladly complied, she thanks him effusively. "Now," she adds, "I will show you how *I am going to do it!*" Whereupon she slithers, slides, and insinuates herself into an embrace the seductiveness of which is only exceeded by the real authority and beauty of her conception. The Acting Manager smiles wanly and has to admit she is an apt pupil, take it by and large.

That scene progresses toward its climax, which is never reached. Over and over again the action is

built up to within a hair's breadth of the peak, only
to be whistled back to the beginning again. Merely
watching it makes one feel in the throes of some
nightmare wherein one climbs a glass mountain
vainly, always slipping back just as the last step is
reached.

"How can they do it?" murmurs the visiting
prima donna, mentally and irrevocably scrapping a
contract which lies waiting at home for her signa-
ture. "Where is the incentive, the reason, the reward?"

Thaïs looks over the shoulder of the bored
Nicias and makes a cabalistic sign in the air, a capi-
tal S pierced by two spears rampant. An answer
which, if unworthy, is the only one she has discovered, to date.

This, however, may have been blue Monday on
"the lot," for other prime donne, notably Geraldine Farrar, have found the movies pleasant as well
as profitable. No one denies that it is hard work;
but what is that to the thirty-six-hour day preva-
lent in the opera house? The real answer is that
they *are* prime donne, and movie queens are "something else again." Mary Pickford, had she a voice
among her other charms, might make a lovely Marguerite, but after one or two excursions upon operatic paths, would be sure to slip back gratefully to
the dear, comfortable old studio—rich in money
and experience, but glad to be "home again." So
Garden and Farrar, while still doubtless pocketing

pleasing royalties from the shadows of Carmen, and Thaïs, prefer to present those ladies in substance and song with all the familiar glamour of footlights, audience, and applause—and we certainly prefer to have them.

CHAPTER XIV

TWINKLING TOES

A FAMOUS *prima ballerina* once said, in a moment of peevishness induced by what she considered an unfair criticism in the press: "How should that man presume to write of my ballet? He is fat and cannot dance a step!" And she is quite right, if somewhat exacting. Writers certainly should dance, and we hope that if her eye ever chances to fall upon these pages, she will realize that even if our wits may lack some nimbleness, we approach the engaging subject of this chapter with a heart as light as her own pretty feet.

The ballet, although relegated to upstairs dressing-rooms and treated somewhat in the nature of a stepchild at the opera, is really of first importance and has more history, and tradition, and noblesse in its heritage than ever its haughty relative can boast. It was popular in Athens two thousand years ago, and *les grands Monarques* of France would have pawned their crowns rather than have relinquished the pleasures of the pageants and dances which enlivened their courts. From the earliest times composers have given much attention to the writing of ballets; for they realize that, although an interpretive art, like other dramatic forms, it is the only one which is the complete expression of movement—a very enticing thought to a worker in rhythm and tempo. Its chief fascination lies, however, in the simplicity of its appeal. It consists elementally of nothing in the world but the first two things a child instinctively attempts—dancing and miming . . . hence it is youth, and joy, and abandon, and all of those fleeting charms which early escape from average flat-footed lives.

Around the personality of the dancers themselves swing some of those fragrant romantic mists which glorify the prima donna. Especially was this true in former generations. Tales of great dancers have become golden legend. Princes have courted them. Was not the bewitching Fannie Ellsler beloved of that pathetic figure who was "L'Aiglon," Duc de Reichstadt? The great Taglioni had only to choose between a dozen coronets, and more recently the beautiful Cléo de Mérode played havoc with many a noble French pulse. It was at one time quite a common sight to see dignified mayors and aldermen replacing the horses between the shafts of carriages which bore these artists from the scenes of their triumphs.

Unfortunately, however, the morals of these ladies were as notoriously gossamer as their petti-coats. Whole books might be written around the romance of the Ballet Green Room at the Paris Opéra—comedy and tragedy. There was, for example, one young Coryfée who, because of her extreme beauty, was so petted and spoiled by admirers that nothing could exceed her capriciousness. When a certain gentleman protested that anything he possessed was hers, she insolently demanded a front tooth, but as soon as the fatuous lover actually appeared lisping fond vows through a disfiguring aperture in his upper jaw, she merely shrugged petulantly and declared that it was one of his lower ones that she had craved. Whether or not he obliged forthwith is not recorded, but if he did he deserved every pang it cost him.

The tragedies have been more numerous, and none sadder than the fate of the child who caught her gauze petticoats in the gas illuminators which were then used to light the scene, and a few days later died in horrible agony. However, the name of Emma Livry should go down as one of the great martyrs to the cause of Art, for even while suffering her last anguish, she permitted some of the pantomimists to witness her struggles, and tried with all her failing strength to relate her sensations to the composer of a piece in which the heroine is burned to death.

With the twentieth century has come a change, however, which has included more than gas jets; and in most of the big opera houses, especially in America, the *corps de ballet* is as earnest a band of young devotees as ever the optimistic Plato had in mind when he expressed an opinion that dancing should induce the utmost virtue, because it gives vent for the expression of many emotions and allows such unequaled opportunity for getting a great deal out of the system—or words to that effect.

The modern ballet girl is a normal youngster, much more normal indeed than her sister who has, perhaps, not come under such salubrious discipline of mind and body. A visit to the ballet school of the Metropolitan Opera will show of what material to-day's dancers are fashioned. In a big, sunny room far up in the mysterious regions above the stage, the classes hold daily sessions. A group of interested mothers sit at one side and watch with pride the gyrations of their offspring under the tutelage of a very earnest mistress, and to the urge of an insistent piano. The pupils are of all ages and sizes, from the merest tots of six or seven, who look like rosebuds on thick stems, to the first year graduates, just under sixteen, who are now regular members of the "corps," but still come here for their practice. All but the beginners work together. With their brief pink frocks, their long silken legs, their warm glowing faces, and their bobbing curls, they are the gayest of flowers in a rollicking garden.

Yet nothing but the hardest sort of work could possibly have brought about the graceful ease with which they are able to perform some of the most difficult of figures demanded by the dance-mistress. She states her requirements in a foreign tongue, and the youthful Terpsichores obey her as promptly as soldiers. The reason for the French terms, which

are always used for the elements of technique, such
as *arabesques, ronds des jambes, battements,* etc.,
is probably the same as that which causes us to use
the Italian terms of expression upon our written
music.   Out of the country where the art was first
perfected comes the nomenclature of the technical
alphabet, and they have remained, even though dancing, like music, is certainly completely international.
In the school they learn to recognize and perform
all these faultlessly, and even to put one or two in
sequence, so that the great ballets into which they
enter later, and which are but an intricate combination of all these classic elements, are not nearly as
difficult for them as they look to the outsider.

The younger the child who comes to be taught,
the better, for after twelve or thirteen the muscles
are much less apt to stretch properly, and self-con-
sciousness begins to mar the exuberant spontaneity
which is one of the principal requirements in a successful student.   Not all of these whirling, skipping,
spinning little girls will grow up to be *ballerine,* by
any means, for as a career it is probably as merci-
less in its demands as any in existence.

The girl who takes up stage dancing as a profession must have far above the average tenacity of
purpose, capacity for hard labor, and an inexhaust-
ible supply of physical vigor.   Certain builds are
better suited for the work than others, and above
all, certain temperaments. The perfect ballet
dancer really ought to be pretty, but lacking that,

as many an able one does, she should have in its
stead a certain quality which the French call "social
beauty" and which we might interpret as the ability
to make herself seem charming. Her figure will usually take care of itself, if she is normally propor-
tioned in the first place. No conscientious dancer was
ever able to accumulate much surplus flesh. In fact
there is, to illustrate this, an amusing anecdote of a
French Coryfée whose work was so conspicuously
good that she was given a part in a *bacchanale* with
two of the male artists. The director, standing
watching her in the wings, remarked upon her per-
fections to the *première danseuse,* a lady at that time
no longer in her prime and beginning to "thicken."

"Is she not superb, *ma chère?*" he demanded
effusively.

"Bah!" replied the jealous one. "That dance
makes me think of nothing but two dogs fighting
over a bone!"

The children learn the three main divisions of
their art before they are graduated. In other words:
the popular forms of steps, the traditional "toe" of
the classic ballet, and the rhythmic movement and
effect of poise which more nearly approximates the
Hellenic. On this last many modern "schools" are
entirely founded, but the operatic dancer must be
facile in all the styles, and by far the hardest of
these is the "toe."

The hour of leaping, bending, gliding, and the
ever popular *battements*—those swift little twisting

beats of the ankles together before landing which give that fascinating flame-like quality of "twinkle" to the feet when in the air—is at last over. "Change slippers!" cries the instructor; and two score little pink powder-puffs sink on the floor, and drag on tiny satin slippers with stiffened blunt toes. In another moment they are up and posing like so many butterflies along the rail which, waist high, runs about three walls.   With incredible swiftness, each little girl has grown a full six inches taller. They come down the room in a quivering phalanx, waving their frail arms, and laughing for mere joy in their accomplishment; and when they reach the great mirror which forms the entire wall at the end of the room, regard themselves therein with frank admiration.

On one toe, now, with the other leg stiff and waist-high—at the side—then the rear!   Here is test for a fairy's balance.   One or two of the big girls manage it somehow, and the littlest one of all accomplishes it with the utmost perfection, but most of them collapse in merry heaps, from which they rise on eager springs to make another attempt. While they rest, the "jumping girls" come forward, and skimming the floor seem to sail through the air in a series of graceful leaps which almost defy the laws of gravitation.

Suddenly a clock strikes the hour.   The lesson is not over, by any means, but several of the tallest dancers drop out of the ranks, and with a smile from which they can scarcely keep the conscious pride, and a murmured word about its being *Rigoletto* to-night, they slip quietly out and across the great iron bridge which spans the stage. These are the girls who are already in the ballet. The others pause a second to follow them with wistful glances of admiration and envy.

Adored by every one, from the tiniest tot to "that wonderful one who is nearly thirty years old"—a hoary, venerable age in the ballet—is Rosina Galli, première of the Metropolitan for the last eight seasons. A *petite* creature with muscles of iron, and a lovely, piquant face upon which, in spite of all her work and care, no hint of a line is yet visible—who stares very seriously at one with what she is pleased to call her "green" eyes, and has many diverting things to tell. Like her compatriot, the amiable Mr. Scotti, her English is quaint, but quite adequate and very charming.

Nothing but that mysterious inner urge, which gives the born artist no peace until he finds self-expression in his proper medium, is responsible for making Rosina a dancer. Certain it is that she got no help from her parents. Her mother had seriously considered entering a nunnery before Signor Galli changed her plans, and he was a railroad employee completely absorbed in engines and time-tables. Their eldest child, Rosina's brother, played the violin, to be sure; but that meant next to nothing in a country where music is as essential as grammar and arithmetic. The little girl, however, was different. Her wayward spirit seemed to be dedicated to something very special from the moment she scrambled out of her cradle; but, as in most busy, practical Latin families, no one paid very much attention to her childish vagaries and she developed her taste alone and unnoticed.

In the long corridor of the apartment in which they lived at that time were hanging many framed pictures of the artists at La Scala and the theaters of Milan. Most of them were in costume and in dramatic pose. Before she could even read, little Rosa would stand admiringly before these, and in the privacy of her own small room would imitate them by the hour, with who knows what unexplained thrill of prophetic imagination. Then when, on a spring afternoon, the hand-organ man would visit the quiet square upon which their house stood, she would run out madly and dance before him until he tired of turning his crank and went away. No one taught her the steps, yet those who saw them say that they were intricate and graceful, not just the ordinary caperings of a baby. In her own mind she was Mignon, or Carmen, or Nedda, like the pretty ladies in the picture-frames.

One day, however, the Galli family put on its best clothes and went forth to a local hall to witness a costume pageant, in which there were amateur entries, and a prize, and that day marked a turning-point in the career of the tiny girl whose chubby hand was held so tightly in her big brother's. Not quite tight enough, though, careless boy! A great circle was cleared in the center of the floor, and one after the other, the contestants for the prize stepped out and performed such struttings and preenings as they hoped would charm the judges. But it was quite too much for the young Rosina. The only way in which to express her complete scorn was to go out there and show them all something really worth while. Wrenching her hand from the casual clasp of her brother, she sprang into the ring, and there, as the music burst into a gay gavotte, performed as captivating a baby *pas seul* as had ever delighted the eyes of those favored Milanese. The judges capitulated at once, and waited to view no more contestants. In spite of the profuse apologies of her scandalized parents, and the indignant protests of the other entries that she was neither in costume nor had she paid her entrance fee, the prize was given to her unanimously then and there.

A family consultation was held that night, and in spite of her extreme youth she was packed off the following autumn to school, to keep her out of mischief. How much this availed we shall see. For nearly three years she behaved herself with great circumspection, and had nearly succeeded in reëstablishing her parents' confidence, when one day she heard a bit of news which got her so by the ears that she neglected her lessons outrageously. The

girls were all talking about the approaching try-
outs for the Ballet School at La Scala. To the
small Miss Galli this sounded like the gates of
Heaven ajar, and from that moment she never
gave her mother and father one hour of peace.
She had not known that it was possible for a little
girl to be so happy as she upon that day when they
finally yielded, doubtless out of cheer exhaustion,
and she was taken to the big theater with the others,
and was looked over by the ballet mistress and the
directors, very much after the manner in which the
prospective purchaser examines the points of a filly.
Some of the other children passed muster and some
were refused, but when it came to her turn, she felt
no nervousness. She knew perfectly her destiny,
and it was no surprise when she heard the masters
say among themselves: "This one we will take. She
is much too young, but only see how strong is her
back and how straight her little legs. Observe how
her head nods in exact time with the music!"

So she was accepted, and her mother, on hearing
the news, promptly burst into tears. Whereupon,
Mr. Gatti-Casazza, who was then director, and happened to be present, came up to her and offered her
this solace: "Do not grieve, my dear Signora, for
you will see that at the end of the three months'
probation period she will find the work so much too
hard that she will gladly come running home to
you."

Mr. Gatti, however, for once in his life was

wrong; and little Miss Rosina, instead of running home weeping to mother, so distinguished herself in her first few lessons that one day when the director of the dance wanted a child for a character bit in one of the big new ballets he was soon to put on, he came to consult the mistress of the school, and her choice fell unhesitatingly upon this youngest of the new pupils. Little Rosa went down to the rehearsal room very elated, and not in the least frightened. Nothing in the line of dancing possessed any uncertainties for her; it was as natural to her as for a duckling to swim.

When the ballet master bent an amused and slightly dubious look upon this diminutive candidate, and said, "Can you do me a little dance to *polka* time, all the while playing upon this small fiddle?" she replied brightly, "But of a certainty, *Maestro!*" and taking up the violin and holding it as she so often had done at home when mischievously mimicking her brother at his practicing, she tapped her impatient toes, *one—two—three,* and was off, whirling about the big room in perfect step and rhythm, to the utter delight of all the seasoned dancers present. The part was hers without a murmur, and they even added a bit of business here and there because she was so delicious.

But at home she said nothing, and they never asked. What she did at the opera house interested them as little as the schedules of her father's trains concerned her. Her mother, however, did notice

that she always seemed to be humming a certain
little tune, and commented upon its monotony.

"What is that ugly thing?" said she.

"Oh, nothing much!" answered Rosina, although
what should it be but her own beloved little polka?
She was trembling in her boots these days for fear
her parents might hear of her exploitation and in
some way take exception to it and withdraw her.

At last came the night of the first performance,
and the child was given two tickets wherewith to
invite her family to be present. They accepted
them casually enough, without even commenting upon the unusual event. They thoroughly enjoyed the
opera which preceded the dance, and along toward
midnight, when the curtain rose on the finale, they
had not even troubled to look at their programs,
so they wondered a little about a very small person
dressed as a music master, who carried a violin and
led the march of all the dancers. They concluded
that, as its movements were so perfect, it must be
one of those marionettes or automatons that they
had heard about. In a few minutes, however, the
tiny figure stepped out alone and began to do the
prettiest three-step in the world. Then it was that
the mother suddenly recognized her child and almost
fainted. As soon as she had sufficiently recovered
she dashed around to the stage-door. But it was
too late; Rosina had scored a *succès fou*.

The little girl had a thoroughly enjoyable evening altogether. It was the first time that she had

seen the big stage, for in those days at La Scala rules were very strict indeed, and no mere ballet child ever dared to enter the sacred precincts of "the house." The lights, and the vast spaces, and the excitement of having an audience, so stimulated her that she danced as never before. When the applause thundered over and the master cried to her "Do it over again!" she was puzzled. In her previous experience, if one had to repeat, it was because one was "no good." However, here she was, doing it even a third time, to delighted cries of "Brava!" It was all very wonderful.

The next day the family of Galli descended upon the opera to withdraw their daughter. An army with banners could not have torn the child then from her adoring masters, but it took the combined diplomacy of Mr. Gatti and all his lieutenants to persuade the parents of the crime it would be to blight a career of such brilliant promise. So Rosina stayed, and joyfully signed the customary contract which obligated her to study, and give her free services for the period of ten years. Nevertheless, in her case, the first and only exception was made in all the century-and-a-half of La Scala's history, and she was graduated with honors after only six years had passed, leaving the scholars' ranks to become *prima ballerina* of the company. How that girl worked, and how happy she was! Even Papa and Mama, the skeptical, at last began to take a little notice, and brag somewhat to the neighbors.

Then came the inevitable day when an impresario from America sought her out. "But I was only sixteen, and I was much frighten' of that big sea. I was shame' to let 'im know I scar', so I ask 'im so *moach money* maybe he quickly laugh and go away. Now what you think, *hein?* He say, 'Sure, all right, you engaged!'" So Rosina took her mother ("Who do me no good at all, she so seeck") and crossed that terrible ocean, and came to Chicago, where she dazzled local audiences with her youth and beauty and extraordinary technique, until her old friend, Mr. Gatti in New York, could stand it no more. After the war made certain changes possible, he lost no time at all in once more drawing her beneath the shadow of his ægis. The rest is current history. Never has the *corps de ballet* been so excellent individually and collectively, and never has there been, since the brief sojourn of Pavlowa, a première who ranked with the singing stars in popularity.

This brief life history sounds too gilt-edged to be anything but unique; however, Miss Galli claims that it is merely the normal result of a consuming enthusiasm and energy; and that any American girl, with even less natural endowment, could have the same success, if she had an equal amount of loyalty to herself and her teachers. "It make me seeck when you all say, 'Ah, zose wonaireful Russians, zose passionate Italians . . . sure, it is natural for 'im to dance!' No, I tell you, I 'ave seen *stupid*

Italians, *dumb* Russians, and Americans what have *fire*. All kinds in all countries, and dancing she is international. I am awful mad. If I tell lies and say my girls all straight from Moscow . . . Whew, you see some fine notices in the papers, *hein?* I tell you no ballet in all the world is any better than right here. Only they should not so moach chew that gum; and I tell them, 'You go to bed early and read nice book now.' But no, all the time they say they got to go to the Movie!"

She implies perhaps that the life of the American youth lacks discipline. If so, she certainly makes up for it during those hours when the "corps" practices under her direct supervision. "They awful scare' from me!" she confides with a sly wink. "You come and see!"

So to a rehearsal of the ballet in *La Juive* we wend our way upon a day when three other rehearsals are being held in various parts of that vast house. The chorus in the Ladies' Parlor, *Götterdämmerung* in the tea-room, and *Pelléas and Mélisande* upon the stage. The ballet is, as usual, upon the roof. The long room is full of girls, laughing and chattering like a fashionable boarding-school at recess, while along the walls various earnest ones are practicing pirouettes, and helping each other with the difficult business of raising a pointed toe to unnatural heights. They all wear simple dresses of rose color and long silk hose, a pretty contrast from the ballet practice of yesterday, when the "ladies" kept on their street attire above the waist, and the tarlatan below.

Miss Galli appears in a pink silk slip and a sweater; her assistant, Mr. Bonfiglio, like a colonial page, in knickerbockers and white hose. A secretary presents her with a discarded curtain pole, the end of which she brings down on the floor with a bang. A lean gentleman at the piano catches her eye and strikes the keys, managing in some marvelous fashion to produce the effect of a full orchestra. The girls spring to position, and with an incredible absence of confusion are suddenly off in the whirling intricacies of an elaborate country dance. To amateur eyes it seems already the acme of perfection, but the curtain rod beats an angry insistence upon the rhythm with increasing fury. The "green" eyes flash. "Will you please to tell me who is dead that you all look so sorry?" she cries. Or, "Are you so tired then that you must sleep already, my goodness!" There must be sixty revolving figures, but she keeps an eye on each individual performer, and praises or scolds as the case deserves. In the next rest, one young thing who "went to sleep" in the wrong place is dissolved in tears, whereupon Miss Galli puts her arms around the heaving shoulders and kisses the hot cheek until the sun breaks through the clouds again.

Once more the orchestral piano, and the rush of satin slippers. This time a circle is left in their midst and Miss Galli and Mr. Bonfiglio run out for

their *pas de deux*.   It cannot be said that they over-
exert themselves—that will come later during their
private practice—but now, as they scarcely more than
walk through their parts, they nevertheless manage
to give a complete impression of what their dance
is like.   A tilt of the head, a swing of the body, a
turn of the ankle, and we visualize the figures as
clearly as if they were done before our eyes.

Her affair ended, Miss Galli comes back to her
chair beside us, and takes up her pole again.   "But
watch now, you will see something!" she whispers,
and to our delight ten of our wee friends of the
school now appear to take part in this particular
ensemble.   They are evidently little soldiers, and
march and countermarch so prettily that it reminds
us of the anecdote of the famous Taglioni, who upon
one occasion was leading a band of Amazons upon
the stage of the Paris Opéra.   In the nearest loge
sat the distinguished General Bugeaud, and as the
line passed him she heard, or fancied she heard
him murmur words of unfavorable comment.   Being
of an inflammable temperament, she stopped the
maneuvers then and there and invited him, if he
thought he could do it better, to come up and take
her sword.   "Thank you, Mademoiselle, I have
mine!" said he, to her surprise, springing over the
footlights and accepting the challenge.   Then, to
the huge delight of the audience and the chagrin of
Taglioni, he proceeded to put her little army
through a complicated infantry drill.   They scarcely

made a mistake, and at the end, as he returned to his box, he stopped and kissed her hand. "My compliments to La Taglioni, these ladies must have seen military service!"

Miss Galli's little army is quite as disciplined, and her wee soldiers are utterly adorable. Their susceptible hearts being supposedly won by the young ladies twice their size, they proceed to make ardent love after her careful instructions. The younger the child, the more perfect her pantomime. Two of them are inimitable. "They have not yet learne' to look in that mirror, those ones. Tha's why!" she explains. She then proceeds to introduce a little new business in regard to a flower snatched by rival suitors. Her instructions are explicit . . . "Now, you don' like it moach he has that rose. You *ver'* mad—but you little gentlemans. All right —he got it—you make nice bow. See?"

They do see. They interpret with an exactness that is convulsing. The big girls seem almost *gauche* beside them. Gradually, however, as the dance progresses, the correct scale is reëstablished and the graceful creatures weave in and out, dip, sway, and turn in a confusion that is perfect order in their minds. But nothing, of course, that is done is haphazard; every step or change of pose is made to express a particular idea or series of ideas.

It suddenly occurs to us then that some one must have devised all this with actual creative skill, and naturally that some one is Miss Rosina Galli. Not only does she plan and arrange the figures of every ballet in every opera, but she studies beforehand all of the music as carefully as if she were to conduct the piece herself. When the composer thoughtlessly failed to include enough measures for her needs, it is she who must seek out other fragments of his works and adapt and include them, as for instance, in the last act of *Carmen*. "That is hard, too, for in a fourth act public are sleepy. We cannot give 'im waving veils. We got to wake 'im up!"

Then, too, no costume plate goes to the wardrobe department for reproduction before it has been submitted to her. She spends hours with the designer when a new production is to be staged, and has many original ideas which are eagerly seized upon. In devising a ballet, she has not only the general plan to construct, but the detail of the special groups. All the girls are not fitted for every sort of dancing. Some are what she calls "athletic," who do the character and eccentric bits best; others are obviously suited to Russian, Spanish, or Oriental types; some are good in boys' parts, others can only be girls; some are best at pantomime, others excel in classic posturing; although every one has, of course, the same foundation. It is almost as trying as casting a play.

Although only a year or so older than the average among them, she scolds them, and loves them like the old woman who lived in a shoe, and her sense

of humor never deserts her, except when she is afraid
that she is not going to have time for her own
practicing. At five-thirty, with only an hour or so
before she has to begin dressing for the evening
performance, she sends them all scampering off and
really gets down to work. Everything else that
has gone before in the busy day has been but the
divertissement of her profession for her. This
quiet hour of grueling effort is the center of everything to her . . . her Art.

The vociferous piano is still, the room is empty.
Miss Galli has at last her heart's solace, and from
below, as they scurry homeward, floats up the laughter of the Coryfées.

Inexplicably saddened in the aftermath of all this
youth and exuberance, we remember an ancient epi-
taph penned by a bereaved Frenchman who loved
a dancer:

> O terre, ne pese pas sur elle,
> Sur toi elle a si peu pesé!

CHAPTER XV

FROM THE ORCHESTRA PIT

THERE is one beautifully consistent thing about every one of any importance at the opera house. They are all sincerely convinced that their particular department is the mainspring of the institution; and there is no doubt at all that in this very conviction and its corollary enthusiasm, lies that element of vitality and energy which makes a colossal undertaking like opera possible at all. There is something sublime and untrammeled about it, something joyous and serene.

One feels this most keenly when conversing with some of the great conductors. They may go late to bed, worn and fagged with a day of rehearsing followed by an exacting performance, but they set this at naught against the pangs of exquisite spiritual agony which they so gladly suffer every time they take up the baton. Now that absolute monarchy has been swept away, probably nowhere in the world is the divine prerogative so nearly approximated as from the conductor's desk. In order to grasp this in all the fullness of its truth, it is necessary to select the greatest genius of the baton available, and win his confidence.

Tullio Serafin, late of that cradle of our great

importations, La Scala, receives us. French being the only common conversational ground upon which we may meet, an expression in that language by chance starts the ball rolling with an impetus we had scarcely dared hope for.

"Opera from the point of view of the *Chef d'Orchestre!* Ah, now you ask me something difficult!" he protests; but as he has certainly first rights to such a viewpoint, we press the matter, and discover that it is in the French term that he finds much material for discussion, and that he takes violent exception to it. Even "conductor" does not completely mollify him. *Chef,* all by itself, is what a conductor is where he comes from, and what, in his opinion, he should be. Chief, or commander, would be our English equivalent, and without any limitation or classification after it, please observe. Now, as Mr. Serafin is an exceptionally modest man, even poking sly fun at certain "egoisms" among others of his calling, it is a little difficult to reconcile his proud words with his otherwise humble attitude. However, by a convulsive effort of the intuition, we suddenly become aware that he is only exhibiting one of those incomprehensible and admirable qualities of real genius, the ability to think outside of himself, and to disassociate his artistic being from his personality as a man.

Let us consider, then, what his conception is. If a living composer comes to a theater to conduct one of his own works, there can be no question whatsoever as to whose word is final upon any point that may be raised in connection with the performance, from the reading of a passage in the score, to the *mise en scène*, the lights, and the dramatic action. The work belongs to the composer, it is the child of his brain and his imagination, and his word is absolute. This does not mean in any sense that he sets concrete limitations. Quite often he will not only be surprised but gratified to hear one of his phrases, or behold one of his characters, in the hands of an inspired artist, developed and carried above and beyond what he had himself conceived. This growth must always be, however, in accordance, and not at variance, with the lines of the original conception. Now Maestro Serafin (and, he maintains, any conscientious conductor) insists that the author of the piece shall *always* be present at every performance. As this is obviously impossible, being prevented by physical limitations, or in most cases by the black waters of the River Styx, an understudy must take his place. And who, then, if not the conductor?

Following out this theory meticulously, Mr. Serafin dislikes to assume his baton for the interpretation of any opera the author of which is alive and well, without having first discussed with him every minutest detail, and not only learned to know the work through the creator's eyes, but to look even deeper and try to know the man himself. Thus he makes frantic journeys hither and yon, on the trail of everybody from Richard Strauss to Stravinsky. As for the Italian composers, little and big, there is scarcely one of them who has ever set down two notes together on paper that is not numbered among his intimate friends. In regard to those composers who have departed beyond the reach of boat or train, he makes equal efforts at acquaintance and friendship. Before presuming to interpret any of Wagner's works, he collected about himself a veritable library of Wagneriana, and proceeded to dig. Nothing that has been recorded of what that great man said, did, or thought, escaped him, and only after it had all been carefully assimilated did he presume even to read through one of his scores. The same with Verdi, Gounod, Mozart, Beethoven, and Glück. He knows them as they may not have known themselves, and without a doubt, when his turn comes to step on Charon's Ferry, he will find them all grouped about the wharf on the other side, waiting to welcome an old friend.

But this is not all, by any means, which entitles him to call himself Chief. He must have a grasp of the drama as well as the music, for it was in this manner that the composer first went to work. Therefore he once more visits all the libraries to which he has access and acquaints himself with everything pertaining not only to the actual libretto, but to the life and times of the story. When this is accomplished, we may venture to suppose that he has begun to have a hold on the thing, but then comes the study of the words, which he goes into almost as thoroughly as if he were to understudy the entire cast.

All this time he has been delving into the music score, and making delightful discoveries, and unearthing an enormous amount of information, which, in the light of all he knows already, can never really surprise him much. As his study of the orchestration and the ensemble grows apace, he branches out into other fields—for instance, the lighting. He cannot permit a yellow light, when the music is distinctly *blue*. He cannot have dusk arrive while the sun still shines in the orchestra.

This and other analogous matters having been settled to his—or rather, let us say, to the composer's—taste, he is prepared to confront the artists upon the stage. This seems to hold no terrors for him. Wearing, as he does, the shoes of the composer and author, why should he ever expect or dread such a scene as that famous occasion upon which his esteemed colleague, Arturo Toscanini, than whom there is none greater, crossed swords with Geraldine Farrar during a rehearsal of *Butterfly*. The conductor took exception to Miss Farrar's tempo in the reading of a phrase, and she, aghast at the indignity of his presumption in criticizing her, came to the footlights and asked with some asperity, "Are you not aware that I am a star?"

"Star?   Star?" cried he excitedly.   "There are
no stars but those in heaven, Signorina!"   But that
brief repartee opened a breach which took long
months to heal, and the great *Maestro* saw to it that
the American soprano did not soon again appear
under his baton.

Serafin forestalls any such *contretemps*, not only
by a primary insistence on his absolute authority,
but also on a frank admission that the orchestra is
there in an opera for the express purpose of ampli-
fying the action on the stage, and that its only purpose is to sustain, accompany and interpret the work
of the singer.   This is indeed a radical departure,
at least in acknowledged policy, if not in actual performance, from the usual proclamations of the orchestra leader who loves to enlarge upon the advantages of giving a great work like *Tristan und Isolde*
without the encumbrance of any voices at all.   (This
is where Serafin interjects "Rank egoism!")   So he
is not only author, composer, *regisseur*, but diplomat; and if you doubt it, you have only to go to one
of his performances and, sitting where you can watch
his activities, observe that his attention is fixed
quite as closely upon what goes on upon the stage
as in the pit below him.   "I must hold the entire
ensemble in my hands," he explains.   "And furthermore, I must make them all feel, through my energy
and my personality, that I am supremely capable of
doing it!"   Any one who would presume to doubt

it in the face of such whole-souled conviction, and such appallingly earnest and fundamental endeavor, would be a pert and negligible upstart.

He believes, however, in encouraging individual enterprise in the singing actors, and will support original interpretations to the utmost degree, if he feels that they are the result of a single-hearted artistic growth. But with the exploiting of self he has no sympathy; no one is quicker to chop off with brutal indifference a tenor's "linkèd sweetness" that is too "long drawn out." In fact, one of this man's striking characteristics is that he always seems hurrying himself and everybody along, even if his actual tempo is sedate. The sweep and swing of the music animates his entire body, and before the first act is half done, his shirt and collar are a complete wreck, and his recalcitrant mop of gray hair is hanging in wet strands over his eyes. Yet in spite of this violence, his conducting is comforting to the ear, and merciful to the voices on the stage.

Conductors vary as to methods of wielding the baton. Most of the Germans, and by that term we include the regular interpreters of German works, indulge in an athletic exuberance which seems to produce a similar response in the instruments—and great is the ensuing din. Bodansky, however, seems to wring the same volume of sound from his band by a system of swoops, and strange serpentine gestures which are utterly fascinating. One conductor at the Metropolitan puts his hand, if it happens to be idle for a second, neatly into his pocket, but he has to withdraw it so often and so quickly that the aperture, in order to outlast a performance, must surely be bound with leather, like those of the bus conductors. Alfred Hertz, a famous leader, once at the opera, and now of the San Francisco Orchestra, was, in spite of his conspicuous lameness, one of the greatest gymnasts who ever wielded a baton; while Toscanini, a little emaciated man who towered head and shoulders musically above all his contemporaries, wrought his mighty works as quietly as if he were embroidering. He is also one of those rare geniuses who memorizes his entire score, and never takes a note with him to his desk. He was extremely susceptible to the artists upon the scene. At a rehearsal one day, the second act of *Tristan* was probably given more wonderfully than ever before or since. A very great Isolde was on the stage, and Toscanini, thankful for this relief after several recent experiences with lesser interpreters, and having utter confidence in her response, let himself go with an unwonted prodigality. The singer felt the electrical contact and opened the floodgates of her entire artistic being. The tide swept the stage, and the waves broke about the conductor's stand. Toscanini, not to be outdone, loosed still further dynamic powers he scarcely knew he possessed; the singer answered with a flight to even greater heights. So they went on, merging their genius and lifting and urging each other, until all the casual listeners and minor directors present felt the almost intolerable strain so strongly that they stopped whatever they were doing, and stood enthralled as if in the presence of a miracle. At the end, Isolde's cheeks were wet with tears, and Toscanini's inscrutable face looked weary. There are few moments like that in a lifetime, even in the opera house; and the members of the orchestra, who fiddle all day and all night and have a right to be bored by almost everything, are still talking about that rehearsal to this day.

It was not long afterward that this same conductor announced that he felt too keenly the restrictions of *musique de théâtre,* and declared his intention of devoting himself exclusively to *musique pure.* Whereupon he left the opera, where he certainly was "Chief" if any one ever was, and took unto himself a Symphony Orchestra. However, according to latest reports, he now finds this less interesting and goes back to the field of his first triumphs.

With Serafin, all forms of real music are equally satisfactory. He "adores" concerts, in which he can have free rein with his deities, Beethoven and Bach, or indulge his flaming interest in the "moderns"; but he "adores" the opera too; chamber music is his delight; he is a distinguished performer upon both violin and piano. But, in his opinion, this is scarcely noteworthy. To be a worthy "Chief," one must have mastered everything over which one may presume to wield authority, and also one must allow oneself very few digressions.

This has been an *"idée fixe"* ever since, as a boy of nine, he first beheld a conductor raise his baton. At that moment he definitely decided what to do with his life and took steps accordingly. Fighting his way up through the intricacies of the piano, the violin, and several other instruments, he at last won a position in the orchestra. From here he progressed to the dignity of a *répétiteur* (or coach, a sort of "general utility" in an opera house) and then became for a while a *régisseur* (one of those minor musical directors who govern the mechanical processes upon the stage). Not satisfied with this much versatility, he studied for and obtained the important post of chorus master, and from there he went back again into the orchestra pit, first as Toscanini's assistant and understudy, and later as his successor.

Thus, and thus only, is the conductor made. The process is going on all the time. Some painstaking young man who holds a score back of the scenes, counts "One, two, three!" and rings a bell at the correct moment, will doubtless one day be out there in that restless cavern, the proud wearer of a collar wilted in the cause of art, while greedy "Symphonies" step in and snatch away the old Chiefs. Damrosch, and Stransky, and Mengelberg, and Hertz, not to mention a dozen others, began in the opera house; but so did Cleofante Campanini, who never left it to the day of his death. For some the witchery of playing like a soloist upon an instrument of strings and winds and drums with human keys; for others the fascination of this same, subordinated ever so slightly to the drama, which in its turn watches so docilely from the corners of its eyes upon the other side of the footlights; and for some, like Tullio Serafin, the glorious joy to be found in every kind of true music under the sun.

The king, however, has subjects, else he would not be a king, and the greatest of these are his henchmen who sit in humility at his feet and who raise their eyes and sweat out their souls at the lift of his hand. Union men all, in this day of commerce, and growing sleek with comfortably filled pockets, yet eking out a slim existence around three cardinal points—the orchestra pit, the lunch counter, and bed. A morning rehearsal, a matinée performance, and the regular evening's work is their average day. What is opera or music drama to them? Merely their job. It is perhaps more exciting or diverting to play under one conductor than another, a trifle nerve-racking to lean on a beginner, a little upsetting to respond to the beat of a newcomer who blithely digs them up out of accustomed grooves; but, take it all in all, a fairly monotonous calling, although every one of them is an accomplished musician in his own right. As for any enjoyment they may derive from the performance upon the stage, one has but to consider the trench in which they huddle, to realize with somewhat of a shock that even if they have time to glance up from their ceaseless occupation, they can see little or nothing, and that some of the 'cellists and bass viols and harps may have been in daily attendance for twenty-five years without ever so much as a fleeting glimpse of any of the great artists performing directly above their heads.

The man who has the finest view of all the proceedings is the prompter, or *souffleur,* as he is called by the initiated, who sits partially downstairs, and partially up, with his head and shoulders on a level with the stage just where he can breathe all the dust. His sufferings may be many, and his compensations few, but one thing he never has is a chill. His little box fits him like a glove, and the heat of the adjacent footlights is not inconsiderable, while his responsibilities keep him in a fever. He dare not lift more than one eye at a time from his page, for if he loses his place, disaster follows swift and sure. It is he who gives every cue to every singer, and just in case they be absent-minded he makes a practice of pointing a long and accusing finger at each one as the moment arrives for them to give tongue. He must be *en rapport* with the conductor in the matter of cuts, and he must know all the special weaknesses in each opera, and the individual stumbling-blocks of the various singers. If tangles occur, it is he who must straighten them out without ever leaving the confines of his coop, and if some stupidity occurs, no matter whose, it is he who must shoulder the blame. So he may have his seat in the front row center as long as he likes, quite uncontested by us.

CHAPTER XVI

THE AUDITION

IN the spring every one knows what happens to the young man's fancy; but there are other symptoms just as reliable. For instance, hurdy-gurdies, and little boys with tops, geraniums on the window-sills, and "auditions" at the opera house.

The property man whistles a cheerful little lay, for his anxious moments are dwindling as the season's end approaches. He directs the placing of a piano on the stage, and offers to the unseen royal family seated out in the darkened house a merry jest concerning his willingness to oblige with a song. He then retires to the wings to watch with callous enjoyment the first performance of the season about which he does not have to worry. Anxiety is one of the chief ingredients which flavors life behind the scenes at the opera, but no moments are more thoroughly fraught with this devastating emotion than these annual voice trials. Here, on a brief April afternoon, the hopes and fears of future Carusos and Melbas are either confirmed or knocked promptly on the head. Teachers shape their whole curriculum toward this very date and hour.

The appointment is set for five o'clock, but fifteen minutes before that time the small foyer leading to the staff offices begins to fill with fluttering candidates. They are of all sizes, types, and of both sexes, although chiefly the female prevails. Their nationality is, however, frankly and predominantly American. They are very dressy, almost without exception, for this is their great moment, you understand, probably the greatest of their lives to date, and they believe in the self-assurance which goes along with one's best apparel. Possibly the ladies go further and faintly hope that a bit of beaded chiffon may charm the eye and influence a decision which the ear repudiates.

But they do not know their audience. The men who are to sit in judgment upon them are so inured to make-up and costume of every extravagant design in the world that the only thing which might possibly win their favorable comment would be the most constrained simplicity. In fact they scarcely even glance at the stage unless something in tone or diction first catches their attention. This audition may be the biggest heart-throb in a young life, but for the director's committee it is a bit of routine business filled with inexpressible ennui.

It cannot, and it *must* not, be said that Americans are given no chance at the opera house. The doors are open to them, let them come in hordes! Nothing in all the world would please the impresario better than to find a pearl, even of great price, in a local oyster. However, long experience has robbed the occasion of much of its stimulation. He and his *aides* face the tragi-comedy before them with what grace they can, feeling only a very mild flutter of expectancy at first, quickly followed by a sense of irritation that in turn gives place to gray despair. Unless, of course, the unexpected happens. . . . Ah, there is a thrill for even these seasoned veterans, when the drabness of the affair is suddenly lifted and shot through with light by the first glorious notes sung by, let us say, a shopkeeper's daughter from Bridgeport, Connecticut. Rosa Ponselle gave these gentlemen such a pleasant shock one spring day that they can never feel the same about "auditions" again.

But to return to the foyer. A young person who has permitted herself far too soon the generous physique which only a seasoned prima donna can hope to carry off successfully, enters attended by two assiduous friends. One of the latter is quite palpitant, considerably more so, in fact, than the heroine. Marching up to the mail-clerk with an air which she imagines to be truly operatic, she announces grandly that "Miss Bean has an appointment to sing for Signor Gatti. Will you please announce her?" But the clerk is unimpressed. "Yeah, just tell her to sit down." The friend bristles just a trifle, and returning to La Bean moans, "My dear, do sit over here out of the draught, and cover your mouth; this smoke is so dreadful for that precious throat!" The glamour of potential stardom is already gilding the ample proportions of this familiar schoolmate.

Others have now come in. A very young girl,
pale but with bravely scarlet lips, has brought
mother along to sustain her, but that indifferent
parent has an evening paper to read and the daily
cross-word puzzle to check up. If her daughter
wants to be an opera-singer, all right; give her
enough rope and she'll hang herself. No one is going to be fool enough to engage that young sheep's-
head. Coming from Germany where operatic artists
are goddesses she knows that her Mitzi is far too
human. She, Mitzi's mother, is only here to get
this thing over once for all and have a "little peace
in the family yet." Now the door opens to admit
an elderly woman, who has been just a trifle too
lavish with the rabbit's foot, and who does not
dream how sweet she would really look if she let
that softening gray show around her temples. She
has a proprietary air, as if the opera house were
her special *pied à terre,* and speaks with a slightly
foreign accent, although one feels somehow convinced that she was born right around the corner.
With her, like a nervous flock of chicks, come four
palpitant girls and one forlorn young man. She
shepherds them all to a bench in the corner, glaring
so at a pale little woman in black who is already
there that she promptly gets up and yields her seat
without question.

The last additions to an already overcrowded
antechamber are a woman just over the edge of her
youth and her escort, a man in spats who looks like

Bond Street, but talks like Michigan Avenue. His lady is excessively agitated, a fact which she tries to hide by a flickering laugh and an air of *camaraderie* with the various employees who pass through the premises. It is obvious that she has been here before, but in what capacity it would be hard to say. "Isn't it just too ridiculous *my* having to sit out here like this! It makes me feel so funny!" she giggles. Drawing off long white gloves, she fans herself restlessly. "Gatti's the one who ought to be nervous, not I. He may lose me yet if he doesn't look out!" Her airy jest falls dead upon preoccupied ears, heads are bent apprehensively over sheets of music. Only the rosy-cheeked girl on the bench beside her looks up with wide eyes. "I don't mind telling the world that *I'm* simply paralyzed!" she announces.

This is, however, merely the *Vorspiel;* back in the darkened house, the ordeal is on.

The stage, set for the first act of *Carmen,* is empty of all but the piano. The curtains are drawn and the footlights blaze full and without mercy upon the shivering candidate who tries to cross that vast platform with some desperate semblance of ease and grace. Some have brought their accompanists as familiar props, but for the others a patient and sympathetic employee of the house is there to see them through. To break the ice, the poor victim usually tries to reach the comparative shelter of the piano and there converse for a moment or two on one pretext or another, just to get used to the feel

of that terrifying stage. The fatal plunge has to
be taken at last, however. The pianist plays the
opening bars of whatever has been chosen by the
teacher as best suited to show the pupil's talents;
the singer swallows, gasps, clenches her hands, and
begins. The poor, misguided creature will almost
infallibly attempt the most florid, difficult, and
famous of arias which even the greatest stars approach with some misgivings. A listing of selec-
tions in one audition sounds like a page from a catalogue of phonograph records. Everything from *Dich
Theure Halle* to the *Pagliacci Prologue* is attacked
with ambitious impartiality, although the youngest
girls are much addicted to *Butterfly* and *Tosca,* as
pleasing visions of Geraldine dance in their heads.

To a student of human nature these auditions are
fascinating. Given a test before which iron nerves
might be excused for trembling, these valiant youths
succeed somehow in presenting at least an exterior
of admirable *sang-froid*. The men are always un-
easy and very pale—and occasionally a young
woman loses her nerve and breaks down in sheer
terror; but after the first horrible moments are past
the average girl is soon in complete control of the
situation. Before her "number" is concluded she is
facing the big auditorium with all the self-confidence
of a prima donna. In fact, many an established
artist is afflicted with more agonies of stage-fright
before every performance or important rehearsal
than one imagines these beginners ever could suffer.

And, lest it should be said that they lack temperament, some of them are very dramatic. They "feel"
their music with every evidence of clasped hands,
arch looks, desperate gestures, and even, upon occasion, realistic sobs. They do more or less as they
have been told, or as they have seen others do; but
alas, few of them do anything because they simply
cannot help it!

Recovery is swift; the piece is apt to end with a
real flourish. Then comes that anxious moment of
silence. With face haggard above the footlights,
the singer looks questioningly toward the spot where
she fancies her judges to be seated. Out of the
black void comes a voice. "Thank you!" it says.
With a bow or a shrug, or complete stolidity, according to her nature, the candidate withdraws, although
some stop a moment to ask in shocked surprise,
"But don't you want to hear the *Habañera?*" One
poised young lady is almost patronizing . . .
"Thank *you* for listening!" says she graciously.

And what then? Usually, *nothing*. In the nearest wing stands the teacher responsible for this particular effort. She probably hides the truth. "My
dear, *wonderful!* Never better! You will see,
something very interesting may happen in a few
days! I am very proud." She need not be, however, for if that fatal "Thank you!" has once
sounded, thumbs are down; it is usually her judgment that has been at fault. Rarely is either the
voice or the general development ready for exhibi-

tion, and she is more responsible for the failure than the pupil, who is, after all, very trusting.

However, there is another side to this as well as to all stories. Once in a while, when the first selection is about half over, the judges will stop their casual chatter and give interested attention. Before the finale is reached their heads are bent together in conference. At the end, "Please sing something else!" takes the place of the mechanical thanks; and then indeed the young singer's heart has a right to miss a beat, for the outer defenses have fallen. Of course the dreaded "Thank you" may have only been deferred, and the disappointment will be all the keener when it comes at the end of the second number; yet in all probability the next utterance will be, "Kindly wait a moment outside"; and one shadowy figure will detach itself from the little group and disappear through the stage-door. Encountering the flushed and almost hysterical teacher with the triumphant pupil in tow, he leads them to an inner office and makes an appointment of momentous possibilities. The chances are good that to-morrow or the next day a contract will be signed, and one more potential nurse, or messenger, or page will have joined the company.

What is there before them, these successful few who enter the gates, or those many others, possibly equally talented and earnest, who have failed? Which are really the fortunate ones? How big are the opportunities for advancement in our local opera houses, and where shall the others turn who did not win this chance? The best person to ask is the one who has been through the mill, whose common sense has been ground exceedingly fine by experience.

Clarence Whitehill, who is more competent to speak with authority than most of our American singers because of his long and varied experiences in the leading music theaters of France and Germany as well as in his own country, takes a rather pessimistic view of things, when cornered one day between rehearsals at the Metropolitan. "The American is up against a thousand difficulties when he wants to go on the lyric stage," says he with a sigh; but so earnest does he become that in all the vast auditorium there is no spot quiet enough for him to unburden his feelings. The ballet ambling before the footlights is too gay and distracting. At last an empty table in the yet emptier foyer becomes his pulpit. Leaning forward gravely, he taps upon this with a well-groomed forefinger.

"This is a very discouraging subject!" he begins ominously; but nevertheless a light of keen interest flickers across his face—upon which, incidentally, whatever worries and struggles he may have borne have left no mark other than to enhance its strength and calm. . . . "First of all, take the matter of temperament. The Anglo-Saxon is taught from ear-

liest infancy to repress his emotions. When as a
boy I blubbered because I fell and bumped my head,
what happened? My mother said at once, 'There,
there, *stop crying;* it is not as bad as all that!' and
my big brothers shrieked 'Shame . . . Shame . . .
Ba-aby!' Out of self-defense, therefore, I soon
learned to suffer in silence. Evidences of temper
were also, quite rightly, suppressed; but then, too,
all demonstrations of affection were apt to be regarded with open scorn. Little French, Italian,
and even Teuton children are of course comforted
when they get their small wounds; but it is not the
weeping and wailing which is objected to . . . unless on account of its noisiness . . . but merely the
cause. The European child is never humiliated because he shows his feelings; consequently he grows
up to enjoy a delightful absence of self-conscious-
ness, and sings, dances, quarrels, and loves quite as
easily in public as at home. From the café and
the boulevards to the stage is an easy transition for
him. He feels no added restraint, perhaps only a
little extra stimulation. And another thing . . . in
foreign opera houses singers perform in the familiar
tongue; the appropriate gestures and poses scarcely
have to be learned, they have been natural from
babyhood.

"Now our problem is different. First of all, we
stand appalled before the emotional splurge which
most of the romantic rôles require; and second, we
have no English opera—that is, no established reper-

toire. The beginner must learn a foreign language
under the most difficult conditions, and oftener than
not sing words he neither pronounces correctly nor
thoroughly understands. One or two of the better
traveling companies may offer him opportunities to
sing standard works in a translated version; but
what good will that do him if he has aspirations,
and hopes some day to belong to one of the two
great companies which produce only in the original?
He will be plunged into confusion.

"No, to Europe he must go, and there begin at
the very bottom. If he, by chance, should begin
too near the top, as I did, it will take him just that
much longer to succeed. At last, when by careful
steps he has advanced to the state where his ability
has been tried, when his assurance has been tested,
when his art is thoroughly grounded—then, and
only then, should he aspire to Chicago or the Metropolitan. They are the ultimate market for finished
wares and not training-schools. The young singer
who gets his first professional engagement in one of
these companies ought to take a pin and promptly
prick his balloon of self-congratulation before he
gets too involved and absorbed, for here the usual
order of things is reversed; the top of the ladder is
the crowded place. The greatest stars in the world,
who have won their spurs on a dozen other stages,
are invited here to sing the big rôles; and no matter how superlatively well Sarah Jones from New-
ark may sing one of the pages in *Lohengrin,* there

is little likelihood of her ever being picked to do Ortrud or Elsa until she has done it somewhere else first.

"Occasionally a singer without much previous training or experience, by some happy combination of circumstances, makes a palpable hit; as for instance Rosa Ponselle or, still more recently, young Lawrence Tibbett. Then it becomes even harder for them. They have that peak, which is far above either their routine opportunity or training to live up to, and the process of steady, slow, thorough growth is that much retarded. It took me almost twenty years before I could be conscious of any real blossoming forth in my work. Twenty years of vigorous stalk and good green leaves, however.

"Europe is the place to *learn*. If you haven't the money, borrow it or wait and earn it. It doesn't take a great deal. Most of us who may perhaps be said to have arrived, starved more or less genteelly during much of the preparatory process. But if conditions absolutely prevent going across, get experience somehow. Go on the stage, any kind of stage, that gives you ease before the footlights and loosens up that awful inhibitive reserve. Learn to walk and talk in the public eye; study languages and music during all the rest of your waking hours, and read everything in the way of history and biography that you can lay your hands on; that's a fairly good home prescription. And one more thing: be as conceited and self-assured as you like. It will get knocked out

of you sooner or later, and you'll need every bit of
it to see you through even the first years. No one
ever got anywhere in the opera world with an in-
feriority complex. Lastly—the successful opera
singer who really will taste glory, should be just
a little mad, I think—"

Stepping nimbly through the dim corridor we
come that same day upon another American singer,
who has recently been setting maidenly hearts aflut-
ter and grim critics to nodding with approval over
his romantic performances of Romeo and Pelléas—
the tenor, Edward Johnson. He sinks wearily into a seat in the orchestra circle, and whispers many
a wise thing in our ears.

"I arrived here via Comic Opera in New York—
Grand Opera in Pavia, Italy—and then Chicago—
and it has been a good road. You probably won't
believe me when I say that I never thought of the
Metropolitan until I was actually signing a contract.
I was naturally elated, for I suppose this is the ultimate in one's career. It is too bad more young
Americans won't realize that. Every one has to
make mistakes and do bad singing at times when he
is learning, but it can't be done here. The only place
where one can serve an apprenticeship is Europe."
This had a very familiar sound; but he proceeded
to explain it in a slightly different way from Mr.
Whitehill.

"In Europe one gets not only experience, but

artistic atmosphere. No matter how small the city of whose opera company you are a member, you can absorb traditions, invaluable for the building of your career. They have always had opera—the boot-black in the top gallery knows your rôles better than you do; he will bring you to time with cat-calls and boos if you offend him. (And, incidentally, what a salubrious thing for American opera houses if we could only import his bad manners.)

"However, don't try to get an engagement as soon as you reach a foreign shore. Earn or save enough money before you go to live quietly for a year or so studying and absorbing language, man-ners, customs. It does not cost as much to live over there, and what is more important, it does not cost as much to go to the opera. The student can attend every day of the week, including Sunday, for the price of standing-room at a single performance here. Above all, there is the language to learn. Think how easy is the road of the foreign artist who comes to the United States; he finds operas put on in his native tongue as if for his special convenience, be-ing curiously better off than the Americans on their home stage. They, poor devils, must go to *his* coun-try to learn *his* language to sing in *their* theater. But also they must learn it to sing in *his.* Trying to get an engagement in Italy or France or Germany without knowing something of the country's speech is a precarious matter. Too much emphasis cannot be laid on languages, and many of them, for every one who aspires even to hold his own in operatic life. If one has a varied repertoire one should be able to talk with native authorities about each type of rôle, and one should know the people and customs of the country in which the scene and the story is laid.

"However, if you hadn't asked me, I should not have begun by talking about the advantages of Europe or any other place. The first step toward the lyric stage, or rather toward success there, is to make sure that you are fitted by nature for this mad career in which one is always in either heaven or hell, but never on any nice neutral ground in between." (Clarence Whitehill said the same thing in another way, you remember.) "There are more qualities than just voice to be considered, and fully as important. This may sound trivial, but *looks* have a great deal to do with it. It isn't necessary to be beautiful, but one must be capable of giving the illusion of beauty. Then there is the flair for the stage —for dramatic action. If that has been left out of your make-up, you have a pretty uphill pull ahead. First, and above and beyond everything else, however, is the question of *health*. The opera singer must be made of steel and india-rubber. Without a tremendous reserve of physical vigor and endurance he could not live through his second season. And enthusiasm . . . but that isn't hard, for in spite of, or even perhaps because of, all these obstacles, this is the most interesting, most inspiring, and, alas, the most transient of careers in all the world!"

These gentlemen, having contributed so much of value, we sought out the only other American member of the cast to get the female slant upon the subject. We caught at the flowing sleeve of Kathleen Howard as she left the stage.

"Tell us, what would you say to the young singer beginning a career?"

"If I happened to be fond of her, I'd say, 'Don't!'" laughed she. "Although I like it fine, myself."

CHAPTER XVII

SINGERS ON THE WING

FULLY half of a singer's life is spent in travel. During spring and fall each year scarcely an ocean liner crosses without its quota of opera folk. Even the members of the chorus, and the leading *ballerine* make yearly pilgrimages, and the impresario, the conductor, the manager, press-agent, and every artist great or small, would no more think of staying on this side—whichever side it happens to be—than of giving up work altogether.

During the winter season, however, the drawing-room in the Pullman car will shelter some well-known musician on almost every trip. Of course, when the entire company goes on its official visits—as near as Philadelphia, as far as Denver—a special train is chartered; but when "guest artists" are loaned, or when they fill their concert engagements here and there, the drawing-room is their refuge. One can usually recognize them by the number of valises, flowers, and reporters about, by the constant ringing of the bell, and the anxious comings and goings of attendants. Although a few of the men sometimes sit out in the general car, with admirable democracy, they soon lose their incognito when they begin to dodge draughts with harried

263

mien and play their own *obbligato* upon the porter's bell with the same amount of enthusiasm as the more secluded prima donna.

They all know, from long practice, how to make themselves thoroughly comfortable, and usually carry along a separate traveling-case full of devices for the purpose—cushions, rugs, thermos bottles, special foods, lounging robes, slippers, fans. One singer has a patented spray, with a solution obtainable only in Vienna, with which her maid keeps the atmosphere fresh; while another experienced traveler hangs damp sheets sprinkled with oil of pine over door and walls to counteract the effect of the dry, sooty air. Some great pianists carry little clavicles, or silent keyboards, upon which they practice during the journey, but singers are never, never separated from the case which holds their music. No maid is entrusted with this; they carry it themselves and sleep with it beside them. If for an instant it is hidden from sight, they are thrown into utter panic. And speaking of maids, here is a career for any young woman who thrives on excitement and variety; but it is no sinecure—the mere management of a touring artist's luggage is an achievement in itself. From two to twenty trunks is the usual freight, and their guardian must be prepared to produce a special pin from any one of them without a moment's hesitation.

Most stage people are superstitious, although few of them will acknowledge it; however, let a nun or a priest travel with them in close proximity and their uneasiness will be ill-concealed. Almost every one has a mascot, inanimate for the most part, but let this object be forgotten or lost, and they are tempted to cancel the trip. Then there is the fetish of numbers . . . certain multiples spelling disaster. This is particularly trying in the Middle or Far West, where there is usually but one "best" hotel, and this more than likely to be in the throes of a Corset-Makers' or Undertakers' Convention. The numbers on the door of the singer's reserved suite total up to one of the dangerous sums—and not another vacant room in the house! What, then, is to be done? Some fortunate undertaker will find himself, to his surprise and delight, in the royal suite, while his late humble bedroom is filled to overflowing with an uncomfortable prima donna and all her trunks, happy although she has made herself unhappy.

The public expects opera singers to splurge, and most of them feel impelled to do so for fear the rumor may be born that they are neither so popular nor so successful as a rival. Although their professional fees are usually enormous, nevertheless, when the expenses of their necessarily *de luxe* existence are deducted, the net profits are not staggering. The great Lilli Lehmann is almost the only one who had the courage to economize in public. She always wore sensible black cotton stockings, and went to and from her performances in the street-

car. Other singers may lead a more or less simple
life in their private family bosoms, but on the wing
the best only is acceptable. The costs mount like
an adding-machine. The prices for drawing-rooms
are exorbitant, and fares are more so. And there
are always several of the latter, for these great ones
rarely travel alone; more often than not they have
a maid, a secretary, and an accompanist. On extended tours they have been known to charter an
entire private car. Geraldine Farrar had one for
her numerous entourage when she went to the coast,
and on her newest venture lives in one for fully half
the year. Alma Glück uses one for all her road
work, rejoicing in the pseudo-domesticity afforded
her in that tiny kitchen to bake cookies for her children. In England a well-known singer has had con-
structed a complete bungalow on wheels, and in it
she lives during most of her professional life, and
motors comfortably about to all her engagements;
but with our vast distances, American singers can
have no such luxury.

Most hotels make a well-known artist what is
called a "special rate," and sometimes it is very
special indeed, several notches higher than that paid
by you or me. Of course a "parlor" is always necessary because of the reporters, when as a matter of
fact personal taste may dictate the humblest bed-
room-and-bath. So it is, also, on the ocean liner.
A *suite-de-luxe* is offered the singer as a matter of
course, and he has to pay for it, not only in cold

cash, but in the matter of that dreaded "Ship's Concert" on the last evening out. Even when the shadows of retirement have fallen softly upon a musical celebrity, he or she must still continue to travel in extravagant fashion, or else some one may say, "Oh, I don't believe Madame Z was as great as they say; why look, she has an inside cabin!"

Another trial of traveling artists is that, no matter how tired, how ill, how let down they may feel, they are always on exhibition. Other folk may peacefully sleep in their deck-chairs with their mouths open, but Lohengrin or Tosca must never relax. In fact very few of them ever visit their deck-chairs at all, because of the battery of curious stares which they must face. To be the observed of all observers is one thing, but to overhear some one say, "Oh, so that's how she really looks!" is quite another. Not only are they stared at but they are subjected to introductionless and often unwelcome interviews from the bolder of their shipmates, while their ingrained desire to please the public prevents them from showing annoyance. They cannot even put on old and comfortable clothes, like other happy human beings, and enjoy themselves; they have to continue always "the glass of fashion and the mold of form."

Rarely are they good sailors; these hybrid products of the nerve factory are the natural victims of uneven seas. The late and lamented Lillian Nordica was one of the best, however, and was the most de-

lightful of traveling companions. She had a pretty
way of coming each morning to the cabin of a suffering colleague with something "distracting to look
at."   One morning it might be a giant orchid, or
again her whole ravishing collection of emeralds, another day some pearls or maybe only a perfect hot-
house peach. It seems sad that this genial, gentle
spirit should have been snuffed out so far from home,
among strangers, a song-bird brought down on the
wing; but, after all, the road is the natural habitat
of the great artist. Olive Fremstad once said, "My
name means *strange city,* and nothing could be more
suitable. It may be a paradox, but I am always
most at home in the midst of the strange and changing."

These talented folk may fuss a good deal about
draughts and the numbers on their doors, or the
color of the wallpaper, but they have never failed
to rise, cool and clear-headed, to a great emergency.
In a wreck or a disaster they can be depended on
to do the reasonable thing. The whole Metropolitan Company was in San Francisco during the earthquake, and none of them lost their heads, although
rumor has it that one or two thought they had lost
their voices and ran about in the confusion, frantically trying their high "C's." A famous Wagnerian singer was snowbound for twenty-four hours
in a heatless, foodless train, on her way from St.
Paul to St. Louis one winter, and as there was nothing any one could do about it, she was intelligent

enough to accept the fact without complaint, even though it probably meant missing her performance. She showed herself one of the least troublesome of all the passengers, and even led them on a tramp over the frozen drifts to an adjacent farm, which they raided for eggs and butter and milk, and had a glorious time.

All this, of course, applies to American travel. In Europe there are so many celebrities drifting about that they almost cease to excite interest. The great Mildenburg and her playwright husband, Hermann Bahr, may camp on the Lido beach in strange gingham *peignoirs* without attracting a passing glance. No one will so much as lift an eyebrow if Cosima Wagner travels second-class. Jean de Reszke could have ridden on a bus or sat in a penny seat in the Tuileries undisturbed. One great advantage these singers have over the rest of us, however—they are never perturbed at frontiers. No matter into what language affairs must be translated, they have it right on their tongue's end. Six or seven is their usual repertoire, and they change from one to the other without the slightest grinding of gears, while most of us are still fumbling for pocket dictionaries.

The late War caused somewhat of a hiatus in the migratory habits of songsters, but there is a vivid picture of Mary Garden which should hang in some gallery of history.

The time is early 1918, and the scene a great ship, painted in camouflage, with guns mounted in her bow, bound for France. She carries a full passenger list; every cabin is crowded to its capacity with earnest men and women going over to help in that great struggle which, as yet, no blessed Armistice has ended. There is noticeable a tense atmosphere, an excitement akin to exaltation, as the vessel glides silently down the harbor; but when the rain and fog close in toward the end of the day, faces become a trifle strained and there is a general feeling of oppression and anxiety impossible to ignore.

The very costumes of the ship's company add to the general gloom; nurses in unrelieved indigo walk the deck in somber pairs, canteen workers in dull gray stand by the rail and gaze over the leaden waters, olive-drab officers discuss the latest *communiqué* in anxious, scowling groups, while down in the bow the steerage quarters overflow with colored troups going over to "win dat man's war." Suddenly, however, a fresh little breeze seems to stir. The odor of bilge-water, rubber, and paint is mitigated by a delightful fragrance, a shaft of sunlight seems to illumine the deck—a jaunty figure appears like a flower in a kitchen garden. Against the neutral background she is very gorgeous: a red velvet suit, a leopard coat, a purple hat with floating white veil, brilliant blue eyes, Titian hair—gaiters, chamois gloves, a cane . . . in short, Mary Garden. What an antidote for the submarine blues! A real prima donna on a transport, a bit of the gay, normal, pleasant world, a link with 42nd Street and Broadway! Already the voyage ahead, with its lurking terror, looms less fearsome.

In a few days the shipload, after the usual custom, shakes down into something more like normality, but the waves are high, the ship is narrow, and many travelers are aboard who never sailed before. The decks are not crowded; only a few courageous ones tramp up and down under the flapping tarpaulin. But watch the groups as they pass a certain window! The steps slacken, the voices are hushed, they listen for a soft little crooning of vague melodies coming from behind the drawn blind, and they sniff with pleasure a haunting fragrance.

Toward sundown the waves relent a bit, and the barbaric leopard-skin and the floating veil appear, and with that inimitable, swinging stride, Miss Garden takes the air. One or two intrepid officers seek and obtain an introduction and lend the support of their manly arms, thrilling to the touch of Mélisande. They cut in on each other like dancing men about a débutante and they consider themselves full of romantic adventure, and try to forget their extreme youth. But Miss Garden remembers it, and where they are going, and why, so she is gracious and friendly and does not try to run away.

Finally there comes a day when the leopard lies all day basking in the sun. The sky is blue and the air balmy—besides, it is at last the dreaded Danger Zone and one prefers to sit where one's eye can scan the waters. Helping a dozen to forget, Miss Garden holds court in her chair.   Earnest clergymen in khaki consult her at length upon the relations of church and stage; leaders of the "Y" cohorts beg for advice and find, instead, a sympathetic listener; pale nurses, on deck for the first time, come to worship and to thrill . . . and go later into the writing-room to tell the folks at home about the real prima donna they know.   To the writer, seeking familiar atmosphere, Miss Garden confides that she always feels ill at sea, that she is going over to promote concerts for the blinded, that this is her sixth war-voyage, and that she has no fear.   We promptly feel a little braver too.

A young doctor goes the rounds of the decks begging fruit for the sick boys in the steerage.   Miss Garden hails him; he ceases to canvass further, and disappears.   The next day we hear the news.   She gave him every package of fruit and candy in her cabin, but that was not all!   Against a dearth of such things in stricken France, she had brought for her own use crates of cereal, chocolate, and sugar; bottles of fresh milk and cream were on ice for her consumption during the voyage.   When she heard that two hundred sick men lacked these things she gave them freely to the doctor.   Not just some of them, but *all* of them, keeping back nothing for herself.

That last night on board, when nerves are stretched to the breaking-point, and one jumps at the sound of a snapping board, Mary Garden comes

into her own. Clad in the loveliest gown she possesses, brought prodigally from the hold for the
occasion, she sings to the men below. Late into
the night she sings, and those anxious forms huddled
in chairs on deck (who "just like to sleep outdoors
on a night like this—oh, no, of course not afraid
of submarines!") hang breathlessly on luscious notes
floating up to them from below, for their lullaby.

The next day the strain is over, the valiant boat
brings us to the safe mouth of the river. All is excitement and bustle, every one for himself and his
luggage. But the jaunty figure with the cane is astir
and not too busy to seek out the writer with mes-
sages for mutual friends at home, and an offer of
seats at the first Opéra Comique performances. A
warm handshake, and a hearty "Good Luck!"—
and she is gone; but surely she has earned and should
be proud of the title the doughboys have given her
. . . "Our little Life Preserver!"

CHAPTER XVIII

THE GENTLE ART OF INTERVIEWING

ONE of the principal nuisances in all artists' lives is the reporter. He claims many of their busiest hours, and yet they dare not say him nay. If he fails to invade their cabin as soon as the boat reaches Quarantine, or to beset them with battalions of photographers wherever they go, they fear at once that their popularity is on the decline. Strangers to our shores are apt to be a trifle resentful just at first, then they are amused, but soon they end by accepting the matter without much difficulty. Quite naturally, however, it must seem odd to them to have so much interest shown in their private lives, and that we should actually care what brand of tooth paste they use, how they eat, sleep, dress, and undress. When they land in our glorious free country they become as much public property as was the royal family of France in a less enlightened epoch, and on the banners with which we welcome them should be emblazoned "Abandon privacy, all ye who enter here!"

Maria Jeritza, when she first came into our midst and took the town by storm, had not the faintest notion how to be interviewed in American style. Although she had been the reigning favorite in Vienna for several seasons, her publicity had amounted to a few dignified articles in local weeklies, press notices by the critics, and a description or two of her life in her summer villa, so she was totally unprepared for the siege which began here the day after her first *Tosca*. A pretty shyness and modesty is one of her most charming endowments, but that, plus the obstacle of a foreign tongue, made a difficult hurdle for the most agile reporter to leap.

The only hope lay in the presence of her husband, the romantic young Baron von Popper, whose elegant and carefully chosen English was capable of conveying the required information, but whose frantic anxiety lest he, too, be written into the interview, was almost pitiful, and decidedly hampering. So the first press exploitation of Jeritza was an anemic thing at best. But in three short years what a change! She has learned to bear the incursion upon her free hours with a fortitude whose outward signs are ease and grace, she speaks the vernacular with only the most pleasing remnant of an accent, and she poses unflinchingly before a battery of cameras, the while flinging succulent morsels of "copy" to a half dozen gentlemen of the press. In time so case-hardened will she become that she may take the same delight in the process as does Geraldine Farrar, who stages her appearances before the reporters as carefully as those before the public, realizing, with her usual cleverness, that it is only another phase of the same thing. Never will she disappoint the most elaborately preconceived idea of what a prima donna is really like.

Her beautiful house, which she furnished so lavishly and occupied during her last years at the Metropolitan, was primarily created as a perfect setting for her personality, and there she shone like a giant diamond perfectly cut and mounted. Worldly success was apparent everywhere, from the moment one entered the front door; but so nicely tempered was it by artistic restraint and a certain romantic and sentimental suggestion that one sat upon the edge of one's chair as in a haunted house of ghosts, listening for the tap of Manon's red heels or the click of Carmen's castanets. Mimi and Tosca, Marguerite and poor little Butterfly seemed palpably lurking behind every screen and curtain, and the echoes of just-finished melodies hung like golden mists around the sacred piano. Now that that house is, alas, no more, she manages by some alchemy, to achieve the same atmosphere in a hotel salon or the drawing-room of a Pullman car.

A suitable time is always allowed to elapse, and then, with a little stir of whispering attendants, the singer appears. It is always very flattering to a humble interviewer to behold how carefully this great and famous woman has prepared herself for the encounter. No detail has been neglected, no trouble nor expense spared. Most beautifully coifed and manicured and cosmeticked, adorned with glittering jewels, and gowned in fabulous loveliness, this beloved Yankee can always be relied upon to give her callers something to look at. One can depend

upon a satisfied ear as well, for publicity has long
been her natural element, and she knows how to
talk. The only real problem is to guide her eloquence into the desired channels. It is an embarrassment of riches, a talk with Farrar, and one staggers rather dizzily away from her ebullient presence,
wondering how on earth a limited number of coldly
printed words can ever do justice to her prodigal
outpourings.

There are other prime donne who are as hard to
catch as hummingbirds but who, once snared, will
provide the most diverting material. Such a one
is Mary Garden, who promptly says "No" to all
ordinary requests, and yet furnishes reporters *en
masse* with some of the most startling stories. She
needs no press-agent; she is never at a loss to supply
an agitating fillip to the public imagination; her
inventive genius and her dramatic talent are phenomenally mated. Yet she is extremely approach-
able from another standpoint, and her dressing room
is always thronged by admirers old and new. She
is cordial and kind to every one she meets, and never
forgets a face; she distributes portraits and autographs generously but she simply *will not* grant an
interview which is tagged as such—proving herself
thereby and all told, one of the most astute ladies
before the footlights of to-day.

These three famous singers are scarcely typical,
however, of what one encounters whose profession

it is to hound celebrities and ruthlessly expose them, captive, to the reading public. The demands of American audiences, who are not content with the play, and the music, and the spectacle which is legitimately theirs for the price of a pasteboard, but wish to be regaled in subsequent hours of ease with personalities and piffle concerning their favorites, have given rise to a small army of eager sleuths, who pursue their calling on relentless feet. To be in this army and yet not of it, to reconcile one's ideals of tact and good breeding with what often seems but impertinent and vulgar curiosity, here is a problem! To give the public as much as it has a right to, and yet convince it that it is getting all it wants—Quixotic! If one could call upon Jeritzas and Farrars and Gardens every day, the life would be exhilarating indeed, but these are the cream, and there is much skimmed milk.

There is the broken or forgotten appointment. Arriving jubilantly at the scene of the engagement, one is met with the perfectly blank statement that Madame X is not at home. Further investigation discovers not even a message of explanation has been left as a palliative. That means that all the long and painful process of remaking this appointment must somehow be gone through again; but, oftener still, it means that a special scoop for a writer, which depended largely on its timeliness for its value, is irretrievably lost. Secretaries should obviate such *contretemps,* but oftener secretaries do far worse themselves, particularly if they are of that deadly efficient, self-important type of young female.

Often, after days of perseverance and hours of anxious anticipation, when you at last nail an appointment, and at the time specified appear, eager and avid, you are met at once by the secretary, who informs you in patronizing tones that, "Signora Bla is so worn out by the strain of her performances and the constant rehearsals that she simply must save her strength—she has asked me to talk to you instead!" The secretary plainly enjoys the substitution; in her eyes there will be no loss to the public. She presents you with methodical memoranda and a photograph or two. . . . You go away snarling.

Another sore trial is the careful artist who insists on seeing a copy of your article before it goes to press. He cannot be refused, for he is within his rights—his photographer submits proofs as a matter of course, why not you? However, once in his hands, it is a safe bet that your brain-child will perish then and there, or else emerge from the ordeal so changed that you will gladly strangle it in its cradle. Wives, sisters, mothers, all have a finger in the pie, to say nothing of the above-mentioned secretary. The odds are distinctly unfair.

Another *bête noire* is the artist who captures all the guns at the first encounter and turns the battery on the interviewer. One clever singer who was to be written up on her unique War work interviewed *me* instead, on how much I got for an article, how much I paid for my apartment, the name of my tailor, where I got my maids, my opinion of opera-singers in general, etc., etc. This is quite a common phenomenon, and a difficult hazard, but not as bad as the artist who simply insists on reminiscing when you have come for points on make-up. He shows you albums, old programs, and inscribed ribbons, and introduces you to his sister, who once "played the violin with the *Kölner Damen Simfonie.*"

Then there is the celebrity who apparently thinks of you as a walking newspaper of the theater, and is peeved that you cannot feed her ears with spicy bits of gossip. But she usually takes pity on you, and herself supplies this lack, so that you need not go from her in the barren state in which you came. Akin to her is the facetious creature who gives you all the wrong answers, and who laughs immoderately at his little joke about being a lonely bachelor, when you are slightly startled at the return from the park of his wife, wheeling the twins in their go-cart.

The little ingénue, whose knowledge of the household arts is confined to squeezing oranges and cracking ice, is apt to receive you in her kitchenette, where she looks simply adorable in a big pink linen apron and cap, with just a coquettish dab of flour on her nose. She regales you with her love of home and mother and all the simple, girlish things. It is she who always talks most freely of her consecration to her Art and her ambition to live up to what her Dear Public expects of her. At least she is more diverting than that other type, usually a dramatic soprano, who raves of Uplift and tries to convert you to New Thought. This is very hard to bear.

There are others, however—thank God for them!—who are real people. They receive you in home or hotel, just as they would any other caller, politely, without frills or furbelows, and speak simply and naturally about whatever phase of their work you require. Sometimes they introduce you to their families, if they happen to be in, or if it nears lunch time and you have a lean and hungry look, they urge you to stay. Again, they may take you out in the big car for the space of the interview. They are full of pleasant suggestions. But, alas, they are not usually . . . sometimes, yes, a golden few, but not often . . . the famous ones. What inexorable urge imprints upon the growing artist's subconsciousness the need of developing the erratic? With the fullness of their artistic stature comes the perfect flowering of what is wrongly called Temperament, a recognized emblem of Genius, to be sure, a by-product of subtle value— and they all know it. When it is imitated it is tawdry, but when it is real, it is priceless copy and is received with prayer and thanksgiving in the halls of journalism.

This, however, has all been from the interviewer's

side of the fence.   Looking at it from the artist's angle, we realize that they, too, have their trials.   A good interviewer, one who knows his business to the extent of exactly how to make the appointment, when to come, how long to stay, who *never, never takes notes,* asks just the right questions, is properly sympathetic, and who pauses circumspectly on the exact borderland between the personal and the impertinent—this is a Utopian individual who rarely comes their way.

They suffer most when on the road; for each local paper will usually have a representative at the hotel ten minutes after the star arrives, and inconvenient as the time may be, the interview must be granted— it is too valuable an asset in untilled soil.   These hinterland reporters are not apt to be very skillful; there is not enough musical or theatrical business to allow them to specialize and they often have to go straight from the prima donna's salon to cover a fight in Tim Murphy's arena.   They use much the same technique in writing up both.   But even the great metropolitan press is not too careful. Ambitious young women from up-state who are just winning their journalistic spurs are, for some obscure reason, often chosen to visit female celebrities. They can be trusted to give glowing accounts of the interior decorations, the flowers, gowns, and coiffure, but the artist may talk earnestly and entertainingly for a full half-hour without a word of what she really says appearing in print.   If papers would learn to send trusted, trained, and able writers to meet the same caliber of stage-folk, interviewing would immediately mount to a higher plane of literary and educational value, without losing any of its luster as publicity or entertainment.

Some years ago *McClure's Magazine* sponsored what was rather a startling innovation for a literary monthly, and sent Willa Cather, who is to-day one of our foremost woman writers, to obtain some operatic interviews, resulting in a most illuminative and valuable series of essays on Three Great American Singers. The intelligent, poised, and diplomatic way in which she handled the interviews themselves won for her, with at least two of these artists, a lasting and close friendship based on mutual respect and understanding.

Another terror of the interviewed is the mutilation their remarks may undergo at the hands of the enthusiastic copy-writers. When Carl Van Vechten was on the *Times,* he came one evening to talk to Olive Fremstad during her idle second act of *Tannhauser,* about old times and new. She regaled him with a series of delightful reminiscences, which enlivened the more serious trend of her conversation. One of the less important anecdotes was concerned with a benefit which she once organized in Munich during her early days, in which she impersonated "Topsy," sang American darkey songs to a ravished audience, and incidentally wore some bright green stockings. . . . She went on to talk of other things. What was her horror to perceive, the following morning at breakfast, this flaming headline ornamenting a column of her favorite sheet: FREMSTAD IN TIGHTS! The eye of the copy-writer, trained to sensationalism, had hit upon the green hosiery as the most striking matter of the whole story. As the singer was then in the zenith of her career as an exponent of the most majestic and sublime of operatic rôles, and was famous for her dignity, seriousness, and aloofness, this was, to say the least, disturbing. Many apologies ensued, but the fact remained, to justify the real culprit, that that interview was very widely read.

The insatiable demand for information extends even to questionnaires submitted by efficient gentlemen compiling symposiums. "What is your favorite color . . . food . . . book . . . rôle?" etc., they usually read, and it is a wise celebrity indeed who promptly puts all such cold-blooded intelligence tests in the waste-basket.

Another and dangerous usurper upon privacy and valuable time is the shameless impostor, who, motivated by curiosity alone, passes himself off as a representative of some paper, and thus insinuates himself into the presence of the artist, sometimes obtaining free passes to a performance as well. The consummate nerve of this individual passes belief, but all such are eventually exposed, for artists are learning to keep tabs on their publicity and the failure of an article to appear usually causes some

inquiry. They have learned, also, to honor first
those demands which come with credentials and
upon official letterheads. Of course, once in a while,
a bona-fide interview will never see the light of print,
for various causes, first among them being the stale-
ness and flatness of the material garnered, which,
being in part the artist's fault, may lead to some embarrassment in the editorial rooms, and a few bitter reportorial tears; but this contingency is rare.

The fake interview is, however, the most infre-
quent of the amateur raids into an opera-singer's
private life. All sorts of passports are offered—
letters, poems, drawings, flowers, and some gifts of
great intrinsic value. A famous Isolde once received, as she entered her dressing-room, a box containing dewy heaps of great single English violets,
while in among their fragrant petals nestled a very
wonderful old ring, of purest soft gold crudely
enameled, and set with curious colored stones. It
might have come from a Viking's tomb, or the hand
of some fair Visigoth, but . . . "This seems to belong to you, Isolde!" read the card. The retiring
and imaginative gentleman who sent it never came
to claim the thanks which his charming gift had
earned; but he was one in a thousand. Upon the
slightest pretext, the average lion-hunter will force
his way in.

Some milder ones stand at the stage-door until
their faces become familiar, and sometimes their
persistency is rewarded by a flower, a handshake,

or a personal word of recognition, which seems to satisfy them. Others push through the doors and all but invade the stage in the exuberance of their admiration. One young girl, by her persevering attendance, eager clamoring, and avid letter-writing, did win her way to be a prima donna's secretary for a summer season, but it was achieved through a series of unusual and propitious circumstances.

Singers' mails are enlivened by countless people who desire to keep house for them, paint them, dress them, massage them, or marry them, not to mention the floods of requests for autographs and pictures. Meeting the demand for the latter is a big item on a popular star's expense account, often running into four figures. To all these communications some form of courteous answer is usually accorded. "From offending my Public, Good Lord deliver me!" is the opera-singer's litany, for he knows that, let his voice be that of an angel, his figure Apollo's, and his art outstanding, it will avail him little enough unless the young girls knit him neckties and the gallery gods clamor to know his breakfast menu.

CHAPTER XIX

GRET INTERPRETATIONS

RUSSIAN is an extremely rich and splendid language which, unfortunately, is spoken by very few except those that are born amidst its intricacies. One Anglo-Saxon, however, without any study or preparation, was able to grasp the fine points of an entire and colorful discourse in that tongue with astonishing ease, simply because the speaker was one of the greatest dramatic geniuses the world has ever known, Mr. Feodor Chaliapin. To be sure, there were occasional sojourns upon the common ground of French, and there was also present an enthusiastic and painstaking interpreter, but the meticulous efforts of this latter gentleman seemed to the fascinated listener almost an unnecessary repetition, so vivid was the great baritone's pantomime, so penetrating the electric current of his thought.

The agile leaping of racial and linguistic barriers seemed, however, entirely natural when in communion with an artist whose very name saves the traditions of operatic art. Wherever two or three music critics are gathered together to mourn the deterioration of the lyric stage some optimist has only to interject, "But there's Chaliapin, you know!" to bring back the light of enthusiasm to their eyes.

287

He is certainly the crowned king of that stage to-day, and incidentally as majestic and impressive a figure as one may find anywhere since the delightful days when there were giants abroad in the land.

He was not always, at least outwardly, so fine and regal. Not always did he inhabit hotel suites full of Easter tulips, with two secretaries and a valet in attendance. He was born a peasant, of lowly parents who could do little to help him in his ambitions and did less. However, as he himself said later, in a more impersonal connection—Who can explain how or why a genius is born, or what goes into the making? In the fullness of time one is sent among us, the product of some mysterious psychic chemistry. Time, place, forbears, history, world fermentation—all play their part as ingredients but explain nothing, and the flame is inextinguishable.

Chaliapin grew into his powers without encouragement, without even the average education. He became a shoemaker's apprentice in the very street, according to one biographer, where Maxim Gorky was toiling in an underground bakery, and eked out his slender living by singing in a choir. Later, in some minor capacity, he obtained employment with the local opera company, but it was so unremunerative that he was forced to increase his earnings by acting as porter in the railway station and helping unload the barges along the wharfs of the Volga. This humble interlude in his career served, however, to enhance the brilliancy of a certain jewel in the crown of his later success. No one ever has or ever will sing the "Song of the Volga Boatmen" as he does.

Running away with an itinerant troupe; singing, acting, even dancing when the need arose, he gradually worked his way about the country and into the notice of persons of influence. An inconspicuous operatic début at Tiflis, a progression from company to company, and eventually and inevitably an engagement at the Imperial Opera of Moscow— such, in brief, is the history of his rise to fame. The fact that it took years, faith, courage, and endurance is merely incidental. His genius brought him to the top as surely as the lily finds the surface of the pond. People were soon journeying from all parts of Russia to hear him, and, as is the fate of most great artists, before very long vast journeys began in turn for him. The continent first acclaimed him, then London, and at last America was privileged to share in the plaudits. The hope of the opera-loving public, the despair of his colleagues, he treads the boards, a colossus moving, as one critic puts it, "half in the white sunlight of worship and half in the black shadow of envy."

So much for the man. As for his art, the manner in which he demonstrates his claim not only to interpretive, but to creative, genius . . . a pair of powerful, but utterly eloquent hands protests to us that this is best seen and heard upon the stage, not talked about. However, yielding to the American insistence on personal contact, he is finally induced to say a great many enlightening things, the very opening of which, in order to be fully appreciated, requires a brief digression.

When first the plan for these intimate chronicles of opera was conceived, it was thought that it might prove both diverting and instructive to devote a chapter to the *future* of this noble art. To that end such authorities were consulted as might be expected to speak most authentically upon the matter; in other words, we sought out the biggest stars in the constellation of the "New" or "Modern" school of composers. But, alas, the chapter was never written, for by common consent, separately and in unison, they all rose up and shouted with laughter and derision! We withdrew as gracefully as possible, really quite upset. "Opera has no future!" the fatal words rang out, their echoes sustained by such plausible reasoning, such objective illustration that they almost carried conviction even to the most loyal among the old retainers. The chapter was never written—but nevertheless, a few dubious little weeds grew up in the garden of romance.

With a kindly hand and an eager toss of a leonine head, the giant Chaliapin plucks up these weeds and flings them to the four winds of hope. This is what he says:

"Ever since the beginning of my serious career I have asked of every one the same question, 'Why cannot the great dramas of the world—Shakespeare and the Greek tragedies, for example—be put on the lyric stage complete, exactly as they were written?' I do not refer to *libretti* made from these dramas, and so the answer has always been, 'They are too long!' But I did not believe it; I still clung to the conviction that a composer great enough for the task would some day appear. My dream was realized when Moussorgsky was inspired to set to music an epic from the history of our nation in the opera *Boris Godounoff*. Of course he is only one genius. Who can say when another of such tremendous insight shall be born? But at least every outstanding figure has lesser followers who somehow fill out the time until the next one arrives. However, I feel confident that in just such a work lies not only the future of opera, but of the whole of artistic human effort. By that I mean that eventually all the five great arts, Music, Painting, Sculpture, Poetry, and Architecture will be united in one cumulative achievement which shall be upon a lyric stage. The ideal, the ultimate opera will be the realization of the *painter's* dream in color, costume, and lighting; the *musician's* in orchestral and vocal expression; the *poet's* in rhythm and dramatic utterance; the *sculptor's* in the grace of plastic pose and grouping; and for the *architect* the limitless possibilities in scenic investiture. It is a shining road, this, which spreads before the sincere seeker after artistic truth; but, alas, there is one equally brilliant, one that glitters with gold coin and leads directly away from this goal!"

Mr. Chaliapin's method of preparing his great rôles is an obscure and mystic process within himself. It has been remarked that the characters which he portrays do not seem to be recreated by him, but rather to spring from the spirit world in which they roam disembodied, and eagerly seize upon the responsive instrument of his mortal virility to walk for such brief periods upon the earth. One pictures in an overstimulated imagination the jostling of the pallid shades of history against the sturdier ghosts of fiction: Philip the Second of Spain, elbowing Boris the Czar, yet both thrusting shoulder to shoulder against the onslaught of quaint Don Basilio, who never existed yet has a hundred counterparts in old Seville. They are struggling for places in the line, eager for their turn to live again in the body of the big Russian. Red-hot pitchforks agitate them from the rear. Cowering, they clear a path for the formidable phantom of evil, the Devil, impatient for one more opportunity to be admired.

When questioned upon this matter, Chaliapin agrees quite simply that it must be so, but adds, "They must, however, in order to draw breath, first pass through the fiery crucible of my brain!" He disclaims much reliance upon study and research, although it would be difficult to conceive of such a master-intelligence ignoring the fundamentals of achievement. If he does study, perhaps he does not think it necessary to call it such, for doubtless such explorations as he makes into legend and tradition and technique are but delightful by-paths along the broad road of his imagination. He trusts his instincts even before cold facts, and claims that every real genius has a right to do so. Sometimes an imaginary conception will be artistically more authentic than a copy of what actually is.

When he takes up a new rôle he reads over libretto and music, and for some time proceeds to saturate his being with the whole in some mystic way all his own. If he can avoid it, he never wishes to see a representation of an opera in which he may sometime sing until that time when he is actually a part of it. When the rôle has become one with his mind and spirit and body, and he has thoroughly visualized everything, even to the *mise en scène*, he is ready to rehearse. He is so *in* the thing that there can be no surprises in store for him—that is, none except the stage manager's directions, which often seem startling and irrelevant. Incidentally, we may venture to suppose that the feeling is probably mutual.

A rôle such as Boris is easy, he declares, although this would seem to us a sweeping statement. If it is easy, why then is not every Boris the crushing, overpowering figure of human tragedy and thwarted greatness which becomes so unbearably real when Chaliapin puts on the imperial robes? However, he is Russian. The history of Ivan, and Dmitri, and the royal murderer are as familiar to him from his boyhood as the tale of Washington's cherry-tree is to us. He has groaned with the toiling people, he has worshiped in brilliantly painted cathedrals, he has run shouting beside processions. He has shivered in the bleak cruelty of the northern cold, and he has sweated in the yet more devastating heat. He has sung the songs of peasants, has chanted with vested priests, has shouted for the Emperor. He is acquainted with the tenderness which little children inspire, for he belongs to a race that are children at heart. He knows Russia—he is Russia, . . . why, after all, should he not sing Boris and find it easy? Nevertheless, all those who have been privileged to hear him in this rôle will agree with the critic of a foremost New York paper who declared it to be "the most stupendous impersonation that contemporary drama, lyric or spoken, can boast."

The characterization from the artist's standpoint is, however, one of mood and reaction rather than personality. Be that as it may, the very impact of his physical presence is overpowering. His great size, his regality, the pomp with which he is framed, all tend to sweep up the listener's soul from out the body. His gestures which have from the very beginning the "grace of terrible things," and his magnificent voice making utterances which seem to be extorted from him by the urgency of the moment, rather than learned second-hand, produce an effect

even upon the most insensitive of opera-goers which
they are unlikely to forget for the remainder of
their lives.

With his Mephistopheles it is different. No less
poignant a characterization, it has, he admits, cost
him more labor. Only by a convulsion of mighty
imagination can anything which is essentially fantastic and unbegotten be brought forth as plausible
and emotionally convincing. The Devil Incarnate!
How often have we invoked him, and received his
prompt visitation under innocuous disguise! One
evening seated before the grim specter of Chaliapin
as Bolto's Mephistophele should break us of the
habit. There upon the stage walks the Arch Fiend,
the Lord of Hell, and none other!

He is not the first nor the last singing actor who
has animated this rôle, but one small incident will
show wherein his portrayal glows with sulphurous
flame while the others merely walk in the ray of a
theatrical arc light. In the Bracken Scene we have
the Imperial Satan brooding upon the little World
which he holds in the hollow of his hands. Incidentally it is an occasion upon which the composer
has fastened one of the principal arias. The average singer grasps the globe with impressive dignity,
and holding it before his earnest gaze, advances to
the footlights and delivers himself of his song. Not
so Chaliapin. His terrible throne built of red and
seething rock rises behind him, and from this pin-
nacle he chooses to sing. Clambering up the steep

sides with the powerful movements of a frightful ape, he reaches the summit, and leaning, poised
in arrested might against his throne, lightly tosses
the little earth-plaything from hand to hand as he
muses. At the conclusion he lets fall his cloak and
stands revealed in all the appalling horror of his
evil majesty, towering above the restless writhing of
the lesser demons beneath his feet. In opera houses
less sedate than those of our community, he is shown
there for a moment in gleaming green flesh and
palpable unconcealment, a figure to be graven on
frightened, susceptible minds to the day of death.

Gounod's Mephisto is quite another matter.
Only in the Church Scene, regrets Mr. Chaliapin,
does this rôle in any way approximate Goethe's conception. Otherwise it is mostly cheap and tawdry,
an *opéra-bouffe* devil, overlaid with innumerable
Gallicisms. As such, however, it is far from unin-
teresting. One of the insidious things about evil is
its charming, and often trivial, aspect. If Gounod
wanted a merry red demon whose courtly manners
and delicate graces added a bit of not unpleasant
spice to the Kermess days at Frankfort, Chaliapin
could have given him his heart's desire. One gets
the impression from his French Mephistopheles
that it is Satan off on a holiday, collecting a lost soul
or two along the way almost from force of habit,
but not caring very deeply one way or another. He
is *debonnair* and almost casual, picking up what fun
he can with silly old Martha, saying "Boo!" to the

callow Siebel, and tickling the necks of close-clasped lovers with a daisy on a long stem. Even the incident of the sword-hilt crosses he seems to consider but a passing inconvenience, refusing to cringe, and waiting with what endurance he can until the intolerable things are withdrawn. The dash and verve of his *Veau d'Or* is almost a dance, and the laughter accompanying the foul insinuations of his Serenade seems to express real, if diabolical, humor rather than the grim mirthlessness of derision.

In the fleeting invocation to the innocent flower-beds to do their worst, we catch a suggestive glimpse of the sinister; but only in the brief Church Scene where, as he said, the libretto allows him some approximation of Goethe's original, does he in any sense frighten us with a sense of supernatural power. On the whole, he is more attractive than otherwise, which is doubtless as true a representation of wickedness in the world as the more alarming and easily recognized brand. One thing he does in this rôle, however, is so contrary to tradition that it has set not a few of the critics to carping. He makes this Mephistopheles the chief personage in the opera, a dominant figure which so eclipses the rightful hero and heroine of the piece that we find ourselves regarding them as annoying intruders when they wander about in the garden where they certainly have a better right than he.

On this very subject, that of so-called secondary

or minor parts, Mr. Chaliapin has something to say. One of his greatest successes in this country has been the relatively small rôle of the music-teacher, Don Basilio, in *The Barber of Seville*. When questioned as to his pleasure in such an effort, he becomes almost indignant, hastening to declare with some asperity that a great artist-writer such as Beaumarchais, who did the original book from which the opera was taken, had better sense than to puff up two or three windbags and, labeling them "principals," proceed to stuff a few little sawdust dolls to fill in the space around them, as do the "cheap" commercial librettists. No! Thrice no! Beaumarchais, Shakespeare, Goethe, and such masters, drew only *types* which are as true to life to-day and to-morrow as of the epoch in which they were placed, and which, having little to say, or much, are all equally important in the general picture. He delights in Don Basilio; he paints him in broad strokes of almost Elizabethan farce, not hesitating to make use of slapstick methods when the occasion seems made for them, rightly judging them to be in fact the only true expression of the real, honest clowning which the absurd music-teacher represents in the cast. In this interpretation he discloses lavishly a quality of which we only get a sly and teasing glimpse in Gounod's Mephistopheles, and which seems completely obscured in the personality of the man himself—his delightful sense of fun and drollery.

Meeting him as Feodor Chaliapin and not as any of the characters he has thrust toward immortality, one would judge him to be the most serious of mortals. Filling the eye with his almost overpowering physical presence, and the imagination with the equal preponderance of brain and spiritual force, he is nevertheless almost a quiescent figure as he talks. He does not leave his chair to move about, pose, or pace. He is not restless or nervous, but sits back with an effect of relaxation which we soon discover to be the utmost in forceful concentration. Only his powerful hands are never still, and his face is an illuminated document for all to read, even if for long moments at a time so intense is his thought that he finds it more expedient to shut his eyes. Seriousness, earnestness, contemplation, and an almost judicial weighing of each subject under consideration seem to be the most prominent characteristics revealed to the stranger. Scarcely a flickering of humor, never a swift sally of wit, nor in all the length of an absorbing interview a smile, save of greeting and good-by. Yet this man is a Russian; he knows how to laugh, to sing, to dance, and to make others shout for joy. There is a mystery surrounding him, and indeed all people of real genius, not unlike that which envelops a great mountain and makes us forget all the gay little life of the insects and birds and beasties who run about so familiarly upon its mighty flanks.

It is perhaps a significant thing that in the entire

record of these impressions we have scarcely found
room to mention the chiefest instrument upon which
this artist plays, and without which he would not
be entitled to move at all upon the operatic stage—
his wonderful voice. But it has been an omission
almost flattering in its unintention, for so smoothly
conceived and projected are all his works that no
component part of his superb artistry stands out
above another. His voice seems the natural companion of his acting; his dramatic expression but the
inseparable adjunct to his vocal skill and endowment. Even in concert the exposition is quite as
evenly spread: one cannot take the voice from the
mood, nor the words from the music. An overwhelming conviction of complete greatness satisfies
his public without creating a desire to analyze and
dissect.

America has witnessed the performance of very
few rôles from Mr. Chaliapin's repertoire. He
hazards at a casual count, that nine-tenths are yet
unrevealed; but he modestly refuses to talk about
them.

"I prefer to show you upon the stage some day!"
he declares with a vastly pregnant solemnity.

CHAPTER XX

GERALDINE FARRAR'S IMPROVEMENTS

"Carmen, an operatic fantaisie in 3 Acts—A modern
revised version from the book of Prosper Merimée and
to the music of Georges Bizet."

THUS Geraldine Farrar describes, upon the program, her latest adventure before the footlights.
Whether it is merely a temporarily amusing, un
usual "show," useful as a vehicle for a popular personality, or a real contribution to artistic progress
in the operatic field, is a question which even she
herself, who has opinions on almost everything under
the sun, cannot answer. One thing, however, she
knows; it has passed the experimental stage and is
giving a great many thousands of people, among
whom may be numbered her talented self, a great
deal of pleasure. That, when all is said and done,
is the complete mission of the stage. If you insist,
however, on including "uplift," perhaps this may
fall a little short; but so do many real operas, for
that matter, and she has substituted for it "refreshment," which is more than one can say of all the
latter.

Before dissecting the thing in relation to its
grandmother, the opera, and its maiden aunt, the
song recital, it might be well to know first what we

are talking about, and the best way to do that is to trace it from the birth of the idea. A few years ago, when Geraldine Farrar was the idol of the matinée girls at the Metropolitan, with a "drawing power" second only to Caruso's—when she was singing big rôles on an average of three times a week, and in between was rehearsing, making phonograph records, trying on costumes, and doing the other hundred and one things that make up a popular prima donna's day—she conceived the idea that she was not working hard enough, and used to entertain herself with visions of what a perfectly delightful satisfaction it would be to sing every night in the week. The excitement attendant upon a performance of operatic proportions is so tremendous, and after keying-up one's nerves to the proper pitch, the after-slump is so appalling, that it seemed to her it would be much easier when once up, to stay up. Of course this was decidedly impracticable. Not only did the other artists have to have a chance occasionally, but the exertions of operatic rôles, as written and as given on any "grand" scale, are so terrific that human machines cannot, with the best will in the world, be forced beyond a certain point. However, such characters as Zerlina in *Don Giovanni,* her little cousin, Cherubino, and other not very tragic or exacting parts were such fun to do that she longed to play them more than a scant half dozen times in a season, and kept herself in a general state of unrest.

Then, when her career and popularity were at their brilliant height, she actually carried through an astonishing *coup,* and bade a regrettable, but certainly a spectacular, farewell to the Metropolitan. She had always said when she was forty years old she would leave opera; and the surprise lay not only in her frank admission of that number of years, but that she actually did what she promised. On that diverting afternoon she blithely broke one of the house rules and addressed the audience from the stage; and it was well she did, or they would have remained there clamoring until morning. But what is more to the point, she announced in tones of alluring mystery that she had some very interesting plans up her sleeve, and that she was not by any means saying good-by. One gathered that these plans had to do with Belasco and the legitimate stage; but, although those have not as yet been revealed, others, which must have taken precedence in her heart, have already crystallized into this latest of compressed tabloid musical offerings

During opera days and immediately afterward she, like all other popular stars, had engaged herself for handsome sums to sing in concerts, both orchestral and with piano. She noticed that her audiences listened merely politely while she offered them her heart's blood in the form of the exquisite classic Lieder, turning a much more interested eye upon her gown than ever they bent an ear upon her vocalization. It was only when they came to those inevitable request numbers with which, in a far different setting, she had made her name—"One Fine Day" from *Butterfly,* the "Jewel Song" from *Faust,* and later, of course, the *Habañera*—that they brightened perceptibly. She always felt, however, like a thief or an impostor. What business had Butterfly in a modern ballgown with coiffure à la mode? It seemed a travesty, a sacrilege. If people who could not hear opera, still insisted on having their favorite "excerpts," then something ought to be done so that they could have them *right.* It began by her catching up a mantilla or a fan before she came back for the *Sequidilla* encore. A rose in her teeth, a lilting walk, a sly wink, and there was the arch and provocative Carmen before their eyes. It was just as easy as that, and it gave her food for thought.

The second step was at the movies (of which she is inordinately fond). It was an average small town along her tour, but the theater was a good one and up to date. The bill included a semi-classic overture, a news weekly, a simple little ballet number, and two songs of olden times, with costume and harpsichord. Miss Farrar sat behind a row of typical corner-drugstore young men and bob-haired, gum-chewing flappers, but a chance remark from one of the latter started her thinking. "Gee," said the girl, "don't they give you a lot for 25 cents!" Miss Farrar's own concert had been many times that amount, and what had she given them? Surely nothing for these girls and boys, although she had poured forth her soul in communion with the great masters of music. Well, was it her entire soul after all? Wasn't there a big part of it which yearned to give to just the people who go to the movies— to bring them what they wanted, whether they knew it or not, and in a form they could understand?

Opera is a magic word. It conjures up pictures of brilliancy, wonder and delight, but it is also a frightening word. Watch the average man of the family shy like a balky horse when his wife suggests that he accompany her. "And who can blame him?" asks Miss Farrar. "There are spots that he will enjoy, but they are few and far between. Even I— and heaven knows that I ought to be able to appreciate and love it if any one can—even I feel the tediousness of large doses of chorus and recitative, and lack of action in some of the older operas, and as for the great and wonderful moving ones like *Tristan* and *Meistersinger,* they are so stupendous, so satisfying, that I always leave before they are over for fear I will not be able to assimilate what I have heard. Well, then, why not meet a popular demand? That person who is before the public and does not within his power give it what it wants is a fool. The principal thing is to recognize the want. Ah! If we could always do that, we would be in Paradise! And, although this is not a first consideration, the artist who pretends indifference to dollars and cents is a complete dissembler.

Others can give uplifting performances to empty benches, or sing out their lofty souls in the privacy of their homes if they like, but I for one prefer the S. R. O. sign and the crowd around the stage-door. Not only does it keep me in hair-nets, but I am convinced that it is a fifty-fifty affair, and that if I hadn't something worth while to give them, they wouldn't be there clamoring for it."

All of which seems reasonable enough. Miss Farrar is an artistic cosmopolitan product, but she is first and foremost a Yankee, and she knows herself, her country, and the times in which she lives. She, therefore, clearly recognizes the value of her own magnetic personality and the popular appetite; so with great astuteness, rather than unalloyed philanthropy, she has capitalized this, her greatest asset, and served it to her public upon a gilded platter of a design best calculated to sweeten such a delicacy.

Enlarging upon the understanding of the times in which she lives, she maintains that most great art works were more influenced, and also more fettered, by contemporary demand than the creators realized. Would Glück have developed his leisurely and serene compositions had there been telephones or "last trains" to the suburbs in his day? Would Verdi have bothered with so much choral strutting if the public had not delighted therein? Would Wagner have produced such profoundly passionate and noble works had he not sensed the steadily in-

creasing *Sehnsucht* (soul yearning) in his compatriots? At any rate, Farrar, in her turn, having taken
the national temperature and felt the people's pulse,
has made a big step toward—what? The possibilities are certainly diverting.

The public knows the *Habañera,* the "Toreador Song," the *Sequidilla.* Once or twice people
have heard and admired "Micaela's Prayer," and
the "Flower Song." It is for these bright spots,
presumably, that they sit through four long acts
of *Carmen.* Good; they shall have them all, but
without the bread and butter—they shall have jam!

When her concert season was over Miss Farrar
retired to her country home with a score of *Carmen,*
a blue pencil, Merimée's book, a paste pot, and a
pair of scissors. Later she added a paint-box, bits
of colored silks and an album of Spanish portraits;
and with these utensils she went to work. By autumn she was ready to engage her company and to
give the waiting world a surprise. The *fantaisie*
was not only born, but ready to walk.

Taking the plot from the book primarily and
paring it down to three essentially dramatic scenes,
she then proceeded to fit such bits of Bizet's score
to it as it would bear. Of course all the big arias
were left in, but calmly uprooted from their time-
honored sequence and put in wherever she considered them most effective. "I really don't see why
Micaela's prayer should be any more beautiful sung
while stumbling about on pasteboard rocks than in

the streets of a busy town, so she sings it there; and I have taken the card scene up by the roots and practically opened the play with it." Needless to say, very little of Carmen herself has been cut out. She is on the stage practically every moment, but that is where Miss Farrar knows what she is about. The audience comes to see and hear *her*, and they shall have their fill. The spoken word is used a great deal between the numbers, and there are parts where there is some excellent pantomime to the accompaniment of musical comment usually made by the chorus, but here diverted to the orchestra. The production is of the folding pocket variety.

The scenery consists of a curtained arch, with a slightly futuristic back-drop which changes for each scene, and the cast is cut down to the minimum. The toreador, the tenor Don Juan, and Captain Zuniga, Micaela, the gypsy Mercédès, and four dancing girls, that is all. The orchestra represents even stricter economy, and one gentleman, reviewing the affair for his paper, suggests that Carmen's costumes are excessive, and that she might pawn a bracelet or two and hire another violin.

However, here again, La Farrar is clever. She knows that with the public for which this entertainment was designed, the eye is quicker than the ear. Hence she omits nothing that can startle and thus give ocular pleasure. She claims to have contrived and originated all the costumes herself, and they are doubtless the fruit of careful research; but, being a good showwoman, she does not hesitate to use her imagination, and clothes her characters as we would like to have them dress, rather than exactly as they really did. Where and how Carmen got the golden top-hat seems to concern reporters all along the route, but the answer is only that it is vastly becoming and pert, and that is explanation enough. Other critics have said, "If one can overlook the artistic maltreatment of a great masterpiece there are certainly details in the performance which can be thoroughly enjoyed. The difficulty is to avoid a constant comparison of the 'version' with the original."

They are doubtless right from their standpoint, but Miss Farrar vastly prefers such heartfelt and spontaneous critique as the words of the fat gentleman, dragged to the performance by his flapper daughter, much against his will, "You know how I hate opera!" he grumbled as they took their seats; but after the second act he continued, "If they were all like this I'd take a season seat!"

Geraldine herself fairly seethes and bubbles with enthusiasm. It is impossible to sit beside her for ten minutes and watch those earnest blue eyes light up, or listen to her amazing flow of eager words, and not catch fire yourself.

"You are getting a very one-sided estimate, I'm afraid," she declares. "If you don't want hyperbole, then don't start a mother talking about her child. Yes; it is *mine* absolutely from beginning to end. Every one surmises about the librettist, but I don't know why, because I answer to that name, as well as to stage manager, prompter, directress, and star. It took me a long time to select the company, because I insisted not only on voice and a fair amount of dramatic ability, but also on a capacity for hard work. I am sure they privately think of me as a survivor of the slave drivers, for I certainly keep their noses to the grindstone. They can rest as much as they wish between performances, but let me catch one of them napping on the stage for a single instant, and crash—a general rehearsal is called for to-morrow morning. I am such a fanatic about work myself that the only attitude I can tolerate around me is the alert and the keen. Up on his tiptoes goes every one who joins my company, and he never lets down till his work is done, or he doesn't stay long with me. But for some reason they all seem to like me," she adds in a tone of amazed gratification. "We are a happy family. Of course I used to love a great many of my associates at the opera, but I did loathe the intrigue which seethed around us. It made me so miserable that I was often physically ill; but I know now that it cannot be really helped. It is an integral part of the opera world. One breathes it in like the dear funny odor of the stage, and most prime donne, tenors, directors, and conductors simply thrive on it. Certainly I'm a true child of the music theater,

but it just doesn't seem to agree with me, and now
I'm so contented and serene, with no more heart-
burnings, or consciousness of 'dirty' looks fastened
upon me—no more plotting and scheming for precedence. I always tried to be casual and impersonal
and take what came while there, but somehow it
used to get me in the end. However, it is finished.
I'm the 'captain of my soul' and the 'master of my
fate,' and I truly and earnestly believe I'm on the
right road artistically!"

So enamored is she of her idea that she cannot
see why it has never been thought of before. She
declares that if she should hear that Chaliapin, or
Mary Garden, or Olive Fremstad were to visit her
town with versions of some of their great rôles
pruned of extraneous matter and condensed to show
to best advantage their masterly interpretations, she
would sit up all night to get a seat in the front row.
She believes that every really great opera is capable
of being thus converted and that inevitably it will
be in that form that they will live for the ages, and
in no other. She also quoted a most timely and
pertinent letter from the great Lilli Lehmann, her
teacher, whom she regards with something approaching veneration, in which she relates that coincident
with Farrar's American attempt, some old operas
of Händel have recently been unearthed, clipped,
abbreviated, revised, and given with immense success in Berlin.

Miss Farrar has, with all her enthusiasm, a

wholesome mixture of common sense. She knows very well that she is not playing for the edification of the intensely cultured minority. She does not bring her production to New York—not because she is ashamed of it, but quite frankly because it was not designed for cosmopolites. She does not want it dissected by shocked gentlemen with eyeglasses on black ribbons. . . . She made this opera—or rather *fantaisie*—for the dwellers upon Main Street, who are just as much her worthy countrymen, with a right to be pleased in a way that suits their taste, as are those endorsers of Russian gloom and "progressive" iconoclasm, the blasé Intellectuals of Gotham.

Practical details of her enterprise are really interesting. She disclaims any difficulties with copyrights, which are non-existent with *Carmen,* although rumor hath it that some people in Paris are getting very much excited over the liberties they consider she has taken with one of their precious Immortals. What snags she may encounter when—and if—she attempts to revamp *Tosca* or *Butterfly* are yet to be seen. She plays only "one night stands," and usually has six performances a week, with sold-out houses at whatever happen to be local theater rates. "I don't charge fancy prices, because I have just a 'show' like all the rest. I flatter myself it's a very good one, but the audience takes the thing on faith when they buy a ticket, and I'd rather have them say, like the girl at the movies, 'That was a

lot for the money!' than go away feeling fleeced."

So she has her impossible wish of those early years and is at last singing every night. And certainly it seems to suit her admirably, for, although she lives in a railroad car, which is always "parked" in the midst of scenery which is, to use her own expression, "scarcely a fragrant vale," she manages to surround herself with the amenities of life and to eke out a tramp existence far from barren. Her tiny sitting-room boasts a tinier piano, well-filled book-shelves, chintz curtains, a profusion of flowers, bonbons and magazines, while her pet dog reclines at his ease not far from a cage of parrakeets. With her rather startling, but vastly becoming, gray hair, and dressed appropriately for a spring afternoon in a gown of tender verdure, a narcissus and a tulip, it is a very earnest and charming person indeed who concludes a truly stimulating talk by a touch of that wistfulness which proves her the great artist.

"In the first years of my career, what tremendous, serious ideals I had! But I will confess, I sometimes wonder if, after all, they are not still there. How else could one go on?"

CHAPTER XXI

AFTERMATH

AND then what happens?

Do they all live happily ever after, these great singers and little dancers, and all of those other ardent workers in the music world behind the scenes? Their past was so brave and eager, their present is so glamorous and triumphant, that we like to fancy them forever trailing down the paths of glory. . . . The gods and goddesses at last march over the rainbow bridge to a well-earned *Walhalla*—all their retainers and henchmen follow, waving laurel branches—the music dies—the golden curtain falls. . . .

But it is not like that!

The workers with their hands, in the big music mill, are looked after. If their loyalty and interest hold them beyond a certain number of years, pensions are forthcoming. They may then sit in comfort with their grandchildren around their knees, and tell mighty tales of past battles. As for the dancers, their career is as brief as that of a moth about a candle. Few remain beyond the age of thirty-five, although Pavlowa, Adeline Genee, and a few other well-known *ballerine* have managed to keep their muscles supple and obedient well into the

forties. It is a profession, however, in which the marriage rate is very high. Settling down, for one of these sprites, seems as natural as it is illogical. Married or single, they seem to have strong domestic leanings. A famous dancer says: "We save our money and we buy ourselves a home. We like very much little farms!" It is a pleasing thought! Coppélia among the chickens, Columbine on a milking-stool. . . . What a blithesome barnyard that must be!

But the singers' aftermath is not so gay. *Creative* artists, little or big, may fill the world with books, and paintings, and statues as testaments for coming generations, but the *interpretive* artist, no matter how great, is doomed to pass and leave behind only echoes and memories which fade with cruel swiftness. No other career in the world is so spectacular while it lasts as that of the opera-singer, none so acclaimed, so promptly and richly rewarded, but alas, none is so completely and thoroughly over, once the sun begins to set! The glamour of the prima donna fades as quickly as a hot-house rose, as soon as the spotlight rays have turned from her to another; and no matter when this tragic moment comes, no matter how long and insistent the warnings, she is rarely ready for it.

An artist now riding on the flood tide of popularity at the Metropolitan said, with a very twisted smile: "My dear, we dare not even *think* of the future!" And in this lament lies the secret of much of their woe. If they could all bring themselves to think more about it; if they could, like the ballet girls, set their hearts upon "little farms," all might be well.

At the peaks of their careers they are often enormously rich, what with opera seasons in New York, South America, and abroad, phonograph royalties, and excessively profitable concert tours; nevertheless, fortunate are those few who actually save enough in the end to guarantee themselves a fairly comfortable old age. They have learned to spend money almost as rapidly as they earn it. Their constant travel eats alarmingly into their incomes; and the style in which they feel impelled to live, either through the pressure of public opinion or their own rampant desire for all the beautiful things which in their struggling youth were denied them—plus the extravagance of their costumes and general wardrobes—all take out a big deduction from their net profits. Many of them are for years paying back debts incurred during their preparatory training; and, above all, most of them have a little army of "hangers on."

How many fine artists are lost to the world because they happen to be born with silver spoons in their mouths cannot be reckoned, but the fact remains that most of those who succeed may boast of "poor but honest parents." When the brilliant son or daughter swims upward to the bright waters of success what is more natural than a "little help at

home"?   Brothers and sisters, cousins, aunts, even
husbands and wives and in-laws dangle about the
neck of the average opera-singer in appalling numbers.   Burdens gladly borne, for the most part, but
none the less exacting, and inauspicious to the found-
ing of a substantial savings account.

The end comes on shockingly soon, too, when in
any other walk of life they would be just entering
into the fullness of their powers.   Every year of
popularity granted to an opera-singer after fifty is
a dispensation of the gods.   The voice may linger
in much of its glory, breaking little by little, but
the dramatic illusion rarely survives, and the ag-
ing singer inspires in the hearts of even his most
adoring public only an affectionate and loyal re-
gret.

The most sensible thing would seem to be, in
order to avoid this drab finale, to retire in the hey-
day, while still on the heights.   That, however, is
not so easy as it sounds; it is somewhat like going
to a hospital and laying oneself down upon the table
to have one's appendix removed while still in perfect health.   A salary of a thousand dollars or over
for every appearance, a life luxurious, varied, and
intense, a gratifying and wholly unavoidable exaltation of the ego—these are things not voluntarily
relinquished; not to mention that sublime joy of the
real artist in the actual exercise of his art.

A prima donna who has become inured to being
stared at and followed on the street complains about

it perhaps, but never for an instant does she envy you your anonymous appearance. Accustomed, when shopping, to have the saleswoman blush with surprise and delight in recognition of her fame, she can never reconcile herself to the speedy forgetfulness or indifference which now says: "Excuse me, how do you spell that name?" And the last humiliation comes when she demands *prix d'artiste* and is met with a dubious shrug.

So few of them, while busy learning notes, and rôles, and languages, and dozens of wonderful accomplishments, ever really have learned how to live. They may refute this statement. Geraldine Farrar insists that an opera-singer lives fifty years in every five, which is doubtless true; but it is a different life indeed to that homely, uneventful existence made up of give-and-take, easy laughter, small irritations, work and play, which the normal citizen approximates. Besides, and what is more important, they are by no means down-and-out and ready for the chimney-corner when they leave the opera. Having formed the habit of intense activity under pressure, they are wretched until some kindred field of endeavor opens for them. Having traveled incessantly for the greater part of their lives, a rooted and grounded existence appeals only as a brief novelty. They must all be off somewhere, doing something . . . or the distress is acute.

The first remedy is the Concert Field; the second is Teaching; and the third and inevitable one is the

Writing of Memoirs. It usually transpires in just that order.

Of all the adored prime donne of past Metropolitan glory, Marcella Sembrich probably stayed latest and has been remembered best. With her departure began that period of ten years or more known as the "Twilight of the Gods," during which, one by one, the great ones fell away. The company gave her a farewell which was never equaled for elaboration or brilliancy until Miss Farrar's, and which differed from the latter in that it was a function devised by the management. A special performance of *Traviata* was announced, in which the entire company appeared, many of the leading stars delighting to take minor rôles. At the close of the second act every one, chorus, ballet, and all the directors and officials, gathered on the stage and there were speeches, testimonials, and inundations of flowers, with the climax in the presentation of a string of pearls purchased by popular subscription. The much-loved little woman was bidden Godspeed with banners waving and flags flying—yet only just the other day an employee of the theater could not remember her name.

Others do, however, and many artists, no matter to what degree of fame they have already arrived, consider themselves fortunate indeed if they can enroll as her pupils. Even while at the opera she used to make of her concert programs a thing of wonder, which caused serious gentlemen like Krehbiel, Henderson, and Aldrich to burst forth into the most exuberant salvos. Consequently, when it became known that she was available for a price, to supervise and suggest in making the programs of others, loud and constant was the knocking at her door. So instead of flying back for refuge and oblivion to her native Poland she has stayed on contentedly here, for program-making was not the only torch which she was able to pass on. The secrets which had developed her own delightful voice to its smooth and limpid glory she was now ready to impart to a worthy few. Some of her pupils have become internationally known, foremost among them Queena Mario of the Metropolitan, and Dusolina Giannini, the young Italian. Others, like the great Jeritza, were almost as well-known as she herself when they came to her. To be considered by her at all is a big step along the rocky road to success, and her fees, although startling, are gladly paid. Lately, when the Curtis Institute of Music was founded in Philadelphia, she was engaged to fill the chair of Vocal Instruction, and makes weekly trips to review and suggest and plan the work of the teachers under her. So she is one of the busiest ladies in all New York, re-living in her pupils the joys of her own triumphant days; creating again in a new acre of her old field of activity; surrounded by friends, and in demand at all gatherings of the musically social world. But is she happy? One cannot say. One sees a dear little person, simply dressed, who still vaguely suggests the pretty Susanna of long-silent *Figaros,* often sitting in a box at a performance by one of her protegées. Her face is not sad, just a little tired perhaps, but quietly serene. She has memories, and she has compensations, *but* she is writing her memoirs.

Another artist who retired only a few seasons later is Emma Eames, who, after the second act of a performance of *Tosca,* without any warning at all, said a quiet and gracious word of farewell, and from that evening on was heard no more in opera. She sang a concert here and there, but for the most part seemed content to retire to her early home in a Maine town and there to live as unobtrusively as if she had never walked as one among the great of the earth. How she bridged the chasm between the opera house and "way down East" baffles the imagination; and still more extraordinary seems the fact that her gifted Spanish husband whom she acquired in a slightly sensational manner, has also been induced to remain there contentedly, using it as a base from which to make his artistic flights before the public. Almost as beautiful as ever, with who knows what glories of voice still hers, she has, nevertheless made her retirement complete and final.

Very different has been the case of Patti, Melba, and Calvé. The first of these was unwisely persuaded to record her voice for the phonograph when, unfortunately, it could no longer convey any suggestion of its one-time brilliancy. Both of the other singers have made a succession of last tours and final appearances which were but sad reminders of the passage of time and of things temporal. Calvé has a sort of glorified school in her castle of old Provence, where a group of girls goes summer after summer in an effort to learn from her the secret which is not within her power to pass on, teach she never so wisely. Calvé's arch fire and subtle charm are forever inimitable. As for Melba, she will probably drop in harness, which is just what our dear Lillian Nordica did, alone upon a remote island in Oceania. The most striking and tragic instance of death upon the field of honor was that of the basso, Castelmary, who was stricken with a fatal heart attack during a performance of *Marta* at the Metropolitan Opera House during the season of 1897. Of him a famous colleague said, "He was such a true artist that he could not even die until the act was over!" And it was true, for although the attack began during the scene at Richmond Fair, the curtain descended before he fell.

Victor Maurel taught singing in New York for years, almost as eclipsed as if he had never known the footlights, but Jean de Reszke had one of the most famous studios in Paris, where twenty-minute lessons were begun and ended on the ringing of a bell, but in the brief course of which the student— often an artist of established reputation—received more than in an hour with the average master.

It is always quite different in Europe, however,

especially in Germany. So respected and loved are the artists who have endeared themselves to the public in their youth that their old age is tenderly revered, and performances clamored for even when their prime is long since past. Lilli Lehmann, although in her seventies, cannot be said with any degree of certainty to have retired from the stage. She is such an extraordinary person that no affectionate toleration need be wasted on her. She is still singing an occasional *"Gastspiel"* in some of the classic rôles, to the marvel of all beholders. Milka Ternina, however, her contemporary and also a superlative artist who, in spite of a negligible amount of personal beauty, rose to tremendous popularity in America and Europe, so felt the strain of her stage career that she became the victim of a disfiguring nervous affliction of the face and was forced to seek seclusion in her own little peasant village of Croatia. She has quite recovered now, and is teaching a little in Munich, but all through those years of her absence, the Müncheners never ceased to talk about her as "our Ternina."

How different from New York, which let Olive Fremstad and Geraldine Farrar depart, in glory perhaps, but without any sign of civic uprising! Both of these artists showed great perspicacity in retiring while still at the top; one can only hope it has not cost them what it has cost the public! Farrar, to be sure, is with us sporadically in a variety of *divertissements*, but that ardent Brünnhilde, that sublime Isolde is, like Sembrich, thrusting her blazing torch into the hands of pupils. As for Caruso, a loyal friend and colleague of his was heard to say that his death, although it left an irreparable void, was perhaps a fortunate thing. He, knowing no other life but that of the theater, would probably have lingered on, urged and applauded by an irresistible public, but nevertheless remaining past the peak of his talents and well into the pathetic shadows of declining greatness. And so it is with all the others who have once been the darlings of the gods, they are trying hard to learn that there is satisfaction of a sort in life without a tinsel crown.

Sooner or later they turn to the concert field, but their careers there are often brief or intermittent. The sums paid them are certainly considerable, but the total gain is less. Traveling expenses for a small retinue, and a goodly percentage to a manager; thousands in advertising, and an equal amount for circulars, window cards, and posters are big "overhead." Then, as to health, life on a succession of sleeping-cars and in "best hotels" may be diverting, but it does not improve the condition of the inner man, and no experience is more wearing than to sleep in a different bed every night.

The chief deterrent, however, is the concert itself. Your true operatic artist, even upon the bare platform, may sing supremely well and interpret with bewildering subtlety, but his name and heart are linked with the music drama. The public demands "excerpts" with an insistence which will not be denied, and concessions are made. Absurd as are these arias and scenes, divested of scenery, costume, and gesture, still more ungrateful are they if an artist in conventional evening clothes, standing beside a grand piano, oversteps the boundaries of concert tradition and becomes too dramatic. When the artists first begin to give *Lieder* groups, they are usually most enthusiastic over the delicate miniature drama they find in each song—the nuances, the variety they may now express unfettered. But the response of the average audience is, as one noted singer very cleverly puts it, "like talking with animation into a telephone when there is no one on the other end." Besides, the singing actor used to the mighty sweep of the stage will find the *Lieder* style restricted and is bound, eventually, to chafe against meticulous etching when he has been trained to paint on a "seven-league canvas with brushes of comet's hair."

There is the tempting pecuniary advantage of selling a famous name to the vaudeville circuit; but just how the *ci-devant* glamorous Marguerite feels sandwiched in between the trained seals and the acrobats will never be fully revealed. By the profession at large, vaudeville is regarded as the last act just before casket and flowers are ordered, yet Johanna Gadski seemed pleasantly and profitably employed in the two-a-day, and on latest reports is still surviving.

If, however, the King is really dead, why not Long live the King!? What of descendants to keep alive inherited talents, to keep green the laurels around a great name? Hostages to immortality— this would seem the surest way. But, alas, how seldom does it happen! The denial of domesticity is one of the sacrifices most of the great stars feel called upon to make, hence their great loneliness. Large families or any families at all are the rarest of accessories upon the lyric stage, except in the case of the contralto, who goes in for the thing with almost exaggerated enthusiasm. Louise Homer did manage to endow her oldest girl with some of her talent, and it has given many an audience a sentimental as well as an artistic thrill to hear the two Louises in concert together, but no Schumann nor Heink has yet greatly distinguished himself in his famous mother's footsteps. The average child of the artist evinces no more interest in the parent's affairs than Marie Rappold's daughter, who used to sit in the dressing-room and read detective stories rather than observe her mother's performance from the wings. Much as they are absorbed in and devoted to their own careers, very few parents influence their children to continue the family traditions, and leave them about all over the world in schools until they have grown up, far away from the smell of grease-paint.

Thus, with posterity an uncertain insurance at best, and an art that is as evanescent as it is great,

what is the declining singer to do but to take his
pen in hand? The writer on musical subjects to-day
must get up very early in the morning indeed, to
catch the worm before he turns, to surprise that
much-interviewed artist into parting with any little
bit of the material he is carefully garnering for
"The Story of My Life." God bless them all, and
may a faithful public applaud with fat royalties, to
deepen the solace of their retrospection! Or, if
this last wish seems a trifle too commercial, may
they remember the happy truth that nothing new is
ever quite so fine, nor half so dear to the heart, as
that which used to be!

CHAPTER XXII

L'ENVOI

THROUGH these pages from time to time has wandered, more or less silently, the Impresario. It is noticeable, however, that we have not harried him in his office nor sought to buttonhole him in a corner of the lobby.

It would scarcely seem polite to tuck him in with the scene-shifters and property man as one of the "Stars in Eclipse," although that title fits him admirably; and he has been given no chapter of his own—it has not seemed necessary. Writers are revealed by their books, artists by their paintings and statues, the architect is represented by his cathedral. Therefore, the Impresario, the mighty heart and brain behind this most fantastic and formidable of undertakings in the world, can best be known by the opera he gives. Sitting at his desk protected by a dozen glorified office boys, or moving spectrally about where one least expects to see him, he is in one sense "The Lord High Executioner," but in every other "The Little Father." Should we ask him for an interview, he would only reply with a benevolent smile: "You have already written it!"

THE END